Nothing More to Declare

by *John Clellon Holmes*

NOTHING MORE TO DECLARE

John Clellon Holmes

E. P. Dutton & Co., Inc.

New York § 1967

Certain sections of this book appeared first, in substantially different form, in the following publications and are included here with the permission of the copyright owner:

Cavalier. THE POP IMAGINATION (1966)
Contact. A FEW LOVES, A FEW DEATHS (1962)
Esquire. THE PHILOSOPHY OF THE BEAT GENERATION. © 1958 by Esquire, Inc.
Evergreen Review. THE LOST CAUSE (1966)
Harper's Magazine. 15¢ BEFORE 6:00 P.M. (1965)
The New York Times. THIS IS THE BEAT GENERATION. © 1952 by The New York Times Company.
Nugget Magazine. FAREWELL TO A BAD DECADE (1963)
Playboy. REVOLUTION BELOW THE BELT (1964) and THE SILENCE OF OSWALD (1965)

Copyrights from which permission to quote have been granted:

Allen Ginsberg. *Kaddish* © 1961 by City Lights Books.
Jack Kerouac. *Visions of Cody* © 1960 by New Directions. Reprinted by permission of the author.
Gershon Legman. *Love and Death* copyright, 1949, by Gershon Legman.

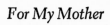

For My Mother

*The death of love, the death
of hope, as we have known them—
out of these we gesture towards a
new sensation or experience, in
which to glimpse ourselves. And
human possibilities.*

Contents

Contents

Foreword

§ § Crossing a frontier involves a passage in time as well as space. Your passport is scrutinized to ascertain just who you are, or (to put it more accurately) who you have *been*; your baggage is searched for that contraband the greedy or the sentimental try to smuggle into tomorrow; and you are asked to make a Customs Declaration of those valuables on which the duty must be paid. For some writers, the age of forty is just such a frontier between the countries of experience.

Poised between the past you can never recover and the future you have yet to achieve, you see things with a curious lucidity. You are leaving the tropics of your youth, and you are leaving them forever. The territory ahead is bound to be chillier, a landscape less exciting to the nerves and more demanding on the mind. The nights and the winters will seem longer there, and you will begrudge the time you wasted once on fools or fun. You will be busier, and glad of it. Whatever paths you take in that new territory are likely to turn inward, and a new insight will come to seem more profitable than a new experience.

My generation—the generation that came of age during, or just after, the Second World War—has reached this frontier also. We are going over into our full maturity, and, hopefully, into our solidest accomplishments as well, and not a few of us, I imagine, are just as happy to pass on the mantle of "The New Generation," which we have worn for over ten years now, to all those energetic kids, with their guitars and placards, who frug and demonstrate so indefatigably everywhere these days.

That a new generation is upon us, complete with its own styles and mores and preoccupations, is immediately apparent when you remind yourself that its Bob Dylans were ten years old when *On the Road* was written, and its Stokely Carmichaels were thirteen when the Supreme Court's desegregation decision was handed down. Whether we like it or not, a new vision is abroad in the land now, a vision that was fathered by my generation's attitudes and antics, a vision that perhaps can best be understood by understanding *us*.

As a writer, I have always found the young more interesting than the elderly (it is an American idiosyncrasy), and now that people of my age no longer comprise "The New Generation," it seems the proper time to collect between covers the various articles I have written that deal with what we were like when we did. I don't expect to speak of my contemporaries as a distinct and separate group again, so this collection is by way of being a Declaration of the few items on the matter that seem valuable enough to take across the frontier into forty-one.

A word or two about those items.

The first, "Representative Men," is made up of a quartet of character sketches of old friends, whose experiences and interests were typical of the times. My choice of these four rather than any other four was made on the basis of affection as well as representativeness, but I am satisfied that these men embody some of the traits that were characteristically ours.

It seemed right that something of my generation's common adolescence should be included here as well, and perhaps nothing had so widespread an influence on our imaginations as the movies. "A Decade of Coming Attractions," then, is a valentine to the vanished phantoms of the Saturday afternoons of long ago.

The next section, "Generationing," is designed as a summary look, in terms of my own involvement, at that by now almost quaint phenomenon, the Beat Generation. It was a task I took up as a responsibility I owed the record. Certain gaps in that record needed filling, and I have tried to be as exhaustive as possible, even at the risk of reprinting parts of two old articles of my own on the subject. Still, the Beat Generation was part of the cultural history of the times (just how much a part, I have tried to indicate), and this section may prove to be more useful in fifteen years than it is today.

"The Silence of Oswald," on the other hand, was written primarily to lay a troubling ghost in my own head. But it is also an analysis of a type of human being—the alienated youth torn between idealism and violence—that our experience peculiarly equipped us to understand; and, as an exercise in what has been called "existential politics," it may suggest one of the ways in which our ideology-stormed psyches responded to history and its crimes.

As for the sexual revolution, described in "Revolution Below the Belt," it need only be said that it is the one revolution in which most of my generation, in this era without utopias, have been enlisted for almost twenty years.

The final piece in the book, "The Raw Materials," is a memoir of sorts, a sampling of the images and ideas out of which the other essays have been written, a personal record of the last two decades as I experienced them, and I felt it belonged in this Declaration because mine was, above all, a first-person generation, with a built in distrust of second-hand opinions and all four estates.

When you go through Customs, when your passport has been stamped, your luggage opened, and your list of valuables checked, there comes a final moment when the inspector looks you gaugingly in the eye, knowing you are impatient to be gone, but vigilant nevertheless, and asks: "Have you anything more to declare?"

On this matter of my generation and its youth, I can honestly say that (for the time being, at least) these are the items on which I am willing to pay the duty.

Representative Men

One:

§ § They say that a writer's vision, his particular quality of mind, is shaped by what happens to him before he is 25. Thereafter he is engaged in post-mortems, explications or extensions. If he is resolute, and lucky, he will capture more and more areas of the larger reality, and put them to his use, but the specific way in which he deals with his experience will probably be ordained by a point of view that was already fixed at the time of his young manhood.

If this is true (and I think in America it mostly is), the long, muggy July 4th weekend in 1948 must be reckoned as a crucial date in my personal education. I was 22, and just beginning to publish, and I suppose I was indistinguishable from three hundred other young intellectuals in New York in those days. We all read the same "little magazines"; we all had first novels underway; and the same secret confusion (about the drift of the times) lay behind our individual ambitions to be the first to strike the "dominant note." In one sense at least, the lessening of my own confusion began that weekend. For all in two days I met four men who profoundly altered my life and mind; vastly different men, one from the other, who nevertheless have come to seem to me as representative of my generation and some of its preoccupations as any four very dissimilar individuals can be. There was something special about each of them that was outrageous, idiosyncratic, and against the grain at the time; a unique view of the world which, a decade and a half later, has proved to be not so special after all. In any case, each had a share in sharpening whatever pen I wield, defining (in their works and personalities) some of the questions, and a few of the answers, that have plagued my times.

That weekend the streets were sultry, fretful, oddly empty. It was trying to rain, and anyone with any place to go had fled to the country—my wife among them. I had to stay on, because an out-of-town magazine editor, who had just accepted a story of mine, was in New York, and wanted to get together. The magazine was called *Neurotica*, and copies of its second issue had been stacked on the tables of the Gotham Book Mart and the Four Seasons for the past week.

The editor was named Jay Landesman, he lived in St. Louis, and I think I was fully, dismally expecting that he would turn out to be a nervous, effete young man, some Des Esseintes of the Middle West. Anyway, I was not looking forward to the encounter. I discovered him at the top of the Marlton Hotel's stuffy elevator shaft, in a cramped room of landlord blue, dressed in the black slacks, black shirt, yellow tie and desert boots of an affable Marseilles hood, surrounded by bottles of gin, stacks of books and newspapers, and several pretty girls— one of whom (I remember) was going around the country getting arrested so that she could study penal conditions. "I'm going to be committed for delinquency next week," she said complacently when we were introduced.

Landesman was tall, bony, dark and volatile. He sprawled, rather than sat; he spoke to you with easy familiarity, and he laughed a lot, as though encouraging you to say the outrageous or revealing thing you must be thinking. His bright, wary eyes always seemed about to flare with excitement, and there was a decidedly impatient air about him, as if he was listening for the phone to ring, and imagining someone across town dialing his number—someone he didn't even know. My first impression was curiously apt now that I recall it: in a tuxedo (I thought) he would look almost exactly like Robert Alda playing Gershwin in the movies. Just a little off the mark, not quite the genuine article, but somehow engaging and energetic, fully as interesting as the original.

I think we talked about tattooing for the first fifteen minutes: he had just been prowling those parlors around Times Square, in which sailors are decorated with flags, hula girls and pierced hearts, and he thought there might be an article in it. Then he wondered why I shouldn't become the New York representative of the magazine: "I don't see why not. Getting material is the biggest problem I'm having. And you probably know everybody." Then pastrami sandwiches arrived, and more girls.

He talked and talked, despite his sandwich. He was looking for tougher material than the "green armpits" poetry he had been publishing; he had put out his first issue on $600 and gotten most of it back. He thought he would eventually bring the magazine and himself to New York, and had been arranging publicity squibs in the *Saturday Review* and *Newsweek* toward that end: "They'll stress the personal angle, of course. You know, 'Antique Dealer Edits "Sick" Magazine On Side.' But what the hell. I don't mind being treated like a sore if I can get through to them." And, oh yes, he was just about to leave to go up to the Bronx to see a guy whose stuff on sex and violence had been rejected by every publisher in America. Of course I'd come along.

Of course I did, and by 10:30 that night six of us, armed with bottles, were milling around an empty corner on the dark margin of Bronx Park, to be approached all of a sudden by a small, belligerent facsimile of Balzac—an unkempt walrus moustache almost obscuring arrogantly curled lips, a leonine shock of hair dishevelled on a huge head, with hot quick eyes that were at once inquisitive and repudiating, as if they had "expected no better"—who said brusquely, "I'm Legman," and led us to a three-room cottage on Hornaday Place a block from the park—"Once Charles Fort's cottage," the rasping voice interrupted itself to note, and then took up its torrent of words again.

The hours that followed left me with that peculiar *humming* exhaustion (from being over-stimulated a little too long) that a wild and "historic" jam session produces. I had rarely heard such talk. A researcher on *Time* had told Landesman that Gershon Legman's essays on censorship in popular culture were the most brilliant things of their kind—"Though, of course, *absolutely* unpublishable," and it was this categorical verdict which was the sole reason for that long subway ride to the

Bronx, for such challenges are a tonic to some people, and the whole Landesman is there.

Legman had seen both issues of *Neurotica*, tersely dismissed them as "mostly garbage," and then, narrowing those little eyes, said: "How serious are you, Landesman? What's your reason for publishing a magazine anyway? You got any real guts, or are you just another dilettante finking out to the culture?"

Landesman said something about the creative expression of the anxious man being archetypical of the age, to which Legman snorted: "Yeah, yeah, yeah—but what's *your* reason? If we're going to work together, let's get down to cases. . . . Me—I'm arrested-oedipal, probably sado too—though at least I beat up on Them, rather than *her*," indicating his silent wife, sitting shyly in a corner, whose only words had been the hesitant announcement that there was no ice. "Now what's *your* excuse?"

Within half an hour, it became clear that Legman was precisely the Someone whom Landesman had hoped would someday dial his number. I drank warm whiskey, and watched them circling around each other. Legman was incensed by comic books, murder mysteries and trashy novels—all of which substituted violence for sex, killing for creation, death for love. His spiel (and he *was* spieling, for behind the fatalism of remarks like "Listen, there isn't an honest publisher in America —why do you think you're any different?" clearly lay the hope that perhaps something might be done with this lanky, laughing fellow who had turned up out of the night)—his spiel was headlong, iconoclastic, funny, rash, irresistible. It was like listening to a Mencken version of a Lenny Bruce routine. You laughed through your wince.

He hurled comic books at us broadside; he quoted Freud on homosexuality, annotating as he went along; he demolished Hemingway in an epigram; he threw Supervia and Leadbelly records on the phonograph; he expatiated on typography—"I'm going to set up my own stuff if I have to. *Someone's* got to do it," gesturing toward a desk top piled with trays of type. And finally he tossed a sheaf of manuscript at Landesman and said indifferently: "There it is. Take it with you. You'll probably be arrested if you print it."

It was the typescript of what would be published a year later as *Love and Death*—that intemperate, brilliant, purging classic that became something of a personal cause to a few of us in the cultural underground of those years. We read it in an empty subway car racketing along under the deserted streets of four A.M. Manhattan, Landesman passing pages to me as he finished them, erupting into amazed laughter, and exclaiming over and over again: "This stuff is dynamite! This guy's a crazy genius!" to which the girl penologist only said: "Well, I think he's a Commie, if you ask me. I'll bet he's even a card carrier." But no one paid any attention to this, for the mind that steamed up off those sheets was clearly too far-ranging to fit into such stunted categories.

At 5:30, limp over cups of coffee, we sat under the dismal fluorescents of the Waldorf Cafeteria on 6th Avenue and 8th Street finishing up the last, by now smudged pages—pages of such power that they struck me, even through my weariness and all the stale cigarette smoke, as the most fiercely beautiful polemic that I had read since Marx on the working day. And all these years later I can still see Landesman looking up from his sprawl, hair rumpled by the excitement of his thoughts, that absurd tie askew, and hear him say with astonishment: "Good God, do you realize? I've met an honest man!"

I think that this remark was my first glimpse of the serious point of view that was mostly hidden behind the Wisecracking Editor that Landesman was then, and the Saloonkeeper, Playwright and Television Personality that he became later on, for anyone who prizes an honest man to that degree has certainly brooded on the hypocrisy of his times. But of Landesman later. And of Allen Ginsberg and Jack Kerouac (who had brooded in quite a different way, and whom I met for the first time the next night) later too. First, Legman.

Two: The Lost Cause

§ § When you came through the door of Legman's house, you found that you were in the bedroom. It was also the library, the study and the living room. The first things you noticed were books. Books everywhere, books overflowing the shelves on every available wall, books stacked under the desk, cartons of books, books lining the window sills, books in *back* of books.

A glance made clear that this was the carefully assembled library of a scholar and bibliographer; a closer look revealed that this scholar's dominant preoccupations were sex and language. I, for one, have never seen so many dictionaries, lexicons, thesauruses and indexes. Nor so many books on every imaginable aspect of the sexual life. A further glance around the room—almost bare of furniture, the bed serving as a couch by day, boxes making do as end tables, everything giving off a vague air of having been retrieved from the street just ahead of the sanitation trucks, and carefully and expertly rebuilt by hand—made it clear that this collection of rare and expensive books had been accumulated, volume after precious volume, by a man who lived almost literally from hand to mouth. Later I learned that Legman would sometimes work, more or less as a journeyman-carpenter, for the booksellers along lower 4th Avenue to pay for a rare volume he simply "had to have." His edition of *The Collected Papers of Freud*, for instance, running to many volumes, had been "liberated," a book at a time, for hardearned cash from a Greenwich Village bookseller. It was also clear that this was a working library. No frivolous fiction, no pretty poetry, nothing to wile away a rainy morning. This was a command post, this was an arsenal, and from that overflowing desk, a species of war was being carried on with the world that lay just outside the handsewn drapes, the weed-overgrown front yard, and the paintless picket fence.

Beyond this room was the kitchen—large, and plain, and pleasant. Also inundated with books. Also more than likely to be a-fume with the dizzying stench of animal entrails being converted into a stew, for Legman and his wife, Beverley, lived on next to nothing, and kept alive (as poets and prophets immemorially have) by developing a taste, or at least a toler-ance, for food that no one else would eat. Legman could fill a shopping bag for forty cents; he was the Escoffier of the butcher shops, and his soul took some of its sustenance from the very ingenuity of feeding the two of them on pennies. You were always welcome to sit down with them, but if you did, you were expected to manfully consume your share of whatever gamey, dark brown concoction they were serving, meanwhile being told good-humoredly that you were "robbing the cats," and given a lecture on parasitism that would have shamed the seediest Bohemian.

Those cats—they were everywhere. Under your feet, under the table, *on* the table. A faintly pungent odor of cat shit and sour milk hangs about all my memories of Legman's house. There were always casualties to the traffic in the streets, but there was always a new litter mewling under the sink that more than made up the loss. Somehow there was always another bit of spleen as well, or a leftover scrap of lung, or one more saucer of milk for any new arrivals, and obviously the word got around among the neighborhood felines. I have never understood the connection between intellectual eccentricity, rare-book collect-ing, and stray cats, but that there *is* some obscure connection I have not the slightest doubt, for people of the most fastidious minds, with the most carefully alphabetized shelves, will hap-pily let a mangy tom, with a dog-ruined ear, eat off their dinner plates.

To the left of the kitchen was the Filing Cabinet. In any other house, this would have been the bedroom, because it was of fair size, it was private, and it was near the bathroom. But in

Legman's house space was at a premium, and The Work came first. After all, you could *sleep* anywhere, but the files—the precious files that represented over a decade of effort to preserve every evidence of contemporary sex life, and its debasement—had to have a safe, dry room, and a door with a lock, and a window through which they could be pitched in case of fire. This was Legman's Sanctum Sanctorum, you were not allowed to linger there, or browse through the packing crates where hundreds of comic books were arranged according to degree of atrocity, and reams of erotic photographs (some going back to the camera's earliest years) were motif-indexed under such headings as "Intercourse—Oral—Homosexual" and "Bondage —Masochist—Female." Here, also, Legman's massive correspondence was meticulously filed in wooden cabinets, in which a letter from a lifer describing sex practices in the penitentiary might be sandwiched next to one from the Custodian of the Prohibited Books Section of the British Museum. In conversation, Legman would often get up and disappear into this room, to emerge with some bit of curiosa that documented the point he was making. But the indefinable, watchful purse of his lips as he handed it to you for inspection, and just as quickly snatched it back again, made it very clear that the room itself was irrevocably off limits, even to close friends.

And The Work? By the time I met Legman, The Work and the life were indistinguishable. What fortuitous collision of circumstances and predilections had guided him to his destiny, I never learned to my own satisfaction. Born in Scranton, Pennsylvania, some thirty years before (a fact that somehow seemed as unlikely to me as Pound's having been born in Hailey, Idaho), he was reluctant to supply further information, and somehow you never persisted in your inquiries. But I seem to remember a story about his having had the word "kosher" written on his forehead in horse-shit juice when he was a boy, and I'm almost certain that he had gone to the University of Pennsylvania for a time, and been thrown out for stealing a typewriter. He appeared in that murky demimonde on the margins of literature (where erotica collectors and ghost writers and researchers-into-the-arcane all shuffle together in the stacks) sometime in the mid-thirties, and the ancient rental machine that replaced the purloined typewriter was seldom silent after that. Occasionally he would allude to all kinds of journeyman-writing in the years that followed: out-and-out pornography, comedy scripts for radio, the ghosting of speeches and "auto-biographies"; and I know for a certainty that he was behind the so-called "Mexico City" edition of *Tropic of Cancer* (though he broke with Henry Miller later over Miller's alleged "anti-semitism"), and just as certainly he had worked as official bibliographer for the Kinsey Institute (and then broken with them too after a disagreement over statistical techniques).

By the time I met him, he was engaged in a fistful of diverse projects: projects as esoteric as writing an encyclopedia of sex technique for use in the bedrooms of lovers rather than the offices of marriage counselors (he had gotten no farther at that time than a rousing little volume called *Oragenitalism*); projects as invaluable as a supplement to the Oxford Unabridged Dictionary containing all the banned words (he planned to print this himself in an edition of just enough copies to supply the half dozen key libraries of Europe and America); and projects as frankly rarefied as a massive collection of erotic limericks, and their variants, which was later published in a handsome edition in Paris. I also have the clear impression that he was busy translating Sade's *120 Days of Sodom,* and working on the first of the folklore studies that were finally published as *The Horn Book* in 1964. Though he viewed *Love and Death* as nothing but the opening salvo in his campaign, the banner under which he fought was first clearly flown in that book.

Appalled by the discovery that the increasing violence and sadism of American culture was the direct result of our society's relentless suppression of sex, the stand he took (and took almost alone in those days) was summed up in these words:

"Murder having replaced sex in the popular arts, the glorification of one requires the degradation of the other . . . so that we are faced in our culture by the insurmountable schizophrenic contradiction that sex, which is legal in fact, is a crime on paper, while murder—a crime in fact—is, on paper, the bestseller of all time. . . .

"Our civilization is not yet ready to let love and death fight it out in the marketplace, with free-speech and four-color printing on both sides. Our censors—private and public—are not yet ready to see, in their total concentration on 'impurity,' the breach through which this backwash of unimaginable violence rolls over us. Our publishers are not yet ready to stop telling writers—as they have told me—'Any lousy, rotten thing you want to put on paper is O.K. with the district attorney, but if you put into a novel the description of the ordinary act of sexual intercourse between a man and wife, we will go to jail.' . . .

"The defenders of free speech generally break down at about this point, too. They are all willing to take the chance that murder-comics, murder-magazines, murder-headlines, murder-books, murder-movies, murder-radio & television—strange how respectable all these are, when 'sex-book' is a sneer—murder, murder, murder, murder, a steady total dose of murder, will not harm in the slightest degree the most impressionable child or adult. But no one seems willing to suggest that in that case the plainest pornography would hurt them even less. At least sex is normal. Is murder?

"The admission, so cheerfully made, that children *need* [comic books as] aggressive outlets in fantasy against their parents, teachers, policemen, and total social environment is an admission that this social environment does not have a place for the child. The necessity for the same outlet by adults [in murder mysteries etcetera] then means the social environment has no place in it for adults. For whom has the social environment a place?"

One measure of how far he was ahead of his times is that the clearly reasoned, exhaustively documented book containing these ideas was rejected by an entire alphabet of over thirty publishers in America before Jay Landesman published parts of it in *Neurotica*. And one indication of the prescience the book contained is that the ideas themselves no longer seem so radical or outrageous. To some degree, at least, the world has grown up to them.

But in those days Legman was as alone (in what seemed to him the gathering twilight of our time) as a St. Jerome of the Bronx. Though he had myriads of friends—people as diverse as local furniture movers and physicists from Oak Ridge—I had the strong impression that a lot of them came to him for what Landesman and I used to call "The Purification." For Legman had a curious effect on people. Frankly, an evening with him could be an ordeal. If you had a secret layer of apathy, compromise or dishonesty, he would instantly sniff it out and subject it to a barrage of sarcasms. His intuitive faculty was positively uncanny, and he would sometimes turn those hot challenging eyes on a perfect stranger, who had uttered not a word, and say witheringly: "Oh, I see you're the *skeptic* in the crowd," and, more often than not, he was right. Though he treated most women with an odd combination of familiarity and gallantry, he nevertheless insisted upon talking about the most intimate matters, in the most pointed obscenities, to all of them—even abashed virgins fresh out of Vassar.

I have seen him say to a girl he had just met that evening: "Anything that fouls up the relations between men and women, I'm against. Starting with your pantie girdle, honey. . . . When are you going to give this guy," indicating her delighted swain, "a chance to prove he's a man, instead of a goddamn tennis player. . . . You like him, don't you? Why do you want him to go fag?"

I have seen him tell my divorced mother (talking about a Persian cat she had just had fixed): "That's awful, it's criminal. Let her die, catting around, but at least let her *live* first. What makes you think we have the right to take out our disappointments and frustrations on animals that can't defend themselves? . . . And that's all it amounts to, you know," he would add with a respectful, but pitiless, half-grin.

I have heard him say to the aforementioned physicists: "Don't tell me that someone else would build the bombs if you didn't! You're here because you're guilty, you're here because you know you've sold out to Murder, and you don't like it. . . . Well, I'm not going to tell you you're clean! I'm not going to make you feel better!"

But the curious fact of the matter is that he always did, and therein lay "The Purification." It took me a long time to realize that people went away from Legman—their psyches stripped naked, their defenses in tatters, their nerves in that odd *hum* of exhaustion—feeling somehow incalculably better than they had

felt when they came. For there was an aura of total freedom
about him, of honesty without mercy, of having nothing to lose,
that made you realize that your usual social armor was unnecessary, slightly silly, an impediment—even as he hacked away at it
like some psychiatric Genghis Khan.

It was this strange effect, I think, that made countless young
men of his acquaintance bring girls (with whom they had yet to
score) to listen to him for an evening. The atmosphere around
him was so irreverent, so stimulating and above all so *liberating*,
that the girls were usually pushovers for the pass when they left.
It was this that made me feel disturbed, wearied, exhilarated,
but always more alive whenever I saw him, and for some years
his passionate combination of moral certainty and moral outrage served me as a substitute for the failed political and
religious absolutes that had left me in something of a muddle
just then. When I was depressed, I would often arrange to see
him, because (though it may surprise him to learn of it now) I
was always somehow more cheerful when I took that long
subway ride home.

There was another Legman whom you saw in the streets
downtown, hurrying along (like the White Rabbit) in an
impatient waddle, more than likely wearing a knitted cap, a
couple of threadbare scarves, a length of rope for a belt, and the
huge scuffed shoes of a London dustman. You most often saw
this Legman crossing Cooper Square in a biting wind, his
pockets full of papers, perhaps popping a candy into his mouth,
and clutching a battered old briefcase in his ravelling left
mitten. At first glance, this Legman resembled an anarchist-
theoretician, plotting the overthrow of the Power Structure—
starting in Bayonne, New Jersey; or a vegetarian poet, mumbling disconnected phrases from Rilke with his mouth full of
sea kelp; or any of the dozen other species of quack, outcast and
weirdo that haunted the sleazy blocks below 14th Street on the
East Side in those years.

But in actual fact, this was the Legman who argued with
printers, post-office clerks and countermen when, later, *Neurotica* moved to New York, and we spent days in a loft
downtown packaging up each issue ourselves to save on costs.
This was Legman the Professional, who knew about type fonts,

and bindings, and where to get good bond on the cheap; and who wrote you terse, pedagogical little memos about your grammar, a sample of which might read: "I am writing to express my admiration for your doubly-split infinitive on page 7—'he is content to simply cynically comment upon them.' Since the inexpugnable split in Wilde's *Decay of Lying*, nothing so thoroughgoing by way of anti-grammatical courage has been seen. I hope you want it kept, and not press-corrected to 'content simply to comment cynically' or something equally pedestrian and proper."

This Legman, also, knew every malodorous subway men's room where fags scrawled out their grosser fantasies (he promptly copied them down for a future work on "pissoir epigraphy"); this Legman knew where you could purchase shackles, French ticklers, erotic Rowlandsons and West African fertility ju-jus (he had once unofficially middle-manned in such items between collectors and dealers); this was Legman the Termite, boring from within, undermining the foundations, and vastly exhilarated by the very decadent world he was so busily anatomizing.

This Legman—the nonstop talker over lunch cart hot dogs, the fanatical ranter with the grin of a Cheshire cat, the walking dossier of scandalous info about the sex habits of politicians, actors and Roman Catholic Cardinals—always made me wonder, with Nathanael West, why "all prophets of doom and destruction [are] such happy men." For the public Legman, the Legman of the streets, the Legman with the faint odor of musty bookshops and standup lunches, and proud poverty about him, gave off, as well, an indefinable air of contentment within his own soul—as if he had conquered some dark underlayer of corruption in himself, and thereby earned the right to be an ambulatory rebuke to everyone else.

Did he like people—really? I don't know for sure. Certainly he was gregarious; he hungered for challenges, verbal jousts, the fray; but I think his secret mind was too full of nightmares and Molochs to allow him the luxury of "frivolous" emotions, and I also think that he was somehow uneasy when he wasn't "on the job"—as if he had never had the time to develop any sort of conventional charm, and had little sense of himself outside his chosen role. Like many messiahs of harsh truths, he liked women better than men. He was more patient with them; the puritanical heat went out of his eyes when he watched them; his feeling for them evidenced an aestheticism he had mercilessly suppressed in the rest of his life. He deferred to them, he defended them, and I often had the unmistakable feeling that he was shyly wooing them in a way I never fully understood. But then I suppose there was something feminine in his very thirst for Justice, Justice, Justice (that blindfolded female whose undeviating demands exhaust most men after a while), the other side of which trait was that curious streak of fatalism —he expected the worst, he intended to survive it—that I, at least, have always associated with women.

Every once in a while I caught brief glimpses of a more private Legman. His guard would drop for a moment, and an altogether different man would appear: a Legman who loved Beethoven, and was, I think, as moved by his music and as unsettled by being moved, as Lenin before him; a Legman whose stubby fingers adeptly fashioned Japanese paper-foldings over the coffee cups in cafeterias—creasing, twisting and inverting until all of a sudden a tiny rooster, a barking dog or a little old man materialized before your eyes; a Legman who delighted in Shakespeare (despite describing him as hardly more than "a talented fruit"), and had a beautifully drawn (by himself) panorama of Elizabethan London on his kitchen wall; a Legman who sat sipping tepid root beer, musing about the vineyards in the south of France and peeking mischievously at Beverley; a Legman who once said to me when I offered him two dollars to get them through a particularly bad week: "Yes, I'll take it. I'll take it because we haven't had anything for thirty-six hours, and it would be too *absurd* if we starved. With all the big things working against us, the important things, *starvation* would be laughable. Besides," he added with the crooked little grin that always suggested a mockery of his own motives, "it'll save the cats." But this Legman quickly recognized himself in your eyes, blushed and spluttered and immediately turned himself back into Brann the Iconoclast again.

If he had a secret motto in those days, the sort of phrase that men repeat to themselves when they flag in their chosen struggle, it was probably Burns':

"If there's a hole in a' your coats,
  I rede you tent it:

A chiel's amang you, taking notes,
  And, faith, he'll prent it."

That, I think, was how he ultimately saw himself: as the keeper of the deepest subcellar in the burning Alexandria Library of the age; the subcellar of our secret desires, which no one else was raising so much as a finger to preserve.

Legman is mostly pigeonholed today as a folklorist, or a bibliographer, or a pamphleteer, and he was certainly all of these things when I knew him. He left the United States in the early fifties as a result of Post Office harassment for *Love and Death* and vanished (from my firsthand knowledge at least) into the south of France, where he has doggedly continued to publish further sections of his life work in small and costly editions, only a few of which can be legally obtained in this country. Some of the old evangelical heat has perhaps gone out of him, and, though I can't quite imagine Legman "mellowing," I can well understand how, with the years, he might tend to disappear a little into the thickets of his specialty.

His work, which I always saw in my mind's eye as a vast, stubborn and exhaustive attempt to limn the underwater part of our society's psychological iceberg, an attempt (on the order of Marx or Freud, if on a smaller scale) to bring some overall coherence to the emotional plight of industrial man, and, like all such efforts, at once brilliant and one-sided and better in its parts than in its whole—this work, its hortatory power perhaps diminishing somewhat as it turns more and more to the consideration of minutiae, may end up contributing no more than a fascinating minor footnote to the cultural history of the times. It is far too soon to say.

Certainly Legman was an extremist, and he suffered from the extremist's myopia. Like many of us in those first postwar years, he was possessed by the idea that our civilization was quietly and relentlessly running amok. The war, with its holocausts and massacres, was a personal nightmare that was never far from our waking minds. Little that we saw around us seemed to offer much hope that a measure of sanity had returned with the peace, and Legman's efforts to remain sane in the general confusion, to oppose the brutalization of human beings by a death-drunk world, and to somehow preserve the clear eye of a St. Augustine while Rome staggered toward chaos and barbarism, sometimes led him perilously close to monomania.

He often saw a dire conspiracy where there was really only the dismal complacency of the unimaginative. He tended to forget, in his Cromwellian zeal, that conflict, violence and death have always stirred on the nightside of life and so, inevitably, have had their disturbing innings in art as well. At the bottom of it, I always thought that he tended, paradoxically, to *minimize* sex, to simplify it, to see sex behind every emotion, and so fail to see how many diverse emotional currents were sometimes contained in it. He judged everything from a conception of "normality" that was watertight in theory, but was also based (as Camus would have said) on "a man who does not *yet* exist." This sometimes led him to verbal pogroms against homosexuals, and others, that were no less totalitarian in their implications than similar diatribes against the Jews by Goebbels. A man imprisoned by an idea is a potentially dangerous man, whether that idea is true or not, and many people who ardently agreed with Legman in those days would probably have left the country had he been elected President—as he, himself, did when his absolute Opposite Number ran for the office in 1952.

But it was neither his work, nor the furies in him which it aroused, that had such a lasting influence on me. Though there were many who believed so strongly in the work that they accepted the fury, and others to whom the very vehemence of the fury threw the work into a dubious light, for me it was the attitude of the man, and the man himself, that was most important, most enlarging.

For implicit in everything he did was the conviction that human beings are more creative than destructive; that they are not *born* debauched, but are debauched later; that the values of our civilization are not the *result* of its recent history, but the cause; and, at the last, that only the drive for love, which is in every man, is as strong as the drive toward death that now dements our world. Beyond this, it was Legman's bravely avowed belief in the passional side of the human being, his refusal to equivocate or euphemize in its defense and his insistence that it was "the central mystery and the central reality of life" that spoke so loudly to this young man, and set him thinking about far more than the special, idiosyncratic concerns of Legman's work.

And the man? The man made me realize (paralyzed, as I felt, by that suspicion of powerlessness to affect events which was perhaps the war's subtlest and most damaging legacy to people of my age) that all the causes had not been fatally compromised by neuroses or *realpolitik*. There was one more cause, perhaps the Last Cause of all: oneself (the besieged human person) and the stubborn flower of one's sex that resists, even when nothing else can or will, the dead concrete pavements of depersonalization which our age seems intent on laying over everything.

For here was a penniless David challenging the Goliaths of publishing. Here was a single, obscure individual saying a defiant "no" to the world in the name of its victims. Here was a man who spoke up for cats, who was appalled for children, who made delicate things with awkward and loving fingers. And here was a moustachioed "eccentric" who insisted that a writer's sole responsibility was to indict his time if he found it wanting, never to collaborate with the Enemies of Life (even when they became internalized), and to do all this alone, unaided, and despised by everyone, if need be.

I remember him with fondness now, and some suspicion that he will find this "no better than he expected" if he reads it. But I also remember Landesman saying not long ago: "Legman had a staggering effect on me. He utterly changed my life, and I was devoted to his way of thinking. In those days, he was the only revolutionary around." Which was approximately what he meant to me too—a part of me at least—at a time when I was being shaped more conclusively than I would realize for years.

What I have written here, from the vantage of a very different life than any I could have imagined then, may add up to no more than a message of friendship to an old comrade. But it is no less than that either.

Three: The Pop Imagination

§ § Whenever I met Jay Landesman in a bar in the old days, I always seemed to arrive first. I waited around, and far from being piqued, I discovered that I was experiencing a pleasant little ping-ping-ping of anticipation. What I was anticipating was laughter.

Black laughter. Like the idea of a cigarette smoking a man, or *Dr. Strangelove.* . . . Absurd laughter. Oh—like a camel in sneakers, beaded Art Nouveau lamps that play "Valencia," Andy Warhol. . . . Pertinent laughter. You know, like, "Laugh? I thought I'd *die*," the cobalt bomb, Lenny Bruce. . . . Laughter accompanied by the sound of hot air escaping from reality's punctured balloons.

When I think of things like this, I always think of Landesman. Not because he was a wit. There wasn't a proper epigram in him. Nor one of those living-room Berles, machinegunning everyone with gags. It was that he saw everything on the bias. It was that everything he did had an air of elaborate burlesque about it.

For instance, his six-button jackets with the multiple vents and triple lapels. His stuffed alligator with the lamp in its jaws. His study in St. Louis that was a facsimile of an old Von Sternberg set in all its claustrophobic proliferation of unrelated dreck. *Neurotica*, for instance—so outrageous in its time that you automatically assumed he must have started it for the same reason that other people suddenly decide to throw a wild party. It was like daring the *Partisan Review*niks to go skinny-dipping.

Or ASCA (The Advanced School of Cultural Analysis), with all those spoofing lectures on sports cars, drinking, jazz, conformity and other "aspects," which seemed to be nothing more than a deadpan excuse for Sunday afternoon cocktail parties. Or the Crystal Palace Cabaret Theater in St. Louis, created by Landesman and his brother for the simple reason (one couldn't help but feel) that it didn't already exist, and they needed an arena in which to "make things hot." Or Landesman's musical, *The Nervous Set*, that got to Broadway, perhaps too soon, and died—funny, irreverent, a parody of the Beat Generation. Or was it? You kept remembering lines from it, you kept humming those songs. And you laughed.

You did. You laughed at all this. You said, "Good old Jay. What the hell kind of wild stunt will he pull off next?" You always looked forward to seeing him, and what he pulled off next was always more outlandish than you had anticipated. . . . A Twist Room that must have been one of the first authentic discothèques in America. Or a TV gab-show that opened with a shot of Landesman's firehouse shoes, and then panned up to a wry smile that suddenly admitted, "Talk is cheap." Or a musical version of *Dracula*.

A million laughs, all right. A hip, sardonic mind behind it. No doubt of that. Landesmania, his friends called it. A life style that was a wacky amalgam of Hellzapoppin, Theater of the Absurd, and Pop Art. But serious? You must be kidding. . . . I mean, I once saw him wear magenta Bermudas and a pith helmet. He planned a lecture entitled "Abortive Attempts at Middle-Class Rebellion." He was often heard to say things like, "George Raft in a dinner jacket looks like a stolen Bentley." And take his parties! There was something fiendish about them. . . . Chandler Brossard and James Jones in the same room. Hostility games. Come as your favorite perversion. Confess your first homosexual experience. He was a wrecker, he was frivolous, he was—well, just think of going up to Dorothy Kilgallen on Madison Avenue and saying, "This is Sin Street, Madam, get off it!" Or naming your kids Cosmo and Miles Davis. It was all prankishness, eccentricity, maladjusted *chutzpah*. And yet—

And yet there was that damn underlayer to all of it. His

projects all seemed to have a disturbing half-life that lingered in the mind like Strontium-90 in the bone. His personal preoccupations had the maddening habit of becoming cultural tendencies ten years later. You never took him seriously at the time, and you were never sure that he did either, and then all of a sudden everywhere you went in New York during the sixties there was a sort of public version of Landesmania. But where was Landesman? He had moved to England, and he wrote back mysteriously, "I see a kind of blurring of the sexual lines. . . . But no matter how you slice it, ducks, it's all love. . . . " And you started to keep your eyes open, craftily, for that one to reach the surface.

After knowing Landesman for seventeen years, I still find it difficult to explain him to a stranger. A tall, shambling man, who has the warm, inquisitive dark eyes and the self-mocking smile of a secret idealist; who speaks in a glib, exaggerated *patois* of show biz lingo, psychiatric gobbledegook, and Negro and Yiddish slang, all blended into a contagious argot of his own, Landesman has been variously described as "a puppetmaster with an aggressive *lack* of talent," "the Mike Todd of dying cities," and "a genie with a certain sense of merchandising." There is a bit of truth in all these estimates, but the whole truth is not there.

For myself, I would say that Landesman possessed, years before it was either chic or marketable, what would now be called the Pop Imagination. In a culture where everything is mass-produced, quickfrozen, readymade, precooked or painted-by-the-numbers, he was the first person I knew who refused such a society's categorical choice of either remaining an esthete or becoming a vulgarian. For any and all evidences of a unique and unconventional point of view interested him, and he looked for these evidences in junk shops, movie houses, and newsstands (wherever his own quirky eye led him), as well as in bookstores, art galleries and theaters. In that Stone Age (ten or fifteen years back), when enlightened people sat in their Eames chairs, under their Calders, talking about T. S. Eliot, Landesman was already living in a thicket of Victorian bric-a-brac, and publishing Allen Ginsberg. I suspect his reasons for doing both were very much the same: he believed in indulging his own curiosity, and only things that were counter, wry, eccentric, special and excessive stimulated him.

Having grown up into (and through) a family antique business, Landesman believed that artifacts were sometimes more evocative of their times than ideas. Things had an uncanny aura to him, and clutter made him feel at ease. The first sight that confronted you on entering his New York apartment was a huge sculpture of Noah's Ark fashioned from half the gunwhale of a cat boat. Over his desk in St. Louis hung a spray-painted jock strap in a gilt frame, and he always worked warmly insulated behind mountains of books, magazines, record albums and any other nameless effluvia that had caught his eye. As a consequence, it was impossible to imagine him living for long in the functional Gobi of a modern house, and he could be painfully hilarious when a guest in one.

Equally, eccentricity of attire was evidence of soul to him, and one ceased being surprised when he turned up in "horrible" candy-striped seersuckers and a string tie that hung down to his crotch, or sporting a denim sack suit in an advanced state of rumple. Such props were as expressive of his personal vision of things as anything he said, for, as he once confided with a dim smile, "Every time I see a man in jodhpurs and an opera hat—and it only happens two or three times a month these days, I always go up and speak to him, because that man isn't going to hang you up about the weather." Sometimes this flair for the eccentric was only inches this side of outright perversity ("the three-lapel jacket—yes, that was a very important project"), but most of the time Landesman was that unique phenomenon in a status-drunk society: a man who knew that the only really hip style is the next one, the one that hasn't been established yet.

He had an omnivorous interest in popular culture, and long before it was High Camp to collect back issues of *Batman* and idolize the horror movies of Tod Browning, he was publishing articles that anatomized the one, and scouring the most dismal reaches of Brooklyn for screenings of the other. Like many of us in the late forties, he felt that the fine arts were so tyrannized by one or another version of the New Criticism that they had become little more than lifeless appendages of it, but, unlike a lot of people in later years, he shifted his attention to the popular arts without sacrificing his sense of the culture as a whole.

The idea that there is something intrinsically worthwhile about the soup cans, science-fiction movies, mammoth billboards and electronic noise that inundates our civilization (an extremely fashionable idea just recently) would have struck Landesman as being hopelessly frivolous. These things were interesting to him only insofar as they indicated the condition of our imaginations, a condition that could not be perceived if we celebrated the signs of its poverty merely for themselves. "Popular culture never lies," he used to say. "Not about the people who consume it," among whom I'm sure he would have included Susan Sontag as well as the stenographer down the hall.

For it was popular culture's unconscious embodiment of inner fantasies that attracted Landesman. He revelled in it, he let it stimulate his rarer appetites for the bizarre, but he never patronized it in the manner of Camp, and his ear was always cocked for the psychic throb within it—seismographic evidences of which filled the pages of *Neurotica*.

As its editor, Landesman's greatest gift probably lay in getting other people to track down and amplify the whispers he had heard. This wasn't laziness, nor inability to do the job himself, but simply a canny understanding that what he could best contribute to the magazine was a general intuition about the culture, and a Hawkshaw-knack for ferreting out people who could particularize that intuition into usable knowledge. Though there were several assistant editors, all of whom did most of the comma-shifting and phrase-haggling, the magazine showed little of their influence—with the single exception of Legman. For Landesman knew precisely what he wanted from the start. He wanted articles like "The World of the Borderline Fetishist," and "Psychiatrist: God or Demitasse?" and "The Unique Mores of the Bar and Tavern Social Milieu"—all of which existed in the beginning only as titles, to which the articles themselves were more or less jerry-written by other people later.

Also he knew the audience he was trying to reach. "I'm not publishing for the three dozen hard-core scatologists along 42nd

Street or the little magazine crowd that tells their Shrinks that, of *course*, they consider *Neurotica* too sick to read. I want to get to the five thousand people who really make this society go—the opinion-makers, the guys with the crazy power, the Sell-Outs who are responsible for running the mess in the first place."

It is highly debatable whether *Neurotica* ever succeeded in achieving this aim (despite the fact that, to my knowledge, it is the only little magazine whose entire run of issues was republished in book form a full decade after its demise), but certainly, in Legman, Landesman found someone with the same muckraking appetites, and they worked together like a couple of unemployed dynamiters trying to blow up the Time-Life Building with a firecracker. I tagged along behind them, as did others.

But for all the barefoot crusades of those *Neurotica* days, it is the sheer excitement, the high pitch of fun, that I have remembered longest. It is the laughter that rose through the smoke to the ten-foot ceiling of Landesman's brownstone apartment on West 53rd Street, where we worked together through the late mornings, writing "Alfred Towne's" exposés of homosexuality in American culture. It is Landesman in his undershirt deciding that we should describe "Towne" as "a midwesterner who has left the country," and the afternoons we fueled our gleeful outrage (at what "Towne" humorlessly insisted on calling "the effeminization of values") with lunchtime gin and staggering corned beef sandwiches from the Stage Delicatessen around the corner. It is remembering how laboriously we fashioned our Mile Wide Hints about such-and-such a conductor; and how lecherously we stripped our scandalous aspersions (concerning so-and-so's penchant for drag) down to their last veil; and with what giggling thoroughness we mapped that murky territory of innuendo just this side of libel.

It all seems a little silly today, a little farfetched (though "fearless" articles almost identical to those "Alfred Towne" published in *Neurotica* and *The American Mercury* still appear all these fifteen years later), and yet from those hoarse and smoky afternoons I think we both distilled, for ourselves at least, a sense that we were engaging the real Scene that lay buried somewhere under the glum hypocrisies and lofty nonsense that passed for a serious culture then.

And, anyway, those afternoons led inevitably toward five o'clock, and five o'clock inevitably brought people: Anatole Broyard with that week's facsimile of the Broyard-girl—blonde, tooled, wordless—changing as little, version to version, as Anatole changed from year to year; Robert Lowry as big and bearish in his corduroys as a grizzly with the face of a panda; Marshall McLuhan (when he was in town) improvising ideas like a combination Spengler, Picasso and Mort Sahl; little, zany William Poster with his clear, darting eye for subtle values; Chandler Brossard as difficult to crack as a horse chestnut and just as tart when you did; Paul Mazursky doing his funny Brando imitations while Stanley Radulovich did his serious ones; Carl Solomon yoinking around so frenziedly on a pogo stick that one night he put the end of it right through the floor into the restaurant below—and all their girls, and their friends' girls, and their friends' friends, and even nameless others who may have just heard the hubbub and walked in the door.

These five o'clocks always got to be ten o'clocks somehow, and we found ourselves in Birdland, or up at the Park Palace in Spanish Harlem, or in Glennon's practicing what Landesman called "futility rites," or down at Louis' in the Village. Landesman was tablehopping, or mamboing with great flung feet and stabbing hands. Landesman was ankling off to phone, or being loudly paged by the bartender, having told half a dozen people just where he would be, and when to call.

Mostly, he was always somewhere near the center of a throng of people when I saw him, but one night I found him alone in his apartment, except for a dark-gold girl named Fran, her face luminous with the hip chick's soulfulness; a girl who bore an astonishing resemblance to Zelda Fitzgerald—only lovelier, softer, more remote; a girl who looked as if she had been tagged early, and *become* herself in the act of surviving it; the kind of girl with a certain pang behind her intelligence and her chic; the kind of girl you marry if you know your own hangups well enough. A month or so later, Landesman did just that, and almost immediately they became "Jay and Fran" to everyone who knew them, one name all but unpronounceable without the other.

Soon after this, Landesman grew bored with hunting the culture's various psychic Snarks, for, unlike Legman, he was not imprisoned by a single perception, and world-changing was not his wine. That singular geiger counter in his head was geared to himself and his personal interests (which he took to be representative), and when there was no click in his current life, he always began to look elsewhere.

Also, by 1951, there was Fran, and their marriage; there was a growing need for a setting where the results of an action could be immediately seen, and there was New York that is never hospitable to this need. In one of those abrupt decisions that make us look at our friends through new eyes, Landesman gave *Neurotica* to Legman, and he and Fran moved back to St. Louis.

Thereafter, the trait that had distinguished everything that Landesman had done surfaced in him rapidly, until it became clear that what drove him (and drives the Pop Imagination generally) was an overriding theatrical sense—a sense of how to put a point of view on display, how to isolate a falsehood so that it could be seen, how to reveal a subtle truth through sheer exaggeration. Landesman's need was to enliven life by "staging" it, to strike creative sparks by rubbing people and ideas together, and, above all, to satisfy a curiosity that was as gluttonous as a Dempster Dumpster. To Landesman, existence was a series of Happenings, or he got glum. Ultimately, his need was for a theater, and St. Louis became that theater for him.

What followed was the Crystal Palace ("the most gorgeous saloon in America"), and the plays, and ASCA, and the TV show. What followed were the lyrics that Fran began to write one day that were set to music by Tommy Wolf, Alec Wilder, and Roy Kral (those sad, wry, sexy leider—like "Listen Little Girl," "Fun Life," and "Spring Can Really Hang You Up the Most—" that resembled nothing so much as the fragrant, whimsical, intimate contents of an evening purse, belonging to a girl who is as interesting to talk to as to lie with, spilled out on the dressing table of another, inevitable dawn), and the need for a showcase in which these songs could be displayed. And what followed that was *The Nervous Set*, with book by Landesman, and all the other shows that made St. Louis, for a few brief years, a town that people visited for more than beer and baseball.

When I conjure up such a visit, I am sitting in Landesman's living room, or in the patio behind his house, or in any one of a dozen apartments nearby that he and his brother kept for "their people"; music is providing its throbbing insulation against the discordant world outside (more than likely little-known show tunes, or bossa nova, or good rock); martinis are being stirred in a huge pitcher, making that velvety sound of ice cushioned by gin; there are half a dozen people around, all of whom give off the indescribable air of being members of Landesman's *troupe*; children yodel at a TV program upstairs; later (I know) there will be a dinner party somewhere under a chandelier or among enormous imitation trees, during which everyone will be brighter and wittier and sexier than he really is, and later still, Gaslight Square and the Palace, Lenny Bruce or Samuel Beckett, and crowds of people who seem to know me simply because I know Landesman.

I am sitting there, nicely mulled, astonished by the realization that I am in the midst of a community within a community—a community with its own theaters, bars, restaurants, apartments and galleries, all reflecting the same life style, the same brand of restless and bizarre intelligence. I am amazed, because I have never known its exact like before, but I am also happily expectant (the way I used to be at Billy Wilder movies, the way I still am when I listen to Thelonious), for I know that no matter what happens in the hours ahead, it will be funny, hip, mordant, noisy and meaningful: the stuff of a good memory.

Landesman's sense of theater permeated this whole community, and infected anything he spent five minutes on. He always answered the phone with a crisp, "Jay L-a-n-d-esman here!" lingering sonorously on his own name, as one does every time one says a name like Walther von der Vogelweide. He introduced outlandish soubriquets for everyone, some of them so maddeningly adhesive that they simply absorbed the actual person, like a kind of verbal Venus flytrap. I remember, for instance, a five-foot-two chutney salesman who was known to me only as The Lord God, a buxom flip of a girl from the Ozarks called Dearest Little, and a hip-talking layout man invariably referred to as F. Scott Fredsegal.

The cocktail hour was orchestrated like an *opéra-bouffe*— music, and booze, and just the right mix of jarring people, all of it calculated to produce an unexpected and sometimes scandalous denouement. Gossip flitted around the room in a balletic counterpoint that intensified the odd feeling of theatricality. There was something overheated and incestuous about these liquid twilights, for Landesman believed that strong personalities, acting on one another in an artificial setting, inevitably would generate the kind of drama out of which recognitions came, and he frankly manipulated "his people" toward this end.

There were animosities a-plenty; there was a more or less continual game of musical beds going on; new "stars" were taken up, old ones dropped; games of charades somehow always ended in group therapy sessions; parties quickly became psychodramas; and there are people from those days who probably have no desire to ever hear the name Landesman again. In my opinion, however, Landesman's habit of playing the social Diaghilev was ultimately more creative than destructive (how thin the line!). For its spur was not merely boredom, but rather a desire to break through all the masks, and heighten his sense of life as being openended, dangerous with possibilities, free; a sense that later drew him naturally toward Zen, LSD and consciousness-expansion in general. In any case, people seemed to "perform" a little beyond their usual talents when they were around Landesman. At least, most of them still refer to those days with the unmistakable accents we reserve for the description of an enlarging experience, and Landesman spoke to a vein of ironical decadence which, in those pious, prosperous years, ran deep in all of us. For in the struggle of progress versus decay, Landesman frankly opted for the latter, and this, I believe, was the closest he came to having a guiding principle. It was also the dark secret of his appeal.

Out of the loftiest of intentions, the lust for progress has created the shallowest of worlds, and even the most optimistic of social engineers must sometimes wake up after midnight, disturbed by a vague but persistent nostalgia for something that is not covered in the manuals. As a result, people of my generation instinctively gravitated to the margins, the corners, the backstreets of contemporary experience, hoping to gain a little human time before the automated bulldozers of the future arrived. A lot of us felt twinges of guilt about this, but there was no arguing with the fact that, though we were *for* progress, it profoundly depressed us; and as the steel and glass "environments" went up, we tended to withdraw to whatever "neighborhoods" were left.

Landesman was usually there before us, getting out the gin, and busily poking at the pomposities of a culture so traduced that it equated the Good only with the Useful. This was why he had gone back to St. Louis in the first place, for St. Louis in the fifties was a dying city (hopelessly stratified by outmoded social distinctions, its growth paralyzed by civic ordinances that were as hoary as its architecture), and its prevailing mood can best be compared to the mood of pre-Castro Havana: lethargy, somnolence and a faint whiff of corruption hung in the air that wafted off the big river. It was precisely the sort of scene in which a canny and energetic provocateur could make his move, and almost before they knew it, the burghers and the debutantes found a minor, but authentic, cultural renaissance flourishing under their very noses—*Krapp's Last Tape* instead of the usual *South Pacific*, and "Squareville U.S.A.: A New Look At Main Street" in place of the standard lecture on rubbernecking in Angkor Wat.

For a while a few luxuriant poinsettias bloomed among the crumbling buildings and the blistered streets. But cultural renaissances cannot hold out for long against America's twin fixations of the moment—urban renewal and civic betterment —and St. Louis eventually voted for progress as represented by the wrecker's ball and the touring company. You *knew* a Broadway musical was good (hadn't you read about it in *The New Yorker*?), and every city, with any pride in itself, was erecting those distinctive air-conditioned saltine boxes. But how did you *know* what to feel about the murky and controversial plays the

Landesmans put on? And those old waterfront buildings, some of them going back a hundred and fifty years or more—they were only eyesores that never ceased to remind you that you lived in a backward little city in Hicksville. So as the Saarinen Arch (The Gateway to the West) relentlessly went up, Landesman's flamboyant banner, on which might have been emblazoned the frank admonition, "Onward and Downward!" fluttered to the pavement. And in another of those abrupt uprootings, which were the surest sign that it was never comfort that he prized, but creative *room*, he went east. All the way east. All the way to London.

Landesman chose decay, I firmly believe, because of what he knew. He knew himself, and he knew what interested him, and he knew in what exotic mulch those interests had a chance of coming to full flower. Also, he knew precisely how he had to live to prevent the contradictions in his nature (an artist's nature, even though he sometimes lacked an art—that is to say, a reckless, inquisitive, ultimately unsatisfiable nature) from becoming stalemated in a struggle that he knew he could only *lose*. For underlying his imagination, his theatricality, and his "decadence," was something considerably more rare: a man cursed with a keenly contemporary sensibility and all its exaggerated appetites, living out, in himself, most of the psychic displacements and realignments, which, in this time, often suggest that a new and wider human consciousness is on the road to its Bethlehem to be born.

Beyond this, one can only speculate, but my speculation tells me that it was a radical notion of sex that stood behind most of Landesman's "projects." For when I think of him, I always think of that black, iconoclastic humor that we all possessed, or at least recognized instantly, in those days; that humor which said, "It isn't that way. That isn't the way it is. We all know how it *really* is"; that humor dubbed "sick" by a society so Orwellian that it actually confused the diagnosis with the disease. I think Landesman knew, as well, that in a situation so existentially false that black humor is the only intelligent saving response, that humor always tends to reflect the secret intuition that sexuality is somehow the last sanctuary of the Real; a final frontier that no passports, visas or customs can prevent us from crossing in order to discover (in the danger and the dark on the other side) what it is like to be fully and mysteriously alive. I think Landesman ceaselessly experimented, dared to "act out," engineered new and disturbing situations, and always put *himself* on the line, because he worked at his life the way writers work at a book, and always assumed (often wrongly) that everyone else was as seriously involved in the search as he.

For, above all, I think he *was* serious. He was serious about marriage, for instance—so serious that he tried to discover a new sort of basis on which it could survive in an Age of Splitsville, a basis that would embody *all* the contradictory urges of love and power, ego and self, which (far from representing abnormality in our century) are the very norm from which we must begin; and his marriage to Fran, which survived enough upheavals to wreck any relationship with the slightest bit of deceit in it, was probably the single marriage that I knew about that I would have made book would last. If, as he got older, he was less and less concerned with challenging the powers that be, influencing the age and competing in the arena (hadn't we all seen the "issues" come and go, despite the tireless energy and high hopes that were expended on them?), it was probably because he eventually came to believe that there was no direction left for us to take, except down into the cavern of ourselves where all the "issues" start. And if he became more hedonistic, less success-driven, and occasionally an advocate of avant-garde sex mores, I think it was because he suspected that the most farreaching revolution of our generation would probably turn out to be the Sexual Revolution—predicated, as it was, on a conception of the totally unsuppressed human being, and promising, as it did, an end to the duality of which all the "issues" were only the bitter, cerebral end products.

"What I really want," he once said, "is reasonably simple. I want economic security, I want to be around beautiful women who smell good, and I want to stay creative. It seems to me, more and more, that this means adjusting, not to the society, but to the springs of life itself—insofar as you can know them by knowing yourself. Beyond that, I guess what I want is to do everything twice." Knowing him, there is nothing very unreasonable in this.

To me, Landesman represented a side of my generation, and its experience, that I have only come to fully appreciate as we have all gotten older and less amusing. The game-playing, style-enamoured, pomposity-puncturing side. The side that practiced its "futility rites" with so much energy, and wit, and unconscious courage. The funny, hip, mordant, noisy, meaningful side. Not the deepest side perhaps; too impatient and too facile, too continually *aware* of everything, to pause for the probe to ultimate causes. But a side that lived intensely up to its times, nevertheless.

In any case, on those flawless spring mornings when anxiety or exhilaration makes me feel that only a drink in a sunny, uncrowded, old-fashioned barroom will put an egg in my day, I always think of phoning Landesman, and urging a lunch. The talk won't be solemn or profound, but its surface will shimmer with a mind that knows where we have been, and where we are now; a mind that has always found life interesting and a little absurd, but has never lost its taste for the adventure. The people who will turn up later are likely to be tough-minded, attractive, and up on things. They will carefully consider what to drink, and make the smart decision. They will pull their own weight, and won't have to have anything explained to them. And for a few hours, I will have a very keen sense of all of us there together—heirs of a fairly bad world, who have lived through it with some grace, and not made it any worse.

Sometime during those hours, Landesman is bound to say to me: "We've got us a big talk coming one of these days, Johnnie. . . ," always a sign to me that he is feeling warm, expansive, hurried and affectionate. And I will think (as I always do) that we really have no need of that talk. I know where he is going, and I know why. His restless eye—for the fun, and the nerves, and the girls of his time—has always given him away.

Four:

§ § The second night of the July 4th weekend, 1948, was even sultrier than the first, and the east side streets smelled like a closet that hadn't been opened in a year. The body under the clothes was coated with a thin, oily sweat no matter what you did; there was a hint of siege in the motionless air; and anyone who was left in town deserved to feel like a bona fide survivor. As a consequence, there were a lot of sudden, reckless parties up and down town that night—those unplanned celebrations (created in an hour out of a telephone and a foundation of beer) that are typical of a century with nothing much to celebrate.

We were on our way to such a party in Spanish Harlem— Alan Harrington and I (by then good friends, and both, as it happened, wifeless for the three-day weekend), and as we waited for the bus to move ponderously toward our corner through the empty pools of street light along York Avenue, he told me that "these new people"—people he had met a few weeks before—were giving the party, and had urged him to bring along anyone he wanted. Though "their" crowd (vaguely centered around Columbia and Times Square) had recently moved onto the edges of "our" crowd (warrened along Third Avenue and down in the Village), I hadn't met any of them yet, and only knew that most of them were younger, wilder, poorer and less settled into job and girl than most of *us*.

The midtown avenues, emptied by the holiday and the heat, gradually gave way to the guitars, crowded stoops, damp undershirts and quick angers of those thronging streets (under their haze of frying beans) that no one escapes simply because it is hot, and we threaded our way down the chalked pavements of a particularly active block, wondering if we were on the right one.

"This must be it, all right," Harrington said. "There's Kerouac."

I knew about Kerouac. He had written a thousand-page novel that was being passed around "our" crowd just then in a battered doctor's bag. Everyone who had seen it, and him, was enthusiastic, and five very different people had expressed that enthusiasm to me in curiously similar terms. The book, they said, was unwieldy, overly lyrical, and needed structuring (we talked like that then, and felt very professional), but it was also compassionate, stunningly written and bursting with life. The man—well, the man was winning, and perhaps a little naive; at once a poet and an athlete; a combination of Jack Armstrong and Thomas Wolfe; in short (I gathered), an original. I surveyed the people moving in and out of the sleazy little grocery up ahead (dark, good-looking men in sport shirts, most of them, with bagsfull of beer), but saw no one I would have identified as the author of a novel, weighing twenty pounds in the hand, that was being seriously touted to publishers by people I respected.

But Kerouac *was* one of those men—the one who looked like the serious, tee-shirted younger brother of the others; the brother they were proud of because he played the violin as well as he played basketball; the young John Garfield back in the neighborhood after college, absolutely at ease there, but just as absolutely separated from it now by some weaning knowledge he could not communicate. He was making the run for more beer, he said with a hesitant smile, and, while Harrington bought a contribution of big, brown quarts, he and I talked a little there on the sidewalk.

I don't remember anything we said. It was probably no more than that gauging, neutral chat beneath which young men take each other's measure, but I do remember my first impression. Under the boyish forelock, his strangely tender brown eyes noted me as we spoke, but all the time I felt that he was more

keenly attuned to the tangled life of that street than to anything we were saying. It seemed to distract and stir him; he was
at once excited and somehow emptied by it. Though he was just
as straightforward, personable, buoyant and attractive as I had
been led to expect, there was a curious shyness under his
exuberance; there was the touch of a moody thought around his
mouth (like the reveller's sudden foretaste of the ashen dawn to
come), and, above all, there was that quietly impressive inten-
sity of consciousness. All of which made me understand my
friends' enthusiasm in a flash: he was so evidently on his way
toward some accomplishment, or some fate, that it was impossible not to warm to him immediately.

The three of us climbed dark, smelly stairways through a
hubbub of mambo and Spanish laughter toward the sounds of
bop and English talk. It was a good-size party already, because
already people were drinking in the halls. The apartment
belonged to a Columbia graduate student (there was an enclave
of them in the building), and it was a typical slum coldwater
flat—four or five ill-ventilated, cramped rooms of depressing
blue, opening off a stuffy kitchen; damp plaster, dripping taps,
worn linoleum, soggy couches; collected editions of the seven-
teenth-century poets, a pawnshop cavalry saber and a dusty
typewriter with a page of thesis in it.

I don't remember it as an unusual party. Later, there were
other parties in that same apartment that are indistinguishable
from this one in my memory. Later, too, this same party was
held in other apartments (down in Chelsea or the Village) that
are equally indistinguishable to me now from the one in
Spanish Harlem. For at all these parties, everyone drank with
thirsty bravado, everyone talked in a mad uprush of youthful
egos; all the arguments were harmless, and nothing important
was broken. The bop defined us to ourselves as a special,
afterdark fraternity, and eventually burned away the character
armor that made the day so glum. And somehow those nights
always managed to last beyond the hour of bad dreams.

But all I remember about this particular night is that someone set off firecrackers in the ashtrays, and someone else,
teetering on the fire escape, sailed the empties down through
washlines to the garbage cans below. There were too many

people (most of whom I came to know well in the next year) for me to recall any longer just who was there and who was not. I don't remember any of them, except for the slight, aquiline young man, looking like an inquisitive dormouse in his black-rimmed glasses, his nostrils all but quivering, squirrel-like, with an abundance of awareness and delight, everything about him somehow *charged,* who came out of the crowd, greeted Harrington with exaggerated formality, and said to me, "I'm Allen Ginsberg. Who are you?"—following this with a funny little whinny of a laugh just in case I took it as effrontery.

For an hour or two after that, I assumed it must be his apartment, so naturally did he take on the finding of glasses and the making of introductions, and, now that I think of it, I remember that he was the one with the firecrackers. In any case, I know that at one point I was leafing through the Nonesuch edition of Dryden, trying to deduce (as I still do) the owner's secret preoccupations from his underlinings, when all at once Ginsberg was at my elbow, with a pleased glint in his eyes that suggested he was deducing me from my habit of deduction. He immediately began talking about Kerouac.

"Have you read *The Town and the City* yet? . . . Oh, you must. . . . Get Stringham to give it to you when he's finished. Or I'll see if I can't locate the other copy. . . . It's full of these crazy poems, it's really a big hymn, you see. . . . And *I'm* in it, too. . . . You ought to read it immediately, it's very important."

Though they were obviously close friends, influencing one another back and forth, each catalyzing the other with their very differences, Ginsberg spoke of Kerouac rather as an agent might speak of a client with whom he is personally involved, but never fails to "represent" in the professional sense because of that. I realized, all at once, that he knew that I was a writer too (and so might have usable connections), and he didn't intend to pass up an opportunity to cultivate anyone who might be helpful.

Still, I didn't feel that he was conning me. His enthusiasm for the book was as real as his affection for the man. It was just that he made no separation between the two. His manner implied that because his friends were fascinating, original and talented (they wouldn't have been his friends otherwise, would they?), their books and poems must be fascinating, original and talented as well. Certain Kerouac was an authentic innovator, he served as his advance man as a matter of course.

Beyond this, I liked him. By all rights he should have been as painfully shy, myopic, scholarly and withdrawn as four or five other bespectacled, sallow young men who sulked in the corners of that party, looking like rabbinical students caught in a burlesque show. But instead he was excitable, infectious, direct. He said whatever came into his head, he brought himself frankly out before you, he slyly mocked you by mocking himself, and then he would abruptly ask, "But where's your wife? What's she like? Does she *approve* of you? What would she think of *me*, for instance?"

Soon, he hurried off to light his firecrackers under the party, during the uproar over which Kerouac and I exchanged a glance across the room, an encouraging glance on his part, that urged me to see the "interesting little guy" behind Ginsberg's antics. Later, when we talked, he said, "He always does things like that—just to get things going. But he's a big poet, you know. Oh, yes. He's all involved with visions and apocalpyses."

Each talked mainly about the other that night, a fact that probably accounted for my feeling that they must be part of a new group that was emerging, independent of the established intellectual life of the city, and somehow more vital, more life-engaged for that very reason.

There is the danger of hindsight, of course, but I know that when I left that party some time after three, I was aware that if I remembered it at all, it would be because I had met these two men. I liked Kerouac instinctively. He knew something that I didn't know, he was already himself whereas I was still forming, and I felt strongly that we would be friends. It had nothing to do with his work (about which I knew nothing at firsthand); it had to do with an immediate feeling of kinship between us, which I couldn't have described then, and didn't even properly understand. Ginsberg was easier for me. I suppose I thought that he was probably the better writer. He used that year's prevailing literary lingo, he was aware of the current scene, and this is the basis on which 22-year-old tyros make their famous judgments. But he seemed to have a special eye as well, and I had liked his stumping for Kerouac, taking it as a sign of his *own* seriousness. All in all, they impressed me, they intrigued me. There was a vividness about them, in their different ways, that spoke to me. But certainly I had no suspicion that something had begun that night that is not over yet.

Five: The Consciousness Widener

§ § Energy, a manic verbal energy pouring out of the mouth, a feverish energy of mind with which words cannot keep pace, that inexhaustible *flux* of a consciousness in the act of exploding outward: when I think of Ginsberg, it is this raw, psychic energy that flickers behind my personal images.

I remember him roving up and down the rugless, creaking floor of my apartment at 681 Lexington Avenue, a spare, hunched, tireless shape driving back and forth between me and the soot-smudged windows of a bleak autumn afternoon in 1948, the long, high-ceilinged room an undersea blur of cigarette smoke, his fluent and absorbed voice droning on and on in what I think of now as a single long sentence that trailed behind him in an undulating wraith of words, his mind erupting out of his parched lips with such involuntary convulsions that he kept moving up and down, as if combatting nausea.

His small, quick, lucid eyes glowed yellow behind the glasses; a sudden nasal laugh, at once macabre and frightened, would break into the words now and then, as if he had heard them as I was hearing them, and wanted me to know he knew. Then he would stare expressionlessly out the window, still talking, but all the while watching the traffic that gnashed and roared so witlessly down in the dark cavern of the street, seeing (though I didn't know it then)

"the motionless buildings
of New York rotting
under the tides of Heaven,"

§ 53

against which his mind struggled, like King Canute, to prevent an inundation in his consciousness.

He was only twenty-two then; his face was pinched with coffee and cigarettes and speculation; and perhaps only young men can turn abstract ideas so easily into ecstasies and premonitions as he did that day. He was talking about God, emanations, Blake, corporeality, visions, Cezanne, transfiguration, madness, prophecy. Everything his eye lit on (my pictures, my books, a sudden wan shaft of sunlight that pierced the gloom) instantly became a sinister symbol, a mystical clue, a further scrap of evidence. A baleful atmosphere, like the atmosphere of an Hieronymus Bosch, bathed the twisted images his mind spewed forth; spiritual hunger burned out of his sallow, thralled face as it must have in Dostoyevski's consumptive student, Ippolit; and I recall my growing alarm, as the hours passed, to see that mind gathering itself into a fist of maddened concentration, which a few weeks later (or a few weeks before—I no longer remember) triggered his Harlem Visions—those hallucinations of spirituality and carnality, all intermixed, of which he would write an exact and literal transcription in the poem, "The Lion for Real," and which constituted the defining inner experience of his adult life.

I watched him storm himself with the hurricane of his own thoughts, I watched him helplessly observe himself nearing the brink of some fissure in his soul, and that afternoon, for the first time, I glimpsed the gnaw that has always kept him on his extraordinary adventure. The adventure that has led him, since, to scour the world, travelling on pennies more widely than anyone else I know with dollars, so that whenever I see him he has always just arrived back, or is just departing; that adventure that always makes me place him in my mind's eye in Kenya, Tibet, Peru or Thule; illuminated under the bridges of Paris, pelted with shoes in Oxford, naked in Hollywood, bearded in Saigon, walking the savage roads of the Peloponnesus, masturbating in a hammock in Yucatán, selflessly sampling all *narcotiques du pays*, his own body the *tabula rasa* on which his mind writes; ranging through cultures and mysteries like an insatiable literary jackal, as if the nerves of a Rimbaud were harnessed to the immense, synthesizing vision of a Spengler;

presenting himself (the penniless, ragged hobo-seeker) at the doors of Suzuki, Buber, Castro or Cendrars, as well as countless nameless gurus, sadkis, hashishans, revolutionists and visionaries, to ask them their opinion of the riddle of the universe; noting the crescents of dirt under the fingernails of the odorous Celine, leaving poems for Apollinaire on his grave in Père Lachaise, imagining the clotheshanger in the bleak closet of the room where Vachel Lindsay murdered himself; writing endless, chaotic, relentlessly cheerful letters to everyone, imprecating them to care for each other, to *know* more extravagantly, to be braver than they are; scribbling me (as an example) a note that reached me in the dreary steppes of winter Iowa, begging an act of friendship for a young Calcutta poet, marooned there amid the American corn.

Energy, energy, and under it all those omnivorous hungers that glimmered through the ashen, fixed expression on his face that afternoon: the anguish of mortality at the recognition of itself, the loneliness of the orphaned flesh mired in its stinks and urges, the longing for unified Being back again after these pulverized decades "in the total animal soup of time." I saw how we humans tremble at the prospect of losing the very carapace of ego that has so tortured us that we make the attempt in the first place, I saw it in him. I saw him struggling to escape the pain, the revelation and the responsibility that lie beyond a mystical experience. And, above all, I heard in his obsessed monologue the howl of the divided spirit of our times, times (as he would describe them later) of "tenderness denied."

Later, his Visions would produce a series of poems (few of them published to this day) that were as weirdly compressed as the most enlayered of Donne or Smart; their metaphysic embodied in glassy images, like so many mirrors face to face, that gradually emptied the lines of everything but an enigmatic glitter; poems demented by their very lust for an absolute metric order; poems that were haunted by the awful question, "Am I to spend my life in praise of the *idea* of God?"

Later still, the Visions would drive him down through Times Square in a convertible, perched on the back of the seat like Lear's Fool imitating General MacArthur, declaiming "Sailing to Byzantium" to the drunks and tourists. He would read Blake

nonstop until finally Blake read to him. He would write and
write, and be mostly alone in the Warsaw of his own mind, no
matter how thronged the room.

And later, the poems and the life (and most of all the
promise of "the health of a unity of Being" which the Visions
held out to him, despite his human misgivings) led him to a
crackup, and a clinic, and psychoanalysis—some of the details
of which are described in "Go." The facts (if not the insights)
there are as accurate as one friend dares to be about the inner
life of another, and it only remains to be added that one day
almost a year later, he turned up at my apartment again, those
darting eyes somehow caged, wearing a wistful suit carefully
pressed in Madtown as preparation for the world of bus sched-
ules and logic, to chat idly, quietly for a few minutes, and then
say with a shy, offhand grin, "Oh, by the way, I'm sane. I've
broken into the world of sanity. . . . Yes, this last week all my
fantasies just evaporated into thin air, leaving—" with a small,
embarrassed chuckle, "well, just thin air, and solid objects." He
went on to talk manfully and gravely about the getting of jobs,
and the wooing and winning of girls, all of which he must go
through now "just like any high-school kid"—though he could
not keep a certain edge of loss and bewilderment out of these
resolutions.

Later, there were long talks about the need for "a new
literalness, and thus a new prosody" (he was studying Pound,
Lanier, W. C. Williams with his usual dogged, bone-worrying
persistence), talks which articulated a dissatisfaction with the
mechanical forms and empty ironies of current poetry that I
had been feeling as well—though my solution was to give up
writing verse altogether, while he persevered and finally broke
out of pentameter into speech.

Later, too, there was a sunny noontime meeting in (of all
unlikely places) Newark's city hall, when he came up to me, in
the crowd of Neal Cassady's "wedding party," to whisper with
manful eagerness, "Consummatum est!", having just come back
from a week in Provincetown with a girl.

Still later, the metaphysical speculations ebbed gradually back
again, now shorn of religious overtones, and it was on after-

noons with him in 1953 that I first heard of Zen, and it was during one night together that (unbeknownst to each other) we both asked the *I Ching* if the time had finally come for us to leave New York, receiving a "yes" that sent him off to Yucatán and me to Connecticut.

Years, travels, letters, a meeting now and then—during all of which he managed to jettison enough words to hear the breathing of his own unique spirit in the silence that ensued.

Reading "Howl" into my tape recorder in January, 1957, he sat crosslegged on the floor, rocking back and forth in the firelight, smoking with that sunk-cheek deep suck of his, his voice rising in hypnotic, singsong shrieks that suddenly ceased with the impatient comment, "Well, it goes on and on like that. As you know." There were mad, stumbling games of football with Kerouac and Orlovsky in the knee-deep snow. There was a new calm, almost a mellowness, about him, as if that envelope of human isolation out of which his quick eyes had always peered so hungrily had been pierced at last. There was also the young, drunken girl publicist, travelling with him (and other poets) on a reading tour, who whined over and over in my living room, "Oh, I know what he *says,* I know about Peter . . . But I'm sure I can make the difference, I know it in my own emotions," thereafter growing so teary and addled that Ginsberg finally put her to bed, staying with her through the nausea and the entreaties, and then came downstairs again to sleep on the couch I suppose (though I have never seen him sleep), because the house was full of poets making love. I imagine him sleeping with one eye open, weary and unresting, that mind going on and on. Alone.

So many sad, unhappy people he has outlasted in his nights— for when the rest of us flagged he always went on somewhere: to Harlem, to the Village, to the Ganges; to wake up some scholar, some junkie, some streetboy; to continue until he was burned down to the ashes of consciousness, and knew *one thing.* So much thwarted tenderness he has seen in the baffled eyes of his generation, and been so often, himself, unable to answer to it that many people would scoff at the very idea that

> "—one moment of tenderness
> and a year of intelligence
> and nerves: one moment of pure
> bodily tenderness—"

is what he looks for as an anodyne for our stricken spirits, poisoned by duality. These people see a different man, an imp of the perverse. They react like Verlaine's wife reacted to Rimbaud, recognizing a powerful, essentially virile will that is antithetical to their world.

A doctor-friend of mine (not a psychiatrist), after observing him for ten minutes some years ago, said categorically: "Over-psyched, permissive, under-controlled—I would almost use the word 'evil' if I knew what it meant. Bits and pieces! That's all your friend is. I don't think I want him around my kids." Norman Mailer, exhilarated at the time by that freedom to utter all the nasty words which overtakes the ex-radical like a fever, wrote of him:

> "I sometimes think
> that little Jew bastard
> that queer ugly kike
> is the bravest man
> in America,"

but somehow I don't think any part of that bravery had to do with tenderness in Mailer's view, for it is difficult, even for the most sympathetic observer, to glimpse the starved, resolute heart for which the furious rantings and outraged obscenities of some men are an implicit defense.

A close friend of mine, a novelist generally recognized to be a precursor of today's "black humorists," has always found Ginsberg to be too black for him. "Whenever he turns up, something bad happens to me," this very unsuperstitious man has said. "And, equally, whenever something bad happens to me, *he* always turns up. He has an unerring instinct for other people's disasters. I know that when I'm lying on my death bed I'll look up, and he'll be there, like some malevolent, clacking crow, asking how I'm feeling—obsequious, wanting to be pres-

ent when *It* happens, with his morbid sense of literary history.
. . . Look how he tried to get to Dylan Thomas in his hospital
room at the very end!"—an apocryphal story, but no less "true"
to my friend because of that. It is this same sense of history,
this self-conscious participation in events with a view to pos-
terity, to which Norman Podhoretz was probably referring
when he said: "Allen seems to think he's a latter-day Ezra
Pound. In his letters, I see the epistolary style of Pound, who
was always writing letters to editors, letters full of profanity,
encouraging them to publish his boys."

For myself, I have always felt that Ginsberg's improprieties
and propagandizing had their source, not so much in any
swollen idea of his own importance, much less in the poseur's
trivial morbidities and affectations, but in an absolutely sincere,
even naive belief in the value of friendship and literary work. If
he used to rush to people's bedsides, it was more in the style of
Shelley than Lautreamont, for in those days his sense of formality was at least as pervasive as his nosiness. And if he
endlessly pesters people about the poetry of some raw young
Lorca in Omaha, it is out of a disarmingly traditional notion of
one poet's duty to another, rather than any cabalistic power
play in the murky game of literary politics.

"But that's awful!" he exclaimed when I told him on the
phone that I was separated from my first wife. "Are you all
right? . . . I'll call her up immediately and take her out—
perhaps to the opera. I'll bet no one's thought to call her up."
No one much had, and I knew he did it (they had never been
particularly close) as much for me as for my wife—a civility
that is typical of him, if not of our graceless time.

But tenderness? Yes, for under it all—the insane verbal
avalanche of "Howl," the "scandalous" public disrobings, the
awesome organ tones that sound in "Kaddish," the kissing
of cops in the loveless streets, the doomed, prophetic bongs that
make "America" and "Death to Van Gogh's Ear" such
"hideous spiritual music"—under it all is the insistence on
tenderness again, and if you have not heard this in his work,
you have not heard his voice.

"We must never underestimate the charm of being human,"
he has said, having glimpsed, in the X-ray of the hallucinogens,

how we stir restlessly in the shroud of the ego, how our clocks pound our heads to pieces, how "the cannibal abstract" corrupts our dealings with one another, and yet—and yet, beneath it all he hears "the great call of Being to its own/ to come back out of the Nightmare—divided creation."

He hears it everywhere, like a vast arterial murmur swelling up under our snappish voices and our maudlin weeps. He sees it, as ecstatics immemorially have, behind the weary, hooded eyes hurrying through the atheist cities, and there is as much joy in his discovery of it as there is despair at our failure to heed it, in the exclamation (which breaks from him in "Magic Psalm"), "O Beauty invisible to my Century!" The alert will recognize the accent here, for at the outermost limits of consciousness, where mystics, madmen and those who travel inward atop the booster of chemistry all converge, there is One Tongue, and it always says the same thing—so literal it sounds incoherent, so simple it cannot be believed, and such a consolation that we instantly grow anxious about our precious "personalities": "We're not our skin of grime . . . We're blessed by our own seed . . . Holy the supernatural extra brilliant intelligent kindness of the soul!"

Of course, there are those to whom any such truth will always have the thud of a cliché. Leslie Fiedler, for instance, with the High Camp snobbery of a secretly disappointed man, accuses Ginsberg of having a naive and adolescent view of God, whereas it seems evident to me that Ginsberg has steadily moved beyond the orthodox religious preoccupations of his youth toward consciousness-expansion in general. The two are traditionally close—one always verging on the other, back and forth—and the startling similarity between the insights of mysticism on the one hand and depth-psychology on the other should no longer be news to anyone, including such mavericks in the trackless Montanas of literary criticism as Fiedler.

Religious obsession, consciousness-expansion, hallucinatory drugs: this is the route to revelation which the seekers of today all travel. In a century without an image of God (naive *or* sophisticated), it is the equivalent of the vows and prayers, the monasteries and desert sojourns, that rewarded the God-hunters of devouter times. In Ginsberg's case, this route has relentlessly led him through all the *forms* of transcendental speculation to the very stuff of Being-that-will-not-recognize-itself. As in the Zen koan, mountains have become mountains for him once again, and the core of his meaning is the simple statement: "Widen the area of consciousness." Why? What is the immense question for which this seems to him to be the beginning of an answer?

Abstractly, it might be phrased thus: Despite the fact that our whole civilization is predicated on the idea that man is an anarchy that must be tamed by laws, our deepest natures are more creative than destructive. Freed of all restraints to the discovery of our own being, we would no longer struggle against the harmony in all creation, but instead would live in accordance with it. And yet, in our time the restraints have become internalized. Beyond all laws, it is our own stunted consciousness that imprisons us, and we suffer from a consequent hunger of the spirit for which all our perversions and our politics are only a kind of ugly stomach cramp. How are we to break out of the prison? How let the spirit prosper so that the blistered desert we are making of the world can flower again?

"Widen the area of consciousness."

Concretely, in terms of Ginsberg's personal situation, the question probably phrased itself to him like this: How can I—always Jewish, sometimes cracked, mostly queer, a poet in an age of Newspeak—become whole again? Am I nothing but my Jewishness, my madness, my queerness, my poetness? Or are these things only the distorted surfacings of some buried wholeness in me—like the hairy monsters our beautiful suppressed desires become in the theater of a nightmare? Is this—all this, this life, this suffering, this miserable mortality—is this *all*? How can I see my own true face?

"Widen the area of consciousness."

And so the Blakean mystical ruminations, brought up to date ("Which way will the sunflower turn surrounded by *millions* of suns?"), the pilgrimages to the feet of contemporary sages (Suzuki yelled, "Remember green tea!" and Buber said visions were "unimportant"), the careful ingestion of drugs and the detailed reporting of their effects ("It's the instant of going/ into or coming out of/ existence that is/ important—"), all

instituted to woo the unconscious, and call up the very fears
and anxieties that lie coiled like snakes in the darkness we dare
not illuminate. For at the bottom of it all, he has always willed
to relive the very traumas that have splintered him, and to
relive them through the burning glass of poetry.

Of that poetry, some few things must be said. No one any
longer denies its historical importance. "Howl," though it was
never seriously reviewed anywhere when it was published, made
its own way into the mind of its times on the lips of thousands
of young people, for whom it had the paradoxical effect of all
revelation—it said precisely what they were thinking and feeling
but could not manage, themselves, to heave into words. Of
course, it was more than that. It was the biography of a part of
our era, and in it Ginsberg gathered up the shards of his recent
past (as you would gather up your valuables in a burning building), and saved them from oblivion by a single, superhuman,
nonstop lurch through the falling walls. It was also a new *kind*
of poetry (or, rather, the oldest kind): it was incantatory,
hymnal, purging in its repetitions; it marked the entry of the
Whitman breath and vision, as a major influence, into American poetry at last (and Sandburg me no Sandburgs, Jeffers me
no Jeffers': cock your ear, and listen). But above all it spoke in
the large, inclusive tones of outrage and pity which, in this most
outraged and pitiable time, have had so few spokesmen among
our tea-cup versifiers. It was the first statement of a point of
view that was uniquely ours, and it was also far better poetry
than most of us realized in our first excitement over the fact
that it had been written at all.

But there was more. There was Ginsberg talking, in the
respectable madhouse of America in the fifties, just as if it *was* a
madhouse, mentioning all the unmentionables (the bomb, the
poor, the money, the genitals), and insisting that in this age of
"obsession on property and vanishing Selfhood," it is "time for
prophecy without death as a consequence." There was also
Ginsberg writing poems with absolute fidelity to the *way* in
which the consciousness actually works (zig-zags of simultan-
eity, asides, outcries, giggles): this fidelity to the process of
awareness being the only part of truth we can be reasonably
certain about anymore. There was Ginsberg peeling away the

veils of his mind and life (as drugs dissolved the double-mindedness of Time) with such immediacy, word to word, that if you attend, if you open yourself up thoughtlessly enough to dig, you will actually see the aperture of consciousness focusing and unfocusing:

> "I want to know what happens after I die
> well I'll find out soon enough
> do I really need to know now?
> is that any use at all use use use
> death death death death death
> god god god god god god god the Lone Ranger
> the rhythm of the typewriter
> What can I do to Heaven by pounding on Typewriter
> I'm stuck change the record Gregory ah excellent
>   he's doing just that
> and I am too conscious of a million ears."

For more than anything else, he sees the plight of our consciousness as resembling the mad thrashings of a bird trapped in a darkened room, hurling itself back and forth, and whishing by the ears of the listener; a bird demented by a chink of light and the instinct in its pounding blood to reach the leagues of blue beyond it. Ginsberg hurls himself toward it no less, tireless, maddened, knocking over vases, books, bruising his wings against invisible windows, using his own body as a radar screen, and frenzied by the discovery, there in the dark, of the contours of his prison.

Ultimately, there was also "Kaddish"—part elegy, part biography; part poem, part prose; a forgiveness and a plea to be forgiven. But what does all that really say about this astonishing evocation of his mother's life and death? I know of no modern poem like it. There is an eloquence of emotion in the first section that made me look at my friend, despite the years of knowing him so well, as if I had never really seen him before, realizing that though words are poor things indeed, they are also sublimely adequate to express the unsayable in the hands of a man who dares to know, down to its last brutal throb, precisely what it is he feels. I have seen audiences gulp back tears as he read it, tears of the same sort of scared awareness that must have worn down the stones of Athenian amphitheaters once.

I am quite serious about this. I believe that the black excesses of this poem, the physical horrors that bathe and finally cleanse it, the awful love and anguish that denude it before your very eyes, the immense and austere twilight of its close, will reserve for it a place in contemporary literature that will be a very lonely place indeed, for what other work so terrible, so primitive, so ennobling, so stark in its glimpse of the fix we're in, can be placed beside it?

I wrote to tell him something of this when I first read the whole of it, and my letter followed him halfway round the world, reaching him (fittingly enough) in Athens. His reply came from Bombay some months later: "Your letter was a joy to receive, another of them joys in the void you were premonitioning . . . I'd forgot about "Kaddish" or in revulsion against Me it had lost its glamor & you were so moved in your letter it moved me and I began practically crying for myself in the middle of the Acropolis. Gad won't we ever be done with all this serious joy & gloom?"

There is a clue here, a clue to a drive behind the poem that is essential to any understanding of Ginsberg, and his work. That drive is to throw light on the traumatic surface itself, to compel the consciousness to open its closets, to get beyond by passing through. For Ginsberg's relationship to his mother was probably the wound over which his madness, queerness, and poetness formed their successive layers of scar tissue. Her death reopened that wound, and what flowed out (because he was brave enough to *keep* it open) were the twin poisons of oppressive memory and censored longing, and what flowed back was nothing less than a chance for further life.

For though it started as a memorial, the poem soon became an evacuation, in which everything he remembered, no matter how lacerating, came up in a terrifying retch:

"One time I thought she was trying to make me come
lay her—flirting to herself at sink— . . . dress up
round her hips, big slash of hair, scars of operations . . .
ragged long lips between her legs— . . . I was cold—

later revolted a little, not much—seemed perhaps a
good idea to try—know the Monster of the Beginning
Womb—"

And starting as an elegy, the poem rapidly changed to a
catharsis of those very deadend recognitions we sometimes live
out a whole lifetime trying *not* to re-experience:

" 'Are you a spy?' I sat at the sour table,
eyes filling with tears—'Why are you? Did Louis
send you?—The wires—'
   in her hair, as she beat on her head—'I'm not
a bad girl—don't murder me!—I hear the ceiling—
I raised two children—'
   Two years since I'd been there—I started to
cry—She stared—nurse broke up the meeting a moment—
I went into the bathroom to hide, against the toilet
white walls
   'The Horror' I weeping—to see her again—"

And intending to proclaim an armistice, the poem eventually
turned into a reconciliation with far more than just his dead
mother, and his own bleak youth:

". . . dark boys on the street, fire escapes old as you
   Tho you're not old now, that's left here with me—
   Myself, anyhow, maybe as old as the universe—and I guess
      that dies with us—enough to cancel all that comes—
      What came is gone forever every time—
   . . . There, rest. No more suffering for you. I know where
   you've gone, it's good."

So that when it was finished, something else was finished too.
Having begun to write out of his own distorted emotions for his
mother, he nevertheless persisted beyond them, until he had
achieved her in reality, until she existed in the poem with that
tragic roundness that is encountered more often in fiction than
in poetry; and in the course of this psychic facing-up, some of
his phantoms evaporated into thin air, and some of them

became those solid objects for which a man, awakened from his nightmare at last, can have a certain fellow-feeling. No wonder the poem had lost its "glamor" by the time I wrote to him. No wonder he could allow himself to love the boy who had lived it, and the man who had managed to *re*-live it in poetry. His pen, like a white-hot knife, had cauterized the wound (art's darkest mystery), and he could feel for himself—"all this serious joy & gloom"—as he felt for others, and know the first feeling inevitably feeds the second.

Most of his major poems are attempts, like this, to fuse the traumatic breakthrough, the emotional moulting and the resurrection inward that occur in a man intent on living out, in his own consciousness, all the inner deaths and births that convulse a civilization that suspects it must find a new vision of man or perish. A comparison with Rimbaud—that seismograph of the spiritual bankruptcies and barbarisms that would level cities and decimate millions a few decades after his death—is not at all presumptuous, because, for both, the road to illumination inevitably led through Hell.

When I think of him these days, it is of this willingness to embrace the monsters in the Self that I think, remembering the 22-year-old who once aspired to being "everyone's Monster, the thing they can't bear to face," but whose monsterishness was only a mask for the "Romeo Sadface" that is revealed in all his later poems. When I think of him, I think of his habit of embracing you, even kissing your cheek, when he meets you after a long time, aware what strangers may think, knowing his public image well enough, but too *manly* to be dissuaded by that, as he is too manly for the false shames of the midtown fairy and the university ironist. When I think of him, it is of that certain egolessness that has always existed between us—for we have never competed; we joke, and share the news; we make direct and simple requests that need no explanation; but in some elusive way, we are not crucial to one another. Rather, we are like soldiers in the same army (perennially fighting on different fronts) who sometimes meet on leave.

And when I think of him, I see him in his Lower East Side rooms (twilit, smoky, somehow timeless rooms, like all his rooms through the years), telephoning everyone about Lenny

Bruce's troubles with the law or the legalization of marijuana, chatting with whoever wanders in and out, organizing the day (or night) so that everyone will be "taken care of," his eyes red rimmed and indefatigable and somehow quietly gay—this strange gregarious man, this caricature of a guru, as courtly as he is comic, sitting crosslegged on the floor, sometimes bearded, now going bald, his hands touching you, his intelligence tirelessly finding words, who always makes me think that *this* is the way Chaplin might have played Gandhi—at once harsh and winsome, full of giggles as well as anathemas, but always exuding that curious fascination with, and protectiveness toward, everything living that is the one part of wisdom all Wisemen share.

I suppose I think of him as "little Allen" too (as Kerouac used to refer to him), because, though he has grown large in his accomplishments, my relationship to him hasn't changed very much since those days when, in trying to understand (and re-create him in a book), I first came to realize that we are more than just "our skin of grime," after all. I remember, for instance, the day he checked over my account of his Visions in that book, and glanced up at me toward the end with a pensive widening of the eyes.

"You haven't really caught the way it felt," he said simply. "But you've caught something else. You've caught the solemn, funny little kid I guess I must have been in those days. And all the anguish of corporeality . . . How come you know about that?"

I don't recall what answer I gave him, but I know how I knew.

Six: The Great Rememberer

ʃʃ "A great rememberer redeeming life from darkness": thus Kerouac, self-described. But he is, as well, an American phenomenon as indigenous as a gas station in the Grand Canyon: the athlete-artist, the tramp transcendentalist, the renowned recluse. And despite all the public nonsense about "the King of the Beats," he remains as unique, primal and obscure as Niagara Falls, which has been looked at so often it can no longer be seen.

Though he has already created a larger body of work than any of his contemporaries, to most people his name summons up the image of a carefree do-nothing sensation-hunter. Though that body of work creates a dense, personal world that is as richly detailed as any such American literary world since Faulkner, he is continually thought to be nothing but the poet of the pads and the bard of bebop. And though he is a prose innovator in the tradition of Joyce, whose stylistic experiments will bear comparison with any but the most radical avant-gardists of the century, he is constantly ticketed as some slangy, hitchhiking Jack London, bringing a whiff of marijuana and truck exhaust into the lending libraries. In short, the kind of writer that only America could produce, and that only America could so willfully misunderstand. One has only to remember Melville "the writer of boys' sea stories" and Whitman "the author of 'O Captain My Captain'" to recognize what legacy of national neglect Kerouac has fallen heir to. For ours is a benevolent society. Not for us to doom our Mark Twains to a garret. No, instead we praise them as vaudevillians. And later wonder why they gnashed their teeth.

The life "redeemed from darkness," which Kerouac's books describe, is nothing less than the whole of his *actual* life, and if the man (and it's the man I am concerned with here) can be approached through the work, it is primarily because that work is not so much concerned with events as it is with consciousness, in which the *ultimate* events are images. A montage of that consciousness might unreel like this:

Redbrick alleys of New England. Brown 1930's suppertimes. Loam-rank cellars full of shadows. The boom of sneakers on trackmeet boards. Love's choked throat under the wheeling prom lights. Times Square wartime bars. Hip sneers in neon flicker. October intersections, Butte midnights, Denver glooms. The awesome prairie from a fatalistic truck. Generation parties whooped on beer. Wino flophouse mattresses. Lost reds of twilight on Mexico adobe walls. A junkie's crucifix. Intersections, further intersections. Pacific immensities by the kerosene cabin. Mad hobos of rainy Susquehannas. Then all of it again. Intersections, lofts, bars, woodsy musings. Until God is no more a superstition, and Truth lies in the Buddha's blessed emptiness, and our portion is to moan for man, and meanwhile wait.

That is the burden of the consciousness that invests Kerouac's books (sixteen so far), and to read them straight through leaves you exhausted, bowed-down, baffled, roused, depressed, exulted, riled, amused but above all *silenced*— silenced by that immensity of distance and that eternity of time, which most religious visions and all hallucinogenic drugs hint at as the true nature of Reality. An odd emotion stirs in your throat, the emotion you would experience if, from some great height, you saw a lone figure walking across an empty plain in the dusk. A pang of creatureliness, intensified by awe, would reconcile you at the exact moment that it saddened. Or as Kerouac puts it, daring to use those orphaned accents that actually murmur behind most modern bravado:

"I'm writing this book because we're all going to die—In the loneliness of my life, my father dead, my brother dead, my mother faraway, my sister and my wife far away, nothing here but my own tragic hands that once were guarded by a world, a sweet attention, that now are left to guide and disappear their own way into the common dark of all our death, sleeping in me raw bed, alone and stupid: with just this one pride and consolation: my heart broke in the general despair, and opened up inwards to the Lord, I made a supplication in this dream."

That paragraph could stand as the key to the man. But what sort of man is he? Though few modern writers have embedded themselves more solidly in their books, there is far more to Kerouac than the books suggest, and I have to admit to the difficulties of my writing about him, so much is my adult life entangled in our friendship.

He has awed me with his talents, enraged me with his stubbornness, educated me in my craft, hurt me through indifference, dogged my imagination, upset most of my notions, and generally enlarged me as a writer more than anyone else I know. We have wrangled, and yelled, and boozed, and disliked, and been fond of one another for almost twenty years. He has figured in my books, sometimes directly on the page, but most often standing just off it; and I appear here and there in his, under various names, though usually as a snide, more fortunate, migraine-headache intellectual, who borrows his ideas, makes money from his perceptions, and is always trying to involve him in stifling ego dramas. And yet only one part of his complicated nature thinks of me this way. For the rest of it, we are curiously close. We represent something to one another: everything we are *not* ourselves.

Our minds, which work in opposite ways, have never been entirely compatible. He is freely contradictory, I tend to be trapped by my own consistencies; he absorbs, I analyze; he is intuitive, I am still mostly cerebral; he muses, I worry; he looks for the perfection in others, and finds existence flawed; I am drawn *toward* the flaw, and believe in life's perfectability. But there is, and was from the beginning, a real and generous affection between us, based on a peculiar sense of kinship— puzzling, maddening, indescribable—that has made our relationship oddly fateful for both of us. For his part of it, I think he believes my heart is in the right place, but I bore him after a while. For mine, what follows may suggest a little of what he has meant to me.

We became friends more quickly than I have ever become friends with anyone else. Everything about him was engaging in those days. He was open-hearted, impulsive, candid and very handsome. He didn't seem like any other writer that I knew. He wasn't wary, opinionated, cynical or competitive, and if I hadn't already known him by reputation, I would have pegged him as a poetic lumberjack, or a sailor with Shakespeare in his sea locker. Melville, armed with the manuscript of *Typee*, must have struck the Boston Brahmins in much the same way. Stocky, medium-tall, Kerouac had the tendoned forearms, heavily muscled thighs and broad neck of a man who exults in his physical life. His face was black-browed and firm-nosed, with the expressive curve of lip and the dark, somehow tender eyes that move you so in a loyal, sensitive animal. But it was the purity in that face, scowl or smile, that struck you first. You realized that the emotions surfaced on it unimpeded. Mothers warmed to him immediately: they thought him nice, respectful, even shy. Girls inspected him, their gazes snagged by those bony, Breton good looks, that ingathered aura of dense, somehow *buried* maleness.

He was moody, there were always weathers in his soul. You would see the cloud pass over his sun; you would see the light go out of his face; he would become as dismal as November, and sit there with an odd *heaviness* about him, saying only the perfunctory least, ungiving, dour beyond help of a joke, as gloomy as an old New England house on a rainy afternoon. But, when it came, his smile was as dewy, radiant and optimistic as the first hour of sun on a May morning. He beamed with an irresistible belief in the equity of things, laughing at himself under his breath, playful, warm and giving off warmth, his mind flowing impetuously out of his mouth, his eyes flashing with humors: everything about him exuded his pleasure in you, simply because you were there.

Above all, he had that quality of charisma, presence, undivided flow of being, that is neither character nor charm, but something different, something more elusive and more rare: call it certainty, or daemon; call it a hint of the integrity of the soul that some people give off like an aroma. Lawrence had it, they say. Love him or hate him, he was always *there*—as a cataract is there, or a snake. Kerouac had it too. You always felt the strong pull of his special view of the world. The uniqueness of his ego was magnetic. He was as genuine as a handcrafted weathervane—one of a kind, continually veering in the wind. Such people can be as exhausting as they are fascinating, and this is not because they live at a different pitch, but because they *always* live at it. Still, this quality of *thereness* is hard to resist, and I responded to it in Kerouac as you respond to a recognition which you do not realize you have been awaiting until it comes. For I *had* been waiting, and was more dissatisfied with the attitudinizing of most of my other friends than I knew. I opened up to his exuberance without a moment's thought.

And meanwhile I read his novel alone one night in Alan Harrington's dim, lofty room on East 60th Street (mysteriously full of old newspapers), reaching into that yawning black bag for the succeeding notebooks, all of different sizes, and all filled to the margins with that angular, flowing rush of print that is his handwriting. I read on for hours, enthralled as only fiction, moving deeply and surely toward the achievement of its imagined world, can ever enthrall the reader. I was drawn down into the book, as you are drawn into a volume of Thackeray, or Dickens, or any of those huge, life-size novels of the nineteenth century that simply burst with innumerable, fascinating events —for *The Town and the City* was just such a crowded, essentially idealistic chronicle of many people living furiously, despite the sorrow that tinged its end.

Amazed by the energy of the book, I was also secretly relieved to discover (being an overly critical young man just then, unsure of his own creative gifts) that it wasn't really *contemporary* in the fashionable sense of that term—not soured, anxious, existential or Europeanized, and thus "posed no threat" to the bleakly allegorical novels the rest of us were trying to write. This foolishness was, of course, mainly a sop to my sophomoric preconceptions of the time, which, once thrown, freed me to the excitement that flowed out of the book like rainwater from a spout. Similarly conflicting reactions, on the part of people who should know better, still haunt most of the reviews of Kerouac's work with the unspoken complaint, "Why isn't he something other than he is?"

But more than the work, it was the man who attracted me. He was sympathetic, changeable, unsophisticated, quixotic, canny and madly imaginative. Whenever we were together, we always seemed to end up at dawn, on a streetcorner somewhere, still talking. He was at ease in all the myriad worlds outside my stuffy, bookish rooms, and was already absorbed in capturing, or being captured by, the vision of our generation that would become uniquely his. In little more than two months after our meeting, we were close enough friends for him to entrust his work journals to my eye.

I responded instinctively to the Kerouac I encountered there: the Kerouac who noted down each day's hoard of completed words, and then figured up his overall batting average; who zealously recorded his slumps along with his streaks, and just as zealously pep-talked or remonstrated with himself; the Kerouac, dizzied by the odors of the spring but chained in solitude by the mad endeavor that is the writing of a novel, who actually tried, with frustrated defiance, to *screw* the earth one night, to simply thumb a hole into the loam, and mate with it, so that he could get on with the task; the Kerouac who wanted to blow a lot of Spenglerian wind into the sails of a book that was already under full canvas on its own; who, in those doldrums of midpassage, those horse latitudes that one reaches in the second half of a long, exhausting project, wondered pensively whether his book was "intellectually substantial," after all, but who, nevertheless, could write at the end: "Sept. 9. Tonight I finished and typed the last chapter. Last sentence of the novel: 'There were whoops and greetings and kisses and then everybody had supper in the kitchen.' Do you mean that the folks of this country won't like this last chapter?—or would it have been better if I had said, 'Everybody had dinner in the dining room . . .' But the work is finished." In these journals, I saw the very work problems that were defeating me shouldered toward solutions; I saw my own confusion about the times spelled out, grappled with, forced to its crisis, and clarified in the act of fiction; and, above all, I saw a man, no more fortunate on the surface of it than myself, tirelessly clutching at his special truth—as any writer must.

When I had finished the last notebook, I felt an emotion

unfamiliar enough in me to demand immediate expression, and longed to call him up (though he had no phone, just then, in Ozone Park), for I was filled with prideful idealism in our common craft; a keener sense of what must be given to it than I had ever had before; admiration for the stubborn, tender, lonesome, angry spirit that spoke from those pages; and something else I neither knew how to recognize nor handle: something almost familial, as if in this account of his consciousness my own had recognized a still-unexpressed fragment of itself; as if the impulsive reflex in him, and the wary reflex in me, were responses to an identical feeling about the world; as if he was an older, wilder brother, utterly unlike me, but sharing the same blood, shaped by the same life in the same house, and embodying the other half of a strong and ambivalent family trait. I wrote him a long, meandering letter, trying to tell him this, but lost the feeling in chagrin.

I mark that night as the start of the curious interaction between my nature and his. I mark it, as well, as the night when I began to be a writer in all seriousness. For something had been summoned out of me: I had glimpsed the potentials and the costs of the vocation; I had seen articulated what was still inchoate in my own mouth; I had taken a first step outwards by acknowledging (against my own timidities) that this man's view of the task was a view through which I might somehow come into my own best self as a writer.

In one of Kerouac's books, "Duluoz" writes to "Cody" that he is "haunted in the mind by you (think what that means, try it reverse, say, supposing you referred all your sensations to somebody and wondered what they thought . . . supposing each time you heard a delightfully original idea . . . you immediately slapped it over to check with the CODY THING." For some years, I did just this with Kerouac, checking my ideas, my perceptions, my emotions, and even my braver sentences, with the Kerouac, uncannily astute and inexhaustibly creative, who always looked over my shoulder in my imagination. Every young writer has a catalyst, and he was mine.

Later, his vision and his style would prove as contagious to others as they did to me during those apprentice years. Later, he would be parroted with a literalness that was anything but flattering. What *I* got from him, however, was not a voice, but an eye. "Reality is details," he would say, and you cut as close to the bone of the detail as words would go. A *decrepit* bureau was infinitely creakier, and emptier, and older than an *ancient* one. Rueful was sadness plus regret. Punctuation was the movie-music of prose. Form should be poetically satisfying, rather than mechanically demonstrable. And ultimately the writer's task was to write the book that he, himself, would most want to read, and to amass "a daily heap of words" toward that end. Beyond these rudiments, I tried to develop his instinct for the moment when gravity became pretension, and emotion turned to sentiment. "Always pull back," he would suggest, "and see how silly it all must look to God."

Once I gave him a chapter of which I was very proud at the time, an intensely Dostoyevskian confrontation between two overwrought young men, each of whom finally expresses a truth about himself which the other fails to notice. I was worried about the ending of this chapter because, no matter how I rewrote it, I couldn't seem to erase the tone of false solemnity that turned it ludicrous. Kerouac read the last paragraph several times—impatiently, almost indifferently—and then scribbled down the simple exclamation "Goodness me!" as the final comment by the weariest of the two. "That's what he'd say . . . See, now he retreats, he feels embarrassed, he sees how funny they are, talking like a couple of Raskolnikovs that way." It was precisely the right note, it restored the perspective in a flash, and this kind of warm canniness, this eye for the sad nonsense of life, has gone mostly unnoticed by Kerouac's critics (busily reacting to his material, as most of them are), but it is an essential part of his view, because his compassionate interest in humankind is grounded, at the bottom, in a fond awareness of its follies.

But if my writing was under his spell in those days (the four years difference in our ages put me four years behind him in experience and skill), my life was not. Though our New England backgrounds were somewhat similar, we were drawn in different directions. I was married, and rooted in New York. I was ambitious for fame and money, and had not yet come upon my own themes. Kerouac, on the other hand, was trying to find a fate to which he could consign himself. He was trying to make a soul-choice, for once and all, between the cozy nest of love and work the boy he had once been longed to build (particularly when in revulsion against cities, and city-centerlessness), and the Wild Road of freedom and possibility to which the man he was becoming was so powerfully attracted.

These were the years of his obsession with Neal Cassady (the "Cody" of the books); the Neal he had met a few years earlier, whose raw energies drew Kerouac back and forth across the continent time and time again; in whom he invested for a while all his deep, and deeply thwarted, fraternal emotions; and from whose vagabond joys and woes he created his most vivid portrait of the young, rootless American, high on life. For in the "Cody" books, Kerouac expresses most clearly his vision of America, "an Egyptian land" at once cruel and tender, petty and immense; and in "Cody" himself, he embodies both the promise of America's oldest dream (the unbuttoned soul venturing toward a reconciliation of its contradictions) and the bitter fact of its contemporary debauching (the obscenely blinking police car that questions anyone "moving independently of gasoline, power, Army or police"). As Americans always have, Kerouac hankered for the West, for Western health and openness of spirit, for the immemorial dream of freedom, joy, communion and Oriental Oneness that even Concord-bound Thoreau always sauntered toward, and his peevish indictments of New York (and New Yorkishness) were symptomatic of his feeling that a certain reckless idealism, a special venturesomeness of heart, had been outlawed to the margins of American life in his time. His most persistent desire in those days was to chronicle what was happening on those margins.

But he was not always of one mind. Once, leaving my apartment with two Negro hipsters at dawn, off again across "all that," he glanced ruefully at my crowded bookshelves, my littered desk, the copy of Doctor Faustus I had been reading when he'd rung the bell hours before to say goodbye (all the conventional props of the author's room), and said with plaintive earnestness: "When I come back this time, I'm going to settle down for a while. . . . You know, and read everything again. Like this Thomas Mann, for instance. . . . You'll see,

John. That's just what I'll do." Then he went away, somehow reluctant to depart (I felt), as if he was already living ahead into all the sore-foot, dispiriting complications of penniless travel (for he never romanticized it, and always spoke of "the essential shame of hitchhiking"), half wondering, in the very moment of setting out, *why* in God's name he was doing it. But though he hesitated (and I always fancied that I saw the horror of being stranded in wintertime Butte in his eyes), he never turned away for long from the roaming, searching side of his nature, and the shifting tensions in his books result from the balancing of these ambivalences.

As a passionate believer in his talent, I felt that his ceaseless wandering was only putting off his "proper" work. I was always adjuring him to sit in one place long enough to write another *Town and City*; I lectured him about responsibility; I pelted him with letters detailing *my* vision of the books he should be writing. For a time, my surprising empathy for him deluded me into thinking that I knew him better than he knew himself, and I squirmed with querulous concern every time he came back from another harrowing jaunt to Mexico, his face haggard, his spirit somehow stretched taut, his feet unfeeling in his battered shoes—for all like a man staggering away from a debauch. I never fully understood the hunger that was gnawing in him then, and didn't realize the extent to which the breakup of his Lowell-home, the chaos of the war years and the death of his father, had left him disrupted, anchorless; a deeply traditional nature thrown out of kilter, and thus enormously sensitive to anything uprooted, bereft, helpless or persevering: a nature intent on righting itself through the creative act. But though I was often mystified by the unfoldings in his work during those years, I knew that his temperament was entirely too obstinate, too unique, and too driven to be corralled by anyone. He simply had to dowse wherever his forked stick led him, no matter how parched the acre seemed. And somehow he always found a spring.

But that spring was in himself, not (as I thought) in the outside world he seemed intent on swallowing in a single, Gargantuan gulp; and tapping it was not (as most people still think to this day) simply a matter of sinking down a pipe and

letting the water gush. When off the road in those days, he was
mostly trying to write *On the Road*, finding, through all his
successive attempts, that the traditional, "novelistic" form of
The Town and the City was not fluid enough to contain the
formlessness of the experience he was attempting to set down.
"It's all an overlay," he kept insisting stubbornly. "It's added on
afterwards. That isn't the truth . . . I want *deep* form, poetic
form—the way the consciousness *really* digs everything that
happens."

When he came by in the late afternoons, he usually had new
scenes with him, but his characters never seemed to get very far
beyond the many-layered New York milieu a well-made novel
seemed to demand as a contrast to all the footloose uprootedness to come. He wrote long, intricate Melvillian sentences that
unwound adroitly through a dense maze of clauses; astonishing
sentences that were obsessed with simultaneously depicting the
crumb on the plate, the plate on the table, the table in the
house, and the house in the world, but which (to him) always
got stalled in the traffic jam of their own rhetoric. To me, on
the contrary, the writing was the acme of brilliance—cadenced,
powerful, cresting toward an imminent beach, and I could
never understand why it dissatisfied him so. I would have given
anything I owned to have written such tidal prose, and yet he
threw it out, and began again, and failed again, and grew
moody and perplexed.

Then one day (he was married at the time, living in a large,
pleasant room in Chelsea, doing book synopses for 20th-
Century-Fox, and more remote from the road than I had ever
known him), he announced irritably: "You know what I'm
going to do? I'm going to get me a roll of shelf-paper, feed it
into the typewriter, and just write it down as fast as I can,
exactly like it happened, all in a rush, the hell with these phony
architectures—and worry about it later."

Though anything I wrote off the top of my head was only fit
to wipe shoes on, this method of composition sounded like
good therapy at least, and when I visited him a few days after
that, I heard his typewriter (as I came up the stairs) clattering
away without pause, and watched, with some incredulity, as he
unrolled the manuscript thirty feet beyond the machine in

search of a choice passage. Two and a half weeks later, I read the finished book, which had become a scroll three inches thick made up of one single-spaced, unbroken paragraph 120 feet long, and knew immediately that it was the best thing he had done.

It was not another *Town and City*. The warmth, the hope, the youthful melancholy of that book had darkened, toughened, and matured. The eager chronicler of family suppers had become the fatalistic shambler after a carfull of horizon chasers, and the lyrical, Wolfean tone had grown as urgent and discordant as the times. Though I loved the book, though it awed me, though I felt as protective about it as if it had been my own (and later helped a little in getting it to sympathetic eyes), it disturbed me too, for in it I caught my first glimpse of the Kerouac to come, a Kerouac for whom I was oddly unprepared: a lonely, self-communing, mind-stormed man—still devout, though in a ruin of faiths; persistently celebrating whatever flower had managed to survive our bitter, urban weeds; indefatigable of eye, and fumy of mind; haunted by a reflex of love in the very pit of rude sensation; and, above all, hankering —hankering for an end: for truth to finally end the relativism, for harmony to somehow end the violence, so that peace would come to the young of this era, who were the heirs of both—and, failing that, for death. Something murmured behind the reckless onrush of the prose. It wasn't quite audible, but it accounted for the note of distant, fleeting sibilance that reverberated within the book's headlong syncopations. And for the first time, I suspected that underneath his youthful energy and jubilant thirst for life this man was immeasurably old in his soul.

It is difficult to articulate, but as the years have passed he has seemed more and more an old spirit to me; folk-old, poet-old, not of this world; like a ragged, tipsy old Li Po, thrashing around down there in the river marshes, muttering verses to himself by his fire of twigs in the dusk, allowing reality to pass through him unobstructed, writing messages back from solitude. Perhaps this is why his evocation of every gas tank, railyard, skidrow and streetcorner that he has ever seen is so hallucinatory, so charged with feeling, and yet so strangely muted by the perspective of our common destination. In any case, it has always struck me as curious that no one hears the old man's garrulity, nostalgia, sense-pleasure, stubbornness and resignation behind his work, because in a special corner of my mind he always appears as an old vagabond going West alone.

I think I first spied this inmost Kerouac in *On the Road*, but he did not come fully into view until that book failed to find a publisher, despite the lionizing, evenings at the opera, and good reviews that had greeted *Town and City*, and Kerouac's hopes for a quick career seemed to vanish (as surely as Dreiser's did when *Sister Carrie* was suppressed by the very house that printed it), and there was nothing left for him to do except consign himself, without a lifeline, to that "huge, complicated inland sea they call America," to sink into despondency, like Dreiser, or somehow swim.

Swim he did, though from the shore his efforts sometimes looked like the flailings that help to drown a drowning man. He took a deep plunge into the continent (and himself), a plunge that lasted almost five years, during which he regularly surfaced in San Francisco (for work on the railroad), Mexico City (for writing and kicks), and New York (for the quiet days and drowsing nights of home life with his mother). Stubbornly, he kept writing during this impoverished time. Ironically, he came into full and unique voice precisely during this half decade of anonymity. Paradoxically, it constituted the most fruitful period of his life—a period of explosive creativity (an average of two books every twelve months) that is perhaps unequalled in contemporary American literature, except by the four years during which Faulkner wrote *The Sound and the Fury*, *As I Lay Dying*, *Sanctuary* and *Light In August*.

I saw less of him during those years, but his letters were absorbed in the struggle to throw his net wide enough to snare the feverish vision of his own life that was maturing in his imagination: "When I get to be so pure you won't be able to bear the thought of my death on a starry night (right now I've nothing to do with stars, I've lied so far) it will be when I'll have come to know and tell the truth (all of it, in every conceivable mask) and yet digress from that to my lyric-alto knowing of this land . . . a deep-form bringing together of two ultimate and at-present-conflicting streaks in me." (July 14, 1951)

This feeling that he had "lied so far" had driven him to write *On the Road* as he did; rejection of the book by the publishers made it seem that there was no one to write for but himself, and little sense in writing "novels" that were not wanted anyway; and so he proceeded to dismantle all his hard-learned "artistries," seeking to free the whole range of his consciousness to the page—the consciousness that was one continuous, vivid flow of sense-data, associations, memories and meditations—until by the spring of 1952, he could write to me exultantly: "What I'm beginning to discover now is something beyond the novel and beyond the arbitrary confines of the story . . . into realms of revealed Picture . . . *wild form*, man, wild form. Wild form's the only form holds what I have to say—my mind is exploding to say something about every image and every memory . . . I have an irrational lust to set down everything I know . . . at this time in my life I'm making myself sick to find the wild form that can grow with my wild heart . . . because now I KNOW MY HEART DOES GROW. . . ." Though I didn't always comprehend what he was driving at, I always encouraged him (as did all his friends), because there was simply no distrusting a man who burned as purely as he was burning then.

The letters kept arriving—tortured, angry, pensive, triumphant, bitter with complaints, insistently creative; letters from west coast Mexico, from L. A. slums, from rusty tankers and Washington State lumber towns; letters that traced (for me) the progress of a man gradually sinking out of sight, down into the darks of life and Self, below "literature," beyond the range of its timid firelight. Manuscripts kept arriving too, sent haphazardly across thousands of miles of road, wrapped in brown paper bags, unregistered, uninsured, often with no carbon copy at the other end in case of loss.

I read them eagerly. I read each one at a single sitting. And I always had the same reaction. I was overcome each time by a strange mixture of exhilaration and depression. Some linch-pin had been pulled in those books, some floodgate had been opened, and Kerouac wrote like a man unhinged by his own prescience, as helpless as someone under LSD to control the movement of his consciousness backwards and forwards over his life. I imagined him (a lightning typist since his youth) sitting at the machine, staring into the blankness of the space in front of him, careful not to *will* anything, and simply recording the "movie" unreeling in his mind. Somehow the words were no longer words, but had become things. Somehow an open circuit of feeling had been established between his awareness and its object of the moment, and the result was as startling as being trapped in another man's eyes.

For me, reading those books was like recklessly diving through a surf you have underestimated. At first, the green shimmer of the subterranean world beneath the waves intoxicates you with the daring of your own species; then all at once the power and the reality of the element in which you are trespassing comes home to you, and for one moment the danger and the joy are so absolutely intermingled that something in you shrinks back from going deeper, from knowing more. I shrank back from Kerouac's books. I feared for his mind out there, and sometimes for my own. His eye was like a fine membrane vibrating between the intolerable pressure of two walls of water: the consciousness flowing outward to absorb everything in the drench of thought; and reality flooding inward to drown everything but the language to describe it. My eerie sense of kinship with him gave his work a reality for me that always seemed to overwhelm my own life for a while.

This curious reaction was intensified by my hope that he would write something that would earn him a settled life. But every new book he sent me seemed to beat more obstinately against the literary currents of the time, and I found myself in a paradox that was distinctly uncomfortable for a serious man: so passionately did I long for his work to be given the recognition it deserved, that sometimes I caught myself wishing he would blunt the edge of it a little toward that end. Also, I must confess, I did not always have the courage of my own tastes. I remember, for instance, reading *Visions of Cody* one muggy afternoon, and then going out to walk by the East River, cursing Kerouac in my head for writing so well in a book which, I was firmly convinced, would never be published. To this day, whenever I grow complacent about my own good sense, I recall that river walk. I recall that I cursed *him*, rather than the publishers, or the critics, or the culture itself that was excluding

him. Some years later, I reread *Cody* with a feeling of amazement at my own confusion that was fully as great as my shame,
for it was immediately apparent that it contained prose of an
eloquence that was Elizabethan, in an accent that was indelibly
that of our postwar generation.

Notoriety came suddenly in 1957, and with it money, adulation, TV appearances, interviews, scandals, and another sort of
crucible (the crucible of the public eye) than any Kerouac had
survived already. That notoriety was mostly based on *On the
Road*, a book six years old, written by a man he was only second
cousin to any longer, and yet people invariably looked at him,
spoke to him, and deferred to him, as if he *was* that other man,
for the Beat Generation was news by then, and Kerouac (they
thought) *was* the Beat Generation.

They tended to drive their cars more recklessly when he was
with them, as if he was "Dean Moriarty," and not the Kerouac
who hated to drive and whom I had once seen crouching on the
floor of a car, in a panic, during a drunken, six-hour dash from
New York to Provincetown. They plied him with drinks, they
created parties around him, they doubled the disorder in the
hopes of catching his eye, and so never glimpsed the Kerouac
who once confessed to me: "You know what I'm thinking
when I'm in the midst of all *that*—the uproar, the boozing, the
wildness? I'm always thinking: What am I doing here? Is this
the way that I'm *supposed* to feel?" They peeked at him as if he
was some Petronius Arbiter of cool, detached hipness, and saw,
to their confusion, a man who always turned the volume up,
who tapped his feet and exulted, and loathed the hostility for
which coolness was a mask. They saw the seeker after continuity
who, no matter how rootless his life may seem, has always
known that our anguish is uprootedness. Wherever he went, he
was confronted by that other man. Once in L.A., alone in a
coffee house, he tried to strike up a conversation with the guy
behind the counter, saying, "Hey, I'm Jack Kerouac. Let's have
a talk or something," to which the guy replied with hip disdain:
"Sure you are. They all say that." A few such encounters
produce the bizarre feeling that one is invisible, and there were
many such.

On top of this, he heard his writing praised as "rollicking" or damned as "typing," knowing that both opinions were probably based on a reading of no more than *On the Road*—in some ways his most carelessly written book. *Doctor Sax, Cody, Tristessa, Lonesome Traveler*—all the books in which his voice is most assured and his vision clearest—were either dismissed or ignored, because they did not easily jibe with the image of the adolescent, kicks-hungry yawper that has dogged Kerouac's career as relentlessly as the image of the South Sea Island tale-teller dogged Melville's. He saw the Buddhist reverence for all sentient life, which months alone on mountaintops and years in the glut of cities had only reinforced in him, repeatedly labelled "gibberish" and "nonsense" by men who relegated "reverence," without a qualm, to the religion shelves of their libraries, and then called *him* uneducated. And the man who wrote me fifteen years ago, "Life is drenched in spirit; it rains spirit; we would *suffer* were it not so" (and believes it still), lived to see the books which embodied this credo on page after page used as bibles of hipness by the Beatniks, derided as incoherent mouthings by the critics, and treated as some kind of literary equivalent of rock 'n' roll by the mass media.

The years went by; the books appeared one by one; he moved ceaselessly back and forth between Long Island and Florida; and he went on writing just the same.

In 1960, it became a mystery to me why he did it: he seemed to care less and less about things like "career" and "reputation." All of a sudden, I couldn't understand any longer what made him continue. I remembered Melville (the American writer Kerouac most resembles in temperament); I remembered that something had abandoned Melville in midlife—some unexamined faith, some fruitful illusion, which had cohered in him long enough for the early novels to get written. I remembered, as well, that Hawthorne, sensing its absence in 1856, had sadly reported that Melville had "pretty much made up his mind to be annihilated." And suddenly I felt, with a shiver, that Kerouac would not live much beyond forty. Such voracious appetites, such psychic vulnerability, such singleness of purpose, must (I felt) ream a man out at the end, and the Kerouac I knew was as incapable of turning away from his own consuming consciousness, as he was of living for long once he had been burned out by it. Still (I told myself), eight years after **Haw-** thorne's insight, he himself was dead of the very abandonment he had felt in the other man, while Melville, living on into that quiet obscurity that comes to men who have *passed through* themselves, turned as naturally to poetry as aging men turn to gardening. Perhaps with Kerouac it would be the same.

Whenever we got together, however, I was not so sure. We always seemed to sit and drink—sometimes for a week. In the beginning, we would talk and talk and talk, but then we would grow strangely silent, as if there was no more need to say certain things. During these silences, I caught myself looking at Kerouac, as you look at all tremendously gifted, tremendously complicated men, wondering where in God's name the damned vision comes from.

I saw a man, often quarrelsome, sometimes prone to silly class resentments, as defensive as a coyote on the scent, and as intractable as a horse that will not take a saddle; a man who sometimes seemed positively crazed by the upheavals in his own psyche, whose life was painfully wrenched between the desire to know, for once and all, just *who* he was, and the equally powerful desire to become immolated in a Reality beyond himself. I saw a man who (for as long as I had known him) had undeviatingly pursued his vision of the dislocations and attritions of his generation's experience "in great America," undeterred by failure or despair, so selflessly enlisted in its service that the man and the vision were inseparable; the process by which one fed the other (and vice versa) too organic and too mysterious to comprehend, and the only word inclusive enough to contain the full range of all the gifts, and all the flaws, that vague word, "genius." Looking at Kerouac, I realized he was the single writer I had ever known for whom no other word would do. And yet I could not shake off the premonition that he would vanish suddenly.

Then one day an odd thing happened. A few miles up a bad stretch of road, imperilled by an autumn flood, a few years ago, I drove into Marquette, Iowa, under the bleak Mississippi palisades, in a dismal rain, and there, at the end of the street, saw Burke's Hotel—grimy, plain as coffee grounds, soot-enlayered, in need of paint, redolent of iron bedsteads, damp sheets, forlorn unopened Gideons, smoke-blackened paneling in the shadowy lobby, and corrugated tin ceilings of 1930's cobwebs. There it was, *decrepit* as a bureau under the forbidding, wild escarpment in the river drizzle, with its steamy lunchroom full of greasy smells, and its barbershop of rusty fans: an end-of-the-road hotel, marooned in that rainy Saturday afternoon, in that town of a few woeful beer taverns and hardware stores—the huge bluffs of the awesome river looming over it.

Instantly, I thought of Kerouac, for the place was quintessentially *his* America, the America he knows down to its last stained mattress ticking and its final broken bottle in the railroad weeds; the America he taught me how to see, full of the anxious faces in which his eye has spied an older, more rooted America (of spittoons, and guffawing, and winter suppers), now vanishing bewilderedly behind the billboards and TV antennas; an America whose youths stand around on the street-corners, undecided, caught in the discrepancy between the wild longings they feel and the tame life they get; a land (now in its sour time) which Kerouac goes on evoking in the accents most native to it: "I loved the blue dawns over racetracks and made a bet Ioway was sweet like its name, my heart went out to lonely sounds in the misty springtime night of wild sweet America in her powers, the wetness of the wire fence bugled me to belief, I stood on sandpiles with an open soul." (There's all our uprootedness in that, and all our hungering for roots—what another American writer called our "complex fate": even truer of us now, in a century severed from its faiths.)

The special Kerouac-mood was on that town, and, as I waited for the stoplight, realizing again how eloquently he has spoken for the pang of being young in America in this time, I imagined him there in Burke's Hotel, having a coffee behind the blurred plate glass, baseball-hatted and crepesoled for the road, weary and intent, something spectral and unnoticed about him down the counter there as the waitress gossiped—passing through, years ago, toward the promise of another coast.

I caught myself thinking: he has given this way of seeing to all of us. Then I missed him keenly, and knew for sure he would survive.

A Decade
of Coming Attractions

§ § It has been said that if you would understand the mind of my generation you must start with World War Two, on the theory that a widespread attitude is shaped by a common experience. The war seems a likely enough starting place, and yet in a subtler sense everyone who is now between the ages of thirty-odd and forty-odd had already shared a common experience by the time they entered the armed services. It was an experience that was vastly more formative than the bad circumstances of the Depression or the anxieties of the post-Munich years, because it happened to us on the inside, down in the psyche where the adolescent is most receptive and most vulnerable. It was the experience of moviegoing in the thirties and early forties, and it gave us all a fantasy life in common, from which we are still dragging up the images that obsess us.

When comedian Lenny Bruce snarls, "Don't give me any of those Barton Maclaine takes!" it is more than a face or a role that is evoked in Harvardmen and hipsters alike. It is a whole big-shouldered, thick-faced attitude toward life—the attitude of the spoiler, the strikebreaker, the sadistic warden, the lumberjack bruiser, the smasher of things. The name itself summons up a promise of violence (heavy and unimaginative) that is as different from the psychotic violence of Peter Lorre as Sammy Glick's machinations are from Iago's. When we think of Barton Maclaine, we immediately think of a blunt object about to run amok.

Equally, when poet Frank O'Hara writes an elegy to Margaret Dumont, everyone recalls the grudging respect you had to accord her lofty gentility, besieged as it was by the maniacal Dada of the Marx Brothers. Impregnable in bosom and coiffure she survived their inspired vulgarity with a touch of dignified good humor—rather as you imagined your very proper grandmother might survive a burlesque show; and who can say how much she taught us about a world of social niceties that we would never really know? The point is that at the simple mention of a name we all re-experience the nostalgia, vividness and perception of the same childhood dream, no matter what has happened to us since.

Whether the theater was the smalltown two-hundred-seater (down near the railroad tracks) that seemed eternally drifted in O. Henry wrappers or sticky with Juicy Fruit, the sooty brick building with the fading black and yellow billboard advertising *Photoplays*, where, on Saturday afternoons, an unruly army in corduroys stomped their feet, raced up and down the aisles or pelted disapproving girls with ice cream; or whether the theater was one of those huge, Moorish big-city picture palaces, with arched Scheherazade balconies, stars that twinkled, fountains that played and platoons of uniformed ushers, the images that flickered on the silver screen and the dreams and visions they aroused were identical. The veteran of Iwo Jima may feel a resentful superiority to the veteran of Normandy (the resentful superiority the proletariat sometimes feels for the bourgeoisie), and find himself wondering if they are talking about the same war, but if *Gone With the Wind* comes up both are securely in the same army fleeing Atlanta. One's boyhood experience of the Depression may center around a Hooverville or a house in the suburbs, but one's fantasies of those years are likely to inhabit that carefree world, as shiny and as shallow as patent leather, where Fred Astaire and Ginger Rogers denied all shabbiness and anxiety for a few hypnotic hours. When I think of the midthirties, for instance, an odd image always comes to my mind: the image of a dismal milltown in New Hampshire, complete with shuttered brick factory, rotting bandstand on the green, and NRA stickers in the windows of Woolworth's, over which the outline of a mythical RKO Venice, made of plastic and cellophane, and piped to antic joy by the fleet Astaire, hovers like a double exposure. The quick dream and the dead reality remain so wedded in my memory to this day that it is impossible for me to know how much my particular vision of the world was formed by them.

The power of the film as a molder of mass emotions was recognized within little more than a decade after *The Great Train Robbery*, but it was probably not until the advent of sound, together with the death of vaudeville and the insecurities of the Depression, that moviegoing became as universal a part of puberty as acne and masturbation. If sound produced a lowering of artistic standards, it also made possible a heightening of psychological involvement so persuasive that the gulf between the audience and the image was all but obliterated. In a sense, sound transformed the film from a ritual to an hallucination, and the movies have been more Freudian than Aristotelian ever since. Vaudeville's death multiplied by many thousands the number of darkened theaters in which the flicks could flicker, until there was hardly a town in America that did not have its Orpheum, Bijou or Rex, dispensing the same fable in Bangor and Butte. The idleness and bewilderment of the Depression awakened a hunger for fantasies that would compensate for the impoverishment of reality, and by deceit or cajolery, with permission or without it, most of an entire generation went to the movies two or three times a week, and accumulated, in common, a surrogate reality.

It should be admitted right off that we were indiscriminate. We went to good films and bad films alike, to M-G-M super-spectacles that cost more than the historical events they depicted, and 20th-Century-Fox musicals about as nutritious as Kool-Aid, and Universal horror films that used the same bit of fabricated Transylvania in picture after picture. We would go to see anything that moved, and we probably learned as much from the B-films as we did from the A's. We revelled in their sleazy sets, indifferent acting and skeletal plots; for every Saturday we spent with Gable or Shearer, we probably spent four with Richard Arlen or Arline Judge, and they taught a lot of us to relish the back-of-town, wrong-side-of-the-tracks America where motives were simple and the action was brisk. We still have our favorites—what a friend of mine calls Great Bad Films—and our affection for them is undiminished by the fact that they grow worse with every viewing. I still drop everything whenever A *Message to Garcia* comes around on television, if only to watch Wallace Beery's superbly awful hamming with his torn straw hat.

It would be difficult to calculate the number of hours that people of my age spend simply talking about the movies of those years. The talk is carried on in the sort of shorthand that is all but unintelligible to outsiders, and a snatch of it might go like this: "Name the Lane Sisters, and you're out of the game if you include Gale Page. . . . Remember Henry Armetta with his head askew? Porter Hall the Eternal Conniver? George Zucco's Grey Eminence? Jane Darwell the Earth Mother of Arkansas? . . . Who played opposite Loretta Young in *Zoo in Budapest*? What about O. P. Heggie in *The Count of Monte Cristo*? . . . That wasn't C. Aubrey Smith, it was Sir Guy Standing. . . . Remember the Three Musketeers of Warner Brothers: Allen Jenkins, Frank McHugh, and Edward Brophy? . . . Who can cast *all* the secondary roles in *King's Row*? . . . You're only eligible for the Movie Team if you can name at least three Isabel Jewell films, or Henry Fonda's last line in *Blockade*, or the picture that had a shot of Ann Sheridan without a brassiere. . . ."

Everyone has his favorite William Powell scene (mine is the drunk scene in *My Man Godfrey*), his essential Marx Brothers sequence (I have been torn for years between the end of *Duck Soup* and the stateroom routine in *A Night at the Opera*); and that special film, mostly obscure, often undistinguished, something about which opened the consciousness (that was all ready to flower) to a new perception about life or the world that remains as vivid and evocative as the madeleine in Proust. For reasons which defy description, my awareness of the existential character of modern history was first evoked by a brief scene in a wine cellar from an unimportant 1937 film, *Last Train from Madrid*.

Equally, everyone carries in his head the memory of a special girl, with a special fleeting beauty, that is as graphic and moving today as it was in those years when they pursued that face through film after film until it vanished into death, obscurity or character roles. I know a man who has never really gotten over the death of Thelma Todd, and she exists in his mind, not as the object of Groucho's lechery or as the dumb steno of countless low-budget comedies with Patsy Kelly, but as a fragile ash-blonde wraith, fine-boned and petal-lipped, with that vaguely solemn aura in which some girls, cursed with startling beauty, seem to move. I myself am an Elissa Landi man. I remember her face with the poignance and awe that are reserved for one's first crush on an older woman, and even when I was only ten her beauty seemed to me to be too rarefied, too breathtaking, for this world. I remember watching her as you watch an exotic flower in full blossom, knowing that ahead of such perfection lies only a withering. There are Myrna Loy men (reporters and wits), and Jean Harlow men (sportsmen and boozers), and Marlene Dietrich men (intellectuals and homosexuals); and I suppose we are all Garbo men—at least a little.

Everyone, as well, has a particular star who embodies for him the first full awareness of the rousing eroticism of adolescence, a fantasy love image that initiated him into manhood. Kerouac writes: "My dream has in it a wife beautiful beyond belief, some gorgeous new blonde gold sexpot of starry perfection with lovely lace neck, soft long skin, inturned mouth top—I pictured the gorgeous Gene Tierney—a young beautiful American girl getting excited in your arms." To people of my age, the reference is as precise as the mention of Helen or Hecuba was to classical times, and serves the same purpose. Whether Tierney is your meat or not, you know her, you have considered her, and the leap is made.

For myself, I recall the soft, white, trembling curve of Jean Harlow's breast momentarily revealed (I saw the film three times to be certain) in the seduction scene in Hell's Angels. There it was, unmoored beneath her robe, that object of ceaseless, exhausting midnight speculations. And Ben Lyon was sitting not two feet from her, and it! Not to mention the dozen-odd technicians who were assisting, and whose presence I felt just as strongly, just as thrillingly. I remember her moistly hesitant half smile, which at first I simply refused to believe indicated her acquiescence to *that*. I remember the embrace that followed which, of course, silenced all doubts. And I remember, as well, that I left the theater with my first awareness that women could be more than just reluctant mannequins in the sexual encounter. There are men of my age who have been more or less searching, since those days, for Luise Rainer's gamin smile, or Madeleine Carroll's deep-breasted elegance, or June Lang's indescribably delicate neck, or the buttocks of Frances Farmer, or Ruby Keeler's thighs. In some cases, they have even gone so far as to marry reasonable facsimiles.

The movies were also a continuation of our schooling by other means, and the degree to which they affected our appreciation of literature, for instance, is difficult to overestimate. In almost every case, however, we saw the movie, and only *then* read the book. Though I have been with Tolstoi's *Anna* many more times than I have watched Garbo's, whenever I read the book it is the film star who moves so darkly toward the accelerating railway wheels in my mind's eye, giving the chapters an uncanny third dimension. And is there any way to imagine Mr. Micawber except in the carrot-nosed, garrulous, shabby-genteel figure of W. C. Fields? Is it possible that Sidney Carton did not have the quenched, whimsical eyes and resolute mouth of Ronald Colman? Or that Kipling didn't have Spencer Tracy in mind when he created Manuel in *Captains Courageous?* Not to me. And when I finally plunged into the great English novels of the nineteenth century, I found all of them richly peopled by the likes of Edna May Oliver, Roland Young, Freddie Bartholomew, Basil Rathbone, Montague Love, Herbert Mundin, Elizabeth Allan, Miles Mander, Una O'Connor —indeed, the entire Metro-Goldwyn-Mayer stock company of the thirties, those marvelous Cruikshank-like faces that popped up in film after film, like so many utility outfielders. My first direct exposure to Shakespeare was the Pickford-Fairbanks version of *The Taming of the Shrew* (it was also my first film), and after seeing *The Blue Angel* I struggled through the novel, only to be disappointed. Gary Cooper sent me to Hemingway, and Paul Muni to Zola; and certainly my vision of war was almost exclusively the result of *All Quiet on the Western Front*, which I never would have read at such an impressionable age had it not been for an opportune (?) exposure to the movie at eleven.

The war is a good example of how subtly we were shaped by

those far off Saturday afternoons. Unlike our fathers, we went off to our war with no illusions about "glory and patriotism." Though it was far more worth the fighting than theirs, most of us viewed it (in advance) as an unpleasant, monotonous, dispiriting task that had somehow been shoved on us by the follies of our elders. A large part of the explanation for this lies in the simple fact that we had been exposed to almost a decade of antiwar movies, and the abrupt shift to antifascist films in the early forties could never quite make us forget the image of Lew Ayres, as the young German, begging the bayoneted Poilu to forgive him there in the shellhole, or the obvious meaning of the doughboy-turned-gangster in *They Gave Him a Gun,* or the smashed hopes behind James Stewart's smashed eyes in *Seventh Heaven.* These pictures filled our heads with memories of trench fighting, gas attacks and hopeless years of mud and agony that were no less bitter for being secondhand, and we knew that the only enemy worth struggling against was War Itself. By the time that Hollywood retooled to prove that all Germans and all Japanese were nonhumans, we were incapable of any real enthusiasm for the idea. The war was a fact, a dirty job that had to be done, but very few of us could view it as a crusade or a war to end wars. Could we so easily forget John Gilbert howling like an animal in no-man's land in *The Big Parade?* Or Eric Von Stroheim's sympathetic prison camp officer in *Grand Illusion?*

I remember, for instance, when they reissued *All Quiet* sometime in 1941, with a commentary that attempted to turn it into an antifascist tract. Though I was perfectly willing to be convinced, the images were too stark, too appalling, and no injection of ideology could harness them to the war effort. The futility and simple horror of modern warfare overcame all the sloganizing, and the movie was quickly withdrawn, to be replaced by those numberless films about Nazi atrocities, in which Conrad Veidt, Martin Kosleck and Fritz Kortner made such a good living after Pearl Harbor. But it has always astonished me that almost no one has perceived that one reason that we fought a war (against very real evils) so laconically, with so little rhetoric, and with our eye out mainly for personal survival (not only against the enemy, but against the military system itself) was because we knew that all wars were basically frauds, even just wars. After all, hadn't we learned precisely that in our local movie theater?

The films of the thirties and forties reflected the zenith of the star system, and above all they were vehicles for great person- alities, always somehow bigger than the roles they played, their power commensurate to how completely they embodied an archetype. To my generation, for instance, Humphrey Bogart is not merely Sam Spade in *The Maltese Falcon*, or the cabaret owner in *Casablanca* or the down-and-out prospector in *Treas- ure of Sierra Madre*. Sometimes a hero, sometimes a villain, he is always pre-eminently the Existential Knight, suspicious of sentiment, verbosity and cheap idealism, alike capable of that fatalistic violence which sometimes seems the only way to survive if you have the cruelty of modern cities in your eyes, and that reticent toughness of spirit (which Bogart's famous wince of the upper lip has incarnated forever) that indicates aware- ness of how slim the odds really are, and a besieged personal code. He was Bogey to us, we knew his style and attitudes as well as we knew our own, he taught us something about the world we would inherit that was no less contagious than what Hemingway taught us, and will probably last as long.

I remember, as well, when Carole Lombard died in a wartime plane crash. I was genuinely saddened. It was not that she had ever been an object of romantic reverie to me, or even that I knew (or cared) anything very much about her personally. It was that something witty, madcap, tough, earnest, and even noble had gone out of life, something I would always associate with the thirties: the zany rich girl with the good heart; the honey-blonde broad, with the prominent hipbones, who could drink with the boys; everyone's hip older sister who brought a whiff of the Big World with her when she visited home. She was funny and she was fun; she had something more substantial than glamor; her very name evoked a point of view that I still encounter (and fancy I understand down to its minutest details) in the women of my generation that you meet at cocktail parties, or on the afterdecks of motor-cruisers, or in the executive offices of publishing houses or TV networks.

Since it appeared after the war, everyone has been intimidated (perhaps justly) by James Agee's brilliant piece on silent film comedy, but I'm sure there are many of my generation who, like me, feel that the laughmakers of our era have been sadly neglected as a result. As evidence that great comedy did not die after *The Jazz Singer*, we would offer just three examples, to each of which sound itself was essential.

The Marx Brothers, for instance, are unthinkable without the verbal insanity of Groucho and Chico. Their shameless punning, their deliciously infantile literalness, their eruptions of outright gibberish, drove a decade of Douglas Dumbrilles, Sig Rumans and Herman Bings to the very brink of epilepsy. And can anyone seriously imagine even mute Harpo without his piercing two-handed whistle or the lewd honk of his automobile horn? The adult world of sense, and gravity, and dullness, which the Marx Brothers invaded like a gang of surrealist kids on a perpetual 4th of July, was exactly the pompous, problem-filled world to which we had to return when the film was over, and we went back to it renewed by the knowledge that the Bores could be foiled by the cagey irrationality of Groucho, and the Girls would succumb to Harpo's mysterious and angelic smile when, out of the horrendous ruins of a grand piano, he resurrected a moment of fleeting melody that was like a hint of eternity in a world demented by time. If you looked at it from the vantage of energy and joy, life was absurd, but the absurdity itself was endearing, and the fact that this message was not lost on us can be found in the work of such diverse people as Terry Southern, Gregory Corso and Robert Rauschenburg.

Though they began in the Silent Era, we feel that Laurel and Hardy belong to us, and we cannot imagine Laurel—whey-faced, looking either like a weeping sheep or a grinning horse—without his unmatchable whimper that built so slowly into pathetic sobs, or his droll and somehow tender English accent. Hardy's tiny mouth, and tiny moustache, and tiny eyes in that great runny pudding of a face would always be incomplete to us without his exasperated "*Stan*ley!" delivered with all the prissy impatience of a boy scout master from Georgia, coping with a gang of juveniles in Brownsville. Laurel and Hardy were Outsiders, always broke, somehow innocent, certainly ill-equipped to handle a world of hard facts and solid objects (as much by

Hardy's fastidiousness as Laurel's incompetence), and yet they were always optimistic, no defeat was final, their pretensions were as sweetly naive as their confusions, and the sequence which reoccurred most often in their films found them sitting on the curbstone (having been summarily ejected from the warmth of Life Within), trying to decide what to do next.We often felt exactly the same.

With W. C. Fields, we are on higher ground. Indeed, we are in the realm where mythic figures reside, and Fields probably comes closer to being the secret Dutch Uncle of my generation than any other single artist. To this day, we lapse into the musing, rhetorical, nasal rasp by means of which he sought to evade the hostile world of Una Merkel, Franklin Pangborn and Baby Leroy. I have heard television producers and five-times-busted junkies imitate it with the same uncanny perfection. It is our connection with an older America of frontier gamblers, carnie barkers, talltale tellers; an America now on the con, on the bum, on the sauce; an America heading inexorably for the Grampian Hills, pursued by the Four Horsemen of the Apostasy—moderation, conformity, affluence and humorlessness. In it, we hear train whistles, the click of poker chips, saloon-talk, whorehouse pianos, cars gunning insanely for a light, the shrewd lies that outwit cops and wives, the monologues that can be heard at midnight under the trestle where men, for whom this world is not enough, gather around a can.

We were in immediate rapport with the profounder aspects of Fields' character: the besieged Fields forever menaced by inanimate objects, the impatient Fields trying to get a scoop of ice cream to his mouth by means of two limp soda straws, the outraged Fields finding himself in bed with a goat, the insatiable Fields vaulting out of an airplane after his flask, the fatalistic Fields making for the Black Pussy Café like a wounded elephant lumbering off into the bush. His mouth full of windy jargon, his mordant eye a-scheme, his bulbous nose hinting at thirsts and joys he had managed to thieve from under the very eyes of convention—all this had a lasting influence on us, and what Fields taught us was invaluable, for he was neither merely crazy nor innocent, but a flawed, eccentric man, making out in a reality geared to the silly abstractions of the middle class. One has only to think of such people as Nelson Algren and William Burroughs, their works *and* their personalities, to see the extent of that influence on the generation just before mine. Burroughs, in particular, reflects the Fieldsian accent and point of view, and *Naked Lunch* is probably the way Fields would have rewritten 1984 had he lived. For the rest of us, it is enough to mention the New Old Lompoc House, or Mahatma Kane Jeeves, to start us trading stories back and forth about the same rank-breathed, lying, reprobate old uncle, who passed through all our lives despite the alarums of our parents, leaving a delicious and unsettling aroma of bay rum, whiskey and musty railway depots.

Off the streets where these giants roamed, there was a luxurious room, soundproofed and deodorized, where William Powell, Franchot Tone and Robert Montgomery traded glittering bon mots with Myrna Loy, Jean Arthur and Margaret Sullavan, for sound also brought to our ears (whether they were cocked in Montana or Manhattan) nuances of irony and wit as sibilant as so many cocktail pianos. In this room, Eric Blore spluttered and buttled like a paranoid chipmunk, Eugene Pallette huffed and paid the bills, Billie Burke arrived in a flutter of chiffon, Mischa Auer preened in a rented tuxedo and a bogus title, Edward Everett Horton gabbled like a huge absent-minded rabbit, and Helen Broderick cast a cold, satiric eye on the whole proceedings. Irene Dunne consoled herself with Ralph Bellamy after her misunderstanding with Cary Grant over Gail Patrick, but the orchestra was always ready just out of camera range to supply the lush accompaniment for the reconciliation. People got pixilated, but never drunk. No one worked for a living, and everyone always carried enough cash on their persons to pay first-class passage to Europe when they overstayed the bon voyage party. If the hilarity was irresponsible, the hangover was mostly imaginary. But so was the film, and it was as essential a part of the fantasy life of the thirties as the musicals that made us wonder (as Kerouac has written) "about the world that spoke of beautiful piney islands and Indian love calls and Jeanette MacDonald yet had nothing to show for it but jailhouses, arrested fathers, [and] distant moanings." Who is to say that our sense of the ambiguity of life—a distinctive trait of this generation—did not begin when we watched Nelson Eddy singing "Ah, Sweet Mystery of Life" and then walked home through the bitter hardtime streets of 1935?

We learned so much from the movies, and the lessons were so painless, that I, for one, still associate certain films with the dawning of certain ideas. The social idealism of Frank Capra, for instance, probably reached its apogee in *Meet John Doe,* but it wasn't the betrayed utopianism of the film which impressed me so much as the dangerous heat and dire manipulations of mass politics that it crystallized in three faultless images. Edward Arnold's reptilian eyes behind his pince-nez will always signify for me the desperate lust for power out of which the powerlessness of modern life produces totalitarians. Barbara Stanwyck's gradual involvement in her own Frankenstein still seems to me one of the most succinct examples of how the liberal professional (or vice versa) can be tripped up by trying to walk both sides of the street. And James Gleason, magnificently drunk, attempting to light that memorably bent cigarette, and muttering, "Chalk up another one for the Pontius Pilates," expresses for all time the bitterness and disgust a decent man feels at the debauching of hope by one of Orwell's "smelly little orthodoxies." In the years that followed, when I became attracted to, and then involved with, and finally disaffected from, party politics, the memory of this film (and others like it) had an influence on my decisions and aversions that is incalculable.

But most of what we learned was not this specific. There was the horror film, for instance—a venerable and once-dignified genre which, like the detective novel, has degenerated in these latter days into a moronic comic book of meaningless gore. The thirties were the great years of the horror film—the age of *The Mummy* as well as *Frankenstein, The Old Dark House* as well as *Dracula,* and *Freaks* as well as *The Wolf Man*—but far from merely titillating tastes so jaded by newsreels of Belsen and Dachau that nothing but gouged-out eyeballs in lustful technicolor will serve to jog them, the great classics of our day were specifically films of moral complexity. We sympathized with Dr. Frankenstein's Monster, for his tragedy was the inability to love; we pitied King Kong, for after all wasn't he the visual embodiment of our own overgrown, inarticulate desires for Fay Wray? We knew even Dracula's loneliness before the empty mirror, and his daytime vulnerability there in the coffin. One reason why we became so absorbed in these grisly films was probably the crudity of the photography (the special effects were not as baldly apparent as they are these days), but the deeper explanation certainly lies in the fact that they were fantasies erected on a solid foundation of psychological truth, and not mere *Grand Guignols* to raise the hackles.

We even learned to recognize such esoterica as the difference between the production values of one studio and another, and mine is the last generation for whom the name Cedric Gibbons, for instance, summons up that creamy, middle-tone elegance, that vast spectrum of subtle grays, with which he invested a thousand M-G-M films; a "look" that was as different from the work of his counterparts at other studios as a Cadillac is from an Oldsmobile. Warner Brothers films had the grainy, emphatic alternation between lights and darks that has typified social realism since Goya's day, and 20th-Century-Fox movies were as shiny, confidently vulgar and eye-catching as an electric toaster that will be out of date by next year.

Mine may have been the first generation which produced fans of directors, as well as stars, and I know half a dozen men, none of whom are connected with films today, whose boyhood ambition it was to wield a megaphone. I am one of them. For we knew a great deal about pictures and picturemaking, and I have seen our shot-by-shot re-creations of the movies of the thirties baffle a room full of our elders and our juniors. One night, for instance, I watched the face of a world-famous lady philosopher as two college professors, a poet and a novelist (myself) talked for two solid hours about Bela Lugosi. For the first half hour, she assumed he must be an obscure Hungarian writer, and when she learned the truth, her perplexity at the sight of four intellectuals lavishing on a film actor the sort of enthusiastic analysis that is usually reserved for a Poem or an Idea, brought home to us all, in a flash, how different movie-going in the thirties was from moviegoing before or since.

We were a generation that no longer waited for the Great

American Novel, but that spoke of the Great Hollywood Novel with the same spurious certainty that it would inevitably appear. Hollywood embodied for us the crucial dilemma of American society (the integrity of the individual vision in conflict with the pleasure- and profit-seeking materialism of an industrialized democracy) and the theme, plus its setting, has never lost its fascination for us, though the Hollywood of Scott Fitzgerald and Louis B. Mayer has all but vanished to the four corners of the earth.

But perhaps it was the experience of moviegoing itself that left the deepest impression on us. For moviegoing was sitting in the Plaza Theater in Englewood, New Jersey, with your imagination so heated by images of London or Paris that years later, when you found yourself there, your keenest response was a kind of *déjà vu* that made you round every corner fully expecting to come upon Nigel Bruce or Simone Simon. It was recognizing in yourself, even at thirteen, the anchorless, half bitter, half lyrical, unkempt, rebellious figure of John Garfield in *Four Daughters*—a romantic image of the disaffiliated hobo-artist that has been as difficult for some of us to shake off as the Hemingway sportsman-artist has been for others. It was seeing *Gunga Din* thirteen times with guilty, gluttonous pleasure that was tinged with the wistful knowledge that our world would never be as gallant, rollicking and simple as the one in which Sam Jaffe climbed that golden dome and saved British India from Eduardo Ciannelli. It was coming out of the theater at night, by yourself, and walking home under the summer-heavy trees, the drama continuing to spin on inside your head, so that years later you would realize that it was on those nights that you first learned that the dark is made for fantasies, freedoms and aspirations—unlike the Saturday afternoons of earlier years when the harsh light of day, somehow more graphic and revealing after the hours of darkness, returned you with a jolt to the same old street, the same old houses, with nowhere to take your aroused imagination but home to supper. It was fifteen-cent ticket stubs come upon weeks later in the linty pockets of trousers rolled up at the cuffs; and counting off the minutes until the lights went out with all the impatience of a lover; and knowing the "Coming Attractions" announcement, different in each theater, as well as you knew your own saddle-shoes from those of your best friend.

But it was also the sharing of an initiation rite with your contemporaries (like suffering the same trauma and being supplied with the same clues to its cure), for the movies of the thirties constitute, for my generation, nothing less than a kind of Jungian collective unconscious, a decade of coming attractions out of which some of the truths of our maturity have been formed.

Generationing

The Name of the Game

§ § There was a feeling in the first years after World War Two that is difficult to evoke now. It was a feeling of expectation without reasonable hope, of recklessness without motivation, of uniqueness seeking an image. Probably mine was the last generation to feel that its shared experience had produced an attitude so widespread and so peculiar to us that it could be expressed in a single descriptive term—in other words, the last *postwar* generation. (After the next war, no one is likely to be plagued by terminology.) As writers, we had the example of the twenties to encourage us in this, because the creative renaissance of that decade seemed to have resulted in large part from another postwar generation finding its distinct voice in the act of finding a poetic image for itself. The thirties had produced nothing so good (it seemed to us), nothing so cohesive; and by 1947 the mass-magazines, as well as the literary journals, were alike speculating about the new postwar generation, and its prevailing mood.

We speculated no less. In bars and classrooms and jazz clubs and wild parties, we argued, and joked, about our own identity as an age group. What was produced, while the debate went on, was mostly imitative. The first war novels appeared, but the hand of Hemingway and Dos Passos was so heavily upon them that these books might have been describing *their* war rather than ours (as a comparison of *The Naked and the Dead* [1948] and *Catch-22* [1961] makes immediately apparent). Equally secondhand, our political and social attitudes were almost wholly in the emotional style of the thirties, and the only philosophic insight that seemed to smack exclusively of our time was existentialism—though its bleaknesses and absurdities seemed more suited to a ruined and embittered Europe than to the America we knew, so powerfully flexing itself in its forenoon on the world stage.

Yet we felt our distinctness even if we couldn't describe it. In a few nonintellectual areas, we were already *becoming* ourselves. As an example, one of the key conversion experiences of that time involved Bop, which was not merely expressive of the discords and complexities we were feeling, but specifically separated us from the times just passed, for even our jazz idols of the thirties mostly loathed it. When you "went over" to Bird, when you "heard" him all of a sudden, you were acknowledging that you had become a different sort of person than the Swing or Dixie fan you had been, because, with Bird, you had to *dig* to know; your consciousness had to be at a certain level of evolution; you had to be able to intuit on the bias, to hear music *being* music, to comprehend the difference between the confining intelligence and the soul directly recording its own drift. No one who was not involved in the Bop revolt can know all that it meant to us. If a person dug Bop, we knew something about his sex life, his kick in literature and the arts, his attitudes toward joy, violence, Negroes and the very processes of awareness.

Equally, we felt our distinctness in our immediate attraction to all those far-out experiences, about which society has the most stereotyped aversions: madness, drugs, religious ecstasies, dissipation and amorality. When pressed to explain why these experiences attracted us so, the most we could come up with, even to ourselves, was a feeling that they were somehow "more real" than anything else around. They were still unstained, in our minds, by all that alphabet soup of soggy verbalism and cerebration that we were beginning to find unpalatable. They suggested unexplored territories of consciousness that exerted a pull on us fully as strong and as mysterious as the pull of the Far West a century earlier.

As tyro writers, we sought our distinctness in these things, for writers tend to define their minds against the obdurateness of their material, and so instinctively gravitate to experiences they don't quite understand. This may be the primary reason why American writers in this century compartmentalize themselves into "generations," for American life alters from top to bottom almost every ten years, and each new group of writers is compelled to discover its own America, if it would discover itself. So it seemed only natural that we should seek our identity as a generation in experiences for which there existed no older literary tradition.

Jack Kerouac and I used to sit up most of the night with quarts of beer in my apartment on Lexington Avenue, talking about all these things. Though he knew much more about them than I did, I think I was more concerned than he was with isolating the common element in them. He would tell hours'-long stories about the "wild kids" he had seen everywhere in his travels since the war—all the junkies, musicians, collegian sailors, con men, teen-age Raskolnikovs, parking-lot hipsters, and their rootless, willing girls; stories that excited and disturbed me with a feeling of imminence, stories rich and chaotic with life's improvisations; stories that seemed to be describing a new sort of stance toward reality, behind which a new sort of consciousness lay; stories that struck me just as Gorki's first tales must have struck young Russians in the nineties.

I responded instinctively to these stories. I seemed to know (without *knowing*) the youthful thirst, the restless exuberance, the quality of search, that pulsed in them. I felt it myself. Everyone I knew felt it in one way or another—that bottled eagerness for talk, for joy, for excitement, for sensation, for new truths. Whatever the reason, everyone of my age had a look of impatience and expectation in his eyes that bespoke ungiven love, unreleased ecstasy and the presence of buried worlds within.

I kept goading Jack to characterize this new attitude, and one evening as he described the way the young hipsters of Times Square walked down the street—watchful, cat-like, inquisitive, close to the buildings, *in* the street but not *of* it—I interrupted him to say that I thought we *all* walked like that, but what was the peculiar quality of mind behind it?

"It's a sort of furtiveness," he said. "Like we were a generation of furtives. You know, with an inner knowledge there's no
use flaunting on that level, the level of the 'public,' a kind of
beatness—I mean, being right down to it, to ourselves, because
we all *really* know where we are—and a weariness with all the
forms, all the conventions of the world. . . . It's something like
that. So I guess you might say we're a *beat* generation," and he
laughed a conspiratorial, the-Shadow-knows kind of laugh at his
own words and at the look on my face.

All other legends, rumors and claims to the contrary, this was
how that much-misunderstood and maligned name for our
generation was first coined—in the middle of a long, intense,
only half-serious conversation in November, 1948. The subse-
quent history of the term is a matter of record, and the three
pieces that follow are offered to make clear my personal complicity in, and disagreements with, that record.

The first, *This Is the Beat Generation,* was written at the
behest of Gilbert Millstein. While reviewing my novel, *Go,* he
became intrigued by the phrase (which was casually mentioned
in the book several times), and wondered if I would do an
article on the subject for *The New York Times Magazine.* The
piece appeared on November 16, 1952, thereby earning itself
the dubious distinction of being the first attempt to name the
generation. It caused a ripple of curiosity, prompted a few
hundred letters, and then it was forgotten.

Five years passed, during which "Howl" and *On the Road*
appeared, putting the term back into general circulation again,
and the second piece included here, "The Philosophy of the
Beat Generation," was published in *Esquire* in February, 1958,
and constitutes a deeper and more detailed look at the Beat
point of view as it had solidified since the first article was
written.

Both these pieces, as reprinted in this book, have been
slightly abridged to remove journalistic repetitions.

The final article, "The Game of the Name," was written to
supplement and amend the other two in the light of more
recent developments. It deals with the so-called Beatniks and

their critics. It also attempts to indicate a few of the contributions which the Beat attitude of my generation bequeathed to the generation that has succeeded it.

Try to categorize the experience of one's own peer group (what I call "generationing") is an urge that most fiercely besets you when you are young and the rage for order is at its most intense. I, for one, am not sorry for having given in to that urge. Nor for the fact that it has passed from me now.

This Is the Beat
Generation   (1952)

§ § Several months ago, a national magazine ran a story under the heading "Youth" and the subhead "Mother Is Bugged At Me." It concerned an eighteen-year-old California girl who had been picked up for smoking marijuana and wanted to talk about it. While a reporter took down her ideas in the uptempo language of "tea," someone snapped a picture. In view of her contention that she was part of a whole new culture where one out of every five people you meet is a user, it was an arresting photograph. In the pale, attentive face, with its soft eyes and intelligent mouth, there was no hint of corruption. It was a face which could only be deemed criminal through an enormous effort of righteousness. Its only complaint seemed to be: "Why don't people leave us alone?" It was the face of a Beat Generation.

That clean young face has been making the newspapers steadily since the war. Standing before a judge in a Bronx courthouse, being arraigned for stealing a car, it looked up into the camera with curious laughter and no guilt. The same face, with a more serious bent, stared from the pages of *Life* Magazine, representing a graduating class of ex-GI's, and said that as it believed small business to be dead, it intended to become a comfortable cog in the largest corporation it could find. A little younger, a little more bewildered, it was this same face that the photographers caught in Illinois when the first non-virgin club was uncovered. The young copywriter, leaning down the bar on Third Avenue, quietly drinking himself into relaxation, and the energetic hotrod driver of Los Angeles, who plays Russian roulette with a jalopy, are separated only by a continent and a few years. They are the extremes. In between them fall the secretaries wondering whether to sleep with their boy friends now or wait; the mechanic beering up with the guys and driving off to Detroit on a whim; the models studiously name-dropping at a cocktail party. But the face is the same. Bright, level, realistic, challenging.

Any attempt to label an entire generation is unrewarding, and yet the generation which went through the last war, or at least could get a drink easily once it was over, seems to possess a uniform, general quality which demands an adjective. . . . The origins of the word "beat" are obscure, but the meaning is only too clear to most Americans. More than mere weariness, it implies the feeling of having been used, of being raw. It involves a sort of nakedness of mind, and, ultimately, of soul; a feeling of being reduced to the bedrock of consciousness. In short, it means being undramatically pushed up against the wall of oneself. A man is beat whenever he goes for broke and wagers the sum of his resources on a single number; and the young generation has done that continually from early youth.

Its members have an instinctive individuality, needing no bohemianism or imposed eccentricity to express it. Brought up during the collective bad circumstances of a dreary depression, weaned during the collective uprooting of a global war, they distrust collectivity. But they have never been able to keep the world out of their dreams. The fancies of their childhood inhabited the half-light of Munich, the Nazi-Soviet pact and the eventual blackout. Their adolescence was spent in a topsy-turvy world of war bonds, swing shifts and troop movements. They grew to independent mind on beachheads, in gin mills and USO's, in past-midnight arrivals and pre-dawn departures. Their brothers, husbands, fathers or boy friends turned up dead one day at the other end of a telegram. At the four trembling corners of the world, or in the home town invaded by factories or lonely servicemen, they had intimate experience with the nadir and the zenith of human conduct, and little time for much that came between. The peace they inherited was only as secure as the next headline. It was a cold peace. Their own lust for freedom, and the ability to live at a pace that kills (to which the war had adjusted them), led to black markets, bebop, narcotics, sexual promiscuity, hucksterism and Jean-Paul Sartre. The beatness set in later.

It is a postwar generation, and, in a world which seems to mark its cycles by its wars, it is already being compared to that other postwar generation, which dubbed itself "lost." The Roaring Twenties, and the generation that made them roar, are going through a sentimental revival, and the comparison is valuable. The Lost Generation was discovered in a roadster, laughing hysterically because nothing meant anything any more. It migrated to Europe, unsure whether it was looking for the "orgiastic future" or escaping from the "puritanical past." Its symbols were the flapper, the flask of bootleg whiskey, and an attitude of desperate frivolity best expressed by the line: "Tennis, anyone?" It was caught up in the romance of disillusionment, until even that became an illusion. Every act in its drama of lostness was a tragic or ironic third act, and T. S. Eliot's *The Wasteland* was more than the dead-end statement of a perceptive poet. The pervading atmosphere of that poem was an almost objectless sense of loss, through which the reader felt immediately that the cohesion of things had disappeared. It was, for an entire generation, an image which expressed, with dreadful accuracy, its own spiritual condition.

But the wild boys of today are not lost. Their flushed, often scoffing, always intent faces elude the word, and it would sound phony to them. For this generation conspicuously lacks that eloquent air of bereavement which made so many of the exploits of the Lost Generation symbolic actions. Furthermore, the repeated inventory of shattered ideals, and the laments about the mud in moral currents, which so obsessed the Lost Generation, do not concern young people today. They take these things frighteningly for granted. They were brought up in these ruins and no longer notice them. They drink to "come down" or to "get high," not to illustrate anything. Their excursions into drugs or promiscuity come out of curiosity, not disillusionment.

Only the most bitter among them would call their reality a nightmare and protest that they have indeed lost something, the future. For ever since they were old enough to imagine one, that has been in jeopardy anyway. The absence of personal and social values is to them, not a revelation shaking the ground beneath them, but a problem demanding a day-to-day solution. *How* to live seems to them much more crucial than *why*. And it is precisely at this point that the copywriter and the hotrod driver meet and their identical beatness becomes significant, for, unlike the Lost Generation, which was occupied with the loss of faith, the Beat Generation is becoming more and more occupied with the need for it. As such, it is a disturbing illustration of Voltaire's reliable old joke: "If there were no God, it would be necessary to invent him." Not content to bemoan His absence, they are busily and haphazardly inventing totems for Him on all sides.

For the giggling nihilist, eating up the highway at ninety miles an hour and steering with his feet, is no Harry Crosby, the poet of the Lost Generation who planned to fly his plane into the sun one day because he could no longer accept the modern world. On the contrary, the hotrod driver invites death only to outwit it. He is affirming the life within him in the only way he knows how, at the extreme. The eager-faced girl, picked up on a dope charge, is not one of those "women and girls carried screaming with drink or drugs from public places," of whom Fitzgerald wrote. Instead, with persuasive seriousness, she describes the sense of community she has found in marijuana, which society never gave her. The copywriter, just as drunk by midnight as his Lost Generation counterpart, probably reads *God and Man at Yale* during his Sunday afternoon hangover. The difference is this almost exaggerated will to believe in something, if only in themselves. It is a *will* to believe, even in the face of an inability to do so in conventional terms. And that is bound to lead to excesses in one direction or another.

The shock that older people feel at the sight of this Beat Generation is, at its deepest level, not so much repugnance at the facts, as it is distress at the attitudes which move it. Though worried by this distress, they most often argue or legislate in terms of the facts rather than the attitudes. The newspaper reader, studying the eyes of young dope addicts, can only find an outlet for his horror and bewilderment in demands that passers be given the electric chair. Sociologists, with a more academic concern, are just as troubled by the legions of young men whose topmost ambition seems to be to find a secure berth in a monolithic corporation. Contemporary historians express mild surprise at the lack of organized movements, political, religious, or otherwise, among the young. The articles they write remind us that being one's own boss and being a natural joiner are two of our most cherished national traits. Everywhere people with tidy moralities shake their heads and wonder what is happening to the younger generation.

Perhaps they have not noticed that, behind the excess on the one hand, and the conformity on the other, lies that wait-and-see detachment that results from having to fall back for support more on one's capacity for human endurance than on one's philosophy of life. Not that the Beat Generation is immune to ideas; they fascinate it. Its wars, both past and future, were and will be wars of ideas. It knows, however, that in the final, private moment of conflict a man is really fighting another man, and not an idea. And that the same goes for love. So it is a generation with a greater facility for entertaining ideas than for believing in them. But it is also the first generation in several centuries for which the act of faith has been an obsessive problem, quite aside from the reasons for having a particular faith or not having it. It exhibits on every side, and in a bewildering number of facets, a perfect craving to believe.

Though it is certainly a generation of extremes, including both the hipster and the "radical" young Republican in its ranks, it renders unto Caesar (i.e., society) what is Caesar's, and unto God what is God's. For in the wildest hipster, making a mystique of bop, drugs and the night life, there is no desire to shatter the "square" society in which he lives, only to elude it. To get on a soapbox or write a manifesto would seem to him absurd. Looking at the normal world, where most everything is a "drag" for him, he nevertheless says: "Well, that's the Forest of Arden after all. And even *it* jumps if you look at it right." Equally, the young Republican, though often seeming to hold up Babbitt as his culture hero, is neither vulgar nor materialistic, as Babbitt was. He conforms because he believes it is socially practical, not necessarily virtuous. Both positions, however, are the result of more or less the same conviction—namely that the valueless abyss of modern life is unbearable.

§ § §

For beneath the excess and the conformity, there is something other than detachment. There are the stirrings of a quest. What the hipster is looking for in his "coolness" (withdrawal) or "flipness" (ecstasy) is, after all, a feeling of somewhereness, not just another diversion. The young Republican feels that there is a point beyond which change becomes chaos, and what he wants is not simply privilege or wealth, but a stable position from which to operate. Both have had enough of homelessness, valuelessness, faithlessness.

The variety and the extremity of their solutions are only a final indication that for today's young people there is not as yet a single external pivot around which they can, as a generation, group their observations and their aspirations. There is no single philosophy, no single party, no single attitude. The failure of most orthodox moral and social concepts to reflect fully the life they have known is probably the reason for this, but because of it each person becomes a walking, self-contained unit, compelled to meet the problem of being young in a seemingly helpless world in his own way, or at least endure.

More than anything else, this is what is responsible for this generation's reluctance to name itself, its reluctance to discuss itself as a group, sometimes its reluctance to be itself. For invented gods invariably disappoint those who worship them. Only the need for them goes on, and it is this need, exhausting one object after another, which projects the Beat Generation forward into the future and will one day deprive it of its beatness.

Dostoyevski wrote in the early 1880's that "Young Russia is talking of nothing but the eternal questions now." With appropriate changes, something very like this is beginning to happen in America, in an American way; a re-evaluation of which the exploits and attitudes of this generation are only symptoms. No single comparison of one generation against another can accurately measure effects, but it seems obvious that a Lost Generation, occupied with disillusionment and trying to keep busy among the broken stones, is poetically moving, but not very dangerous. But a Beat Generation, driven by a desperate craving for belief and as yet unable to accept the moderations which are offered it, is quite another matter. Thirty years later, after all, the generation of which Dostoyevski wrote was meeting in cellars and making bombs.

This generation may make no bombs; it will probably be asked to drop some, and have some dropped on it, however, and this fact is never far from its mind. It is one of the pressures which created it and will play a large part in what will happen to it. There are those who believe that in generations such as this there is always the constant possibility of a great new moral idea, conceived in desperation, coming to life. Others note the self-indulgence, the waste, the apparent social irresponsibility, and disagree.

But its ability to keep its eyes open, and yet avoid cynicism; its ever-increasing conviction that the problem of modern life is essentially a spiritual problem; and that capacity for sudden wisdom which people who live hard and go far, possess, are assets and bear watching. And, anyway, the clear, challenging faces are worth it.

The Philosophy
of the Beat Generation (1958)

ſſ Last September a novel was published which *The New York Times* called "the most beautifully executed, the clearest and most important utterance" yet made by a young writer; a book likely to represent the present generation, it said, as *The Sun Also Rises* represents the twenties. It was called *On the Road*, by Jack Kerouac, and it described the experiences and attitudes of a restless group of young Americans, "mad to live, mad to talk, mad to be saved," whose primary interests seemed to be fast cars, wild parties, modern jazz, sex, marijuana, and other miscellaneous "kicks." Kerouac said they were members of a Beat Generation.

ſ ſ ſ

No one seemed to know exactly what Kerouac meant, and, indeed, some critics insisted that these wild young hedonists were not really representative of anything, but were only "freaks," "mental and moral imbeciles," "bourgeois rebels." Nevertheless, something about the book, and something about the term, would not be so easily dismissed. The book became the object of heated discussion, selling well as a consequence; and the term stuck—at least in the craw of those who denied there was any such thing.

ſ ſ ſ

Providing a word that crystallizes the characteristics of an entire generation has always been a thankless task. . . . But to find a word that will describe the group that is now roughly between the ages of eighteen and twenty-eight (give or take a year in either direction) is even more difficult, because this group includes veterans of three distinct kinds of modern war: a hot war, a cold war, and a war that was stubbornly not called a war at all, but a police action.

Everyone who has lived through a war, any sort of war, knows that beat means not so much weariness, as rawness of the nerves; not so much being "filled up to *here*," as being emptied out. It describes a state of mind from which all unessentials have been stripped, leaving it receptive to everything around it, but impatient with trivial obstructions. To be beat is to be at the bottom of your personality, looking up; to be existential in the Kierkegaard, rather than the Jean-Paul Sartre, sense.

What differentiated the characters in *On the Road* from the slum-bred petty criminals and icon-smashing Bohemians which have been something of a staple in much modern American fiction—what made them *beat*—was something which seemed to irritate critics most of all. It was Kerouac's insistence that actually they were on a quest, and that the specific object of their quest was spiritual. Though they rushed back and forth across the country on the slightest pretext, gathering kicks along the way, their real journey was inward; and if they seemed to trespass most boundaries, legal and moral, it was only in the hope of finding a belief on the other side. "The Beat Generation," he said, "is basically a religious generation."

§ § §

On the face of it, this may seem absurd when you consider that parents, civic leaders, law-enforcement officers and even literary critics most often have been amused, irritated or downright shocked by the behavior of this generation. They have noted more delinquency, more excess, more social irresponsibility in it than in any generation in recent years, and they have seen less interest in politics, community activity, and the orthodox religious creeds. They have been outraged by the adulation of the late James Dean, seeing in it signs of a dangerous morbidity, and they have been equally outraged by the adulation of

Elvis Presley, seeing in it signs of a dangerous sensuality. They
have read statistics on narcotics addiction, sexual promiscuity
and the consumption of alcohol among the young—and
blanched. They have lamented the fact that "the most original
[literary] work being done in this country has come to depend
on the bizarre and the offbeat for its creative stimulus"; and
they have expressed horror at the disquieting kind of juvenile
crime—violent and without an object—which has erupted in
most large cities.

They see no signs of a search for spiritual values in a generation whose diverse tragic heroes have included jazzman Charlie
Parker, actor Dean and poet Dylan Thomas; and whose interests have ranged all the way from bebop to rock and roll; from
hipsterism to Zen Buddhism; from vision-inducing drugs to
Method Acting. To be told that this is a generation whose
almost exclusive concern is the discovery of something in which
to believe seems to them to fly directly in the face of all the
evidence.

Perhaps all generations feel that they have inherited "the
worst of all possible worlds," but the Beat Generation probably
has more claim to the feeling than any that have come before
it. The historical climate which formed its attitudes was violent,
and it did as much violence to ideas as it did to the men who
believed in them. One does not have to be consciously aware of
such destruction to feel it. Conventional notions of private and
public morality have been steadily atrophied in the last ten or
fifteen years by the exposure of treason in government, corruption
in labor and business, and scandal among the mighty of Broadway and Hollywood. The political faiths which sometimes seem
to justify slaughter have become steadily less appealing as
slaughter has reached proportions that stagger even the mathe-
matical mind. Orthodox religious conceptions of good and evil
seem increasingly inadequate to explain a world of science-fiction
turned fact, past enemies turned bosom friends, and honorable
diplomacy turned brink-of-war. Older generations may be dis-
tressed or cynical or apathetic about this world, or they may
have somehow adjusted their conceptions to it. But the Beat
Generation is specifically the *product* of this world, and it is the
only world its members have ever known.

It is the first generation in American history that has grown up with peacetime military training as a fully accepted fact of life. It is the first generation for whom the catch phrases of psychiatry have become such intellectual pablum that it can dare to think they may not be the final yardstick of the human soul. It is the first generation for whom genocide, brainwashing, cybernetics, motivational research—and the resultant limitation of the concept of human volition which is inherent in them— have been as familiar as its own face. It is also the first generation that has grown up since the possibility of the nuclear destruction of the world has become the final answer to all questions.

But instead of the cynicism and apathy which accompanies the end of ideals, and which gave the Lost Generation a certain poetic, autumnal quality, the Beat Generation is altogether too vigorous, too intent, too indefatigable, too curious to suit its elders. Nothing seems to satisfy or interest it but extremes, which, if they have included the criminality of narcotics, have also included the sanctity of monasteries. Everywhere the Beat Generation seems occupied with the feverish production of answers—some of them frightening, some of them foolish—to a single question: how are we to live? And if this is not immediately recognizable in leather-jacketed motorcyclists and hipsters "digging the street," it is because we assume that only answers which recognize man as a collective animal have any validity; and do not realize that this generation cannot conceive of the question in any but personal terms, and knows that the only answer it can accept will come out of the dark night of the individual soul.

§ § §

Before looking at some of those answers, it would be well to remember what Norman Mailer, in a recent article on the hipster, said about the hip language: "What makes [it] a special language is that it cannot really be taught—if one shares none of the experiences of elation and exhaustion which it is equipped to describe, then it seems merely arch or vulgar or irritating." This is also true to a large extent of the whole reality in which the members of the Beat Generation have grown. If you can't see it the way they do, you can't understand the way they act. One way to see it, perhaps the easiest, is to investigate the image they have of themselves.

A large proportion of this generation lived vicariously in the short, tumultuous career of actor James Dean. He was their idol in much the same way that Valentino was the screen idol of the twenties and Clark Gable was the screen idol of the thirties. But there was a difference, and it was *all* the difference. In Dean, they saw not a daydream Lothario who was more attractive, mysterious and wealthy than they were, or a virile man of action with whom they could fancifully identify to make up for their own feelings of powerlessness, but a wistful, reticent youth, looking over the abyss separating him from older people with a level, saddened eye; living intensely in alternate explosions of tenderness and violence; eager for love and a sense of purpose, but able to accept them only on terms which acknowledged the facts of life as he knew them: in short, themselves.

To many people, Dean's mumbling speech, attenuated silences, and rash gestures seemed the ultimate in empty mannerisms, but the young generation knew that it was not so much that he was inarticulate or affected as it was that he was unable to believe in some of the things his scripts required him to say. He spoke to them right through all the expensive make-believe of million-dollar productions, saying with his sighs, and the prolonged shifting of his weight from foot to foot: "Well, I suppose there's no way out of this, but we know how it *really* is. . . ." They knew he was lonely, they knew he was flawed, they knew he was confused. But they also knew that he "dug," and so they delighted in his sloppy clothes and untrimmed hair and indifference to the proprieties of fame. He was not what they wanted to be; he was what they *were*. He lived hard and without complaint; and he died as he lived, going fast. Or as Kerouac's characters express it:

"We gotta go and never stop going till we get there.

"Where we going, man?

"I don't know, but we gotta go."

Only the most myopic, it seems to me, can view this need for mobility (and it is one of the distinguishing characteristics of the Beat Generation) as a flight rather than a search.

Dean was the product of an acting discipline known as The Method (taught at New York's Actors Studio), which has proved irresistibly attractive to young actors and has filled the screens and stages of America in recent years with laconic, slouching youths, who suddenly erupt with such startling jets of emotional power that the audience is left as shaken and moved as if it had overheard a confession. The primary concern of The Method is to find the essence of a character, his soul, and the actor is encouraged to do this by utilizing emotions in his own experience that correspond to those in the script. Non-Method actors sometimes complain that disciples of The Method coast along during the greater part of a role, hoarding their emotional resources for the climactic scenes. To which Method actors might reply that only the climactic scenes in most plays and movies have any deep human truth to them, and that the rest is only empty dialogue building toward the moment when the character reveals himself.

An example of this might well be the movie *On the Waterfront*, conceived by its writer, Budd Schulberg, and its director, Elia Kazan, as a social exposé of conditions among longshoremen, centralized in the figure of a young ex-boxer mixed up in a corrupt union. Marlon Brando's electrifying performance of this role, however, so interiorized the character that the social overtones seemed insignificant beside the glimpse of a single human soul caught in the contradictions and absurdity of modern life. It was exactly as if Brando were saying in scene after scene: "Man is not merely a social animal, a victim, a product. At the bottom, man is a spirit." As a theory of acting keyed to this proposition, The Method is preeminently the acting style of the Beat Generation.

Critics constantly express amazement at the willingness, even the delight, with which this generation accepts what are (to the critics) basically unflattering images of itself. It was noticed, for instance, that the most vociferous champions of the film, *The Wild Ones* (which gave a brutal, unsympathetic account of the wanton pillage of a California town by a band of motorcyclists), were the motorcyclists themselves. Equally, most juvenile delinquents probably saw, and approved of, the portrait of themselves offered in *Rebel Without a Cause*, even though they laughed at the social-worker motivations for their conduct that filled the script. One can only conclude that what they see and what adults see are two different things. The standards by which adults judge the behavior portrayed have scant reality to them, for these standards are based on social and moral values that do not take into consideration their dilemma, which might be described as the will to believe even in the face of the inability to do so in conventional terms.

All too often older people make the mistake of concluding that what lies beneath this is an indifference to values of any kind, whereas almost the reverse is true. Even the crudest and most nihilistic member of the Beat Generation, the young slum hoodlum, is almost exclusively concerned with the problem of belief, albeit unconsciously. It seems incredible that no one has realized that the only way to make the shocking juvenile murders coherent at all is to understand that they are specifically moral crimes. The youth, who last summer stabbed another youth and was reported to have said to his victim, "Thanks a lot, I just wanted to know what it felt like," was neither insane nor perverted. There was no justification for his crime, either in the hope of gain or in the temporary hysteria of hate, or even in the egotism of a Loeb and Leopold, who killed only to prove they could get away with it. His was the sort of crime envisaged by the Marquis de Sade a hundred and fifty years ago—a crime which the cruel absence of God made obligatory if a man were to prove that he was a man and not a mere blot of matter. Such crimes, which are no longer rarities and which are all committed by people under twenty-five, cannot be understood if we go on mouthing the same old panaceas about broken homes and slum environments and bad company, for they are spiritual crimes, crimes against the identity of another human being, crimes which reveal with stark and terrifying clarity the lengths to which a desperate need for values can drive the young. For in actuality it is the *longing* for values which is expressed in such a crime, and not the hatred of them. It is the longing to do or feel something meaningful, and it provides a sobering glimpse of how completely the cataclysms of this century have obliterated the rational, humanistic view of Man on which modern society has been erected.

The reaction to this on the part of young people, even those in a teen-age gang, is not a calculated immorality, however, but a return to an older, more personal, but no less rigorous code of ethics, which includes the inviolability of comradeship, the respect for confidences, and an almost mystical regard for courage—all of which are the ethics of the tribe, rather than the community; the code of a small compact group living in an indifferent or a hostile environment, which it seeks not to conquer or change, but only to elude.

On a slightly older level, this almost primitive will to survive gives rise to the hipster, who moves through our cities like a member of some mysterious, nonviolent Underground, not plotting anything, but merely keeping alive an unpopular philosophy, much like the Christian of the first century. He finds in bop, the milder narcotics, his secretive language and the night itself, affirmation of an individuality (more and more besieged by the conformity of our national life), which can sometimes only be expressed by outright eccentricity. But his aim is to be asocial, not antisocial; his trancelike "digging" of jazz or sex or marijuana is an effort to free *himself*, not exert power over others. In his most enlightened state, the hipster feels that argument, violence and concern for attachments are ultimately Square, and he says, "Yes, man, yes!" to the Buddhist principle that most human miseries arise from these emotions. I once heard a young hipster exclaim wearily to the antagonist in a barroom brawl: "Oh, man, you don't want to interfere with him, with his kick. I mean, man, what a *drag!*"

On this level, the hipster practices a kind of passive resistance to the Square society in which he lives, and the most he would ever propose as a program would be the removal of every social and intellectual restraint to the expression and enjoyment of his unique individuality, and the "kicks" of "digging" life through it. And, as Norman Mailer said in the afore-quoted article, "The affirmation implicit in [this] proposal is that man would then prove to be more creative than murderous, and so would not destroy himself." Which is, after all, a far more spiritual, or even religious, view of human nature than that held by many of those who look at this Beat Generation and see only its excesses.

This conviction of the creative power of the unfettered

individual soul stands behind everything in which the members of this generation interest themselves. If they are curious about drugs, for instance, their initial reason is as much the desire to tap the unknown world inside themselves as to escape from the unbearable world outside. "But, man, last night," they will say, "I got so high I knew *everything*. I mean, I knew *why*."

In the arts, modern jazz is almost exclusively the music of the Beat Generation, as poetry (at least until Kerouac's novel) is its literature. If the members of this generation attend to a wailing sax in much the same way as men once used to attend the words and gestures of sages, it is because jazz is primarily the music of inner freedom, of improvisation, of the creative individual rather than the interpretive group. It is the music of a submerged people, who *feel* free, and this is precisely how young people feel today. For this reason, the short, violent life of alto-saxist Charlie Parker (together with those of Dean and Dylan Thomas) exerts a strong attraction on this generation, because all three went their own uncompromising way, listening to their inner voices, celebrating whatever they could find to celebrate, and then willingly paying the cost in self-destruction. But if young people idolize them, they have no illusions about them as martyrs, for they know (and almost stoically accept) that one of the risks of going so fast, and so far, is death.

But it is perhaps in poetry where the attitude of the Beat Generation, and its exaggerated will to find beliefs at any cost, is most clearly articulated. In San Francisco, a whole school of young poets has made a complete break with their elegant, university-imprisoned forebears. Some of them subscribe to Zen Buddhism, which is a highly sophisticated, nonrational psychology of revelation, and wait for satori (wisdom, understanding, reconciliation). Some are Catholic laymen, or even monks, and pray for the redemption of the world. Many of them resemble mendicant friars, or the Goliard balladeers of the Middle Ages, carrying everything they own on their backs, including typewritten copies of their poems to be left, as one of them put it, in art galleries, latrines, "and other places where poets gather." All of them believe that only that which cries to be said, no matter how "unpoetic" it may seem; only that which is unalterably true to the sayer, and bursts out of him in a flood, finding its own form as it comes, is worth the saying in the first place. Literary attitudes, concern about meter or grammar, everything self-conscious and artificial that separates literature from life (they say) has got to go. . . . One of them, Allen Ginsberg, whom *Life* Magazine has called the most exciting young poet in America, has written a long, brilliant and disordered poem called "Howl." It contains a good many expressions and experiences that have never been in a poem before; nevertheless, its aim is so clearly a defense of the human spirit in the face of a civilization intent on destroying it, that the effect is purifying. " 'Howl' is an 'Affirmation' by individual experience of God, sex, drugs, absurdity," Ginsberg says.

The same might be said of *On the Road*. Most critics spent so much time expressing their polite distaste for the sordidness of some of the material that they completely failed to mention that in this world, the world of the Beat Generation, Kerouac unfailingly found tenderness, humility, joy and even reverence; and, though living in what many critics considered a nightmare-jungle of empty sensation, his characters nevertheless could say over and over:

"No one can tell us that there is no God. We've passed through all forms . . . Everything is fine, God exists, we know time . . . Furthermore we know America, we're at home . . . We give and take and go in the incredibly complicated sweetness . . ."

Whatever else they may be, these are not the words of a generation consumed by self-pity over the loss of their illusions; nor are they the words of a generation consumed by hatred for a world they never made. They seem rather to be the words of a generation groping toward faith out of an intellectual despair and moral chaos in which they refuse to lose themselves. They will strike many people as strange words, coming as they do from the lips of a young man behind the wheel of a fast car, racing through the American night, much as Kerouac's reply to *Nightbeat*'s John Wingate seemed strange, when he was asked to whom he prayed. "I pray to my little brother, who died, and to my father, and to Buddha, and to Jesus Christ, and to the Virgin Mary," he said, and then added: "I pray to those five *people*. . . ."

But if this grouping of a saint, a sage and a savior with two twentieth-century Americans seems strange, it is only because many of us have forgotten (or have never known) how real the spiritual experience can be when all other experiences have failed to satisfy one's hunger. The suggestion, at least in Kerouac's book, is that beyond the violence, the drugs, the jazz, and all the other "kicks" in which it frantically seeks its identity, this generation will find a faith and become consciously—he believes that it is unconsciously already—a religious generation.

Be that as it may, there are indications that the Beat Generation is not just an American phenomenon. England has its Teddy Boys, Japan its Sun Tribers, and even in Russia there are hipsters of a sort. Everywhere young people are reacting to the growing collectivity of modern life, and the constant threat of collective death, with the same disturbing extremity of individualism. Everywhere they seem to be saying to their elders: "We are different from you, and we can't believe in the things you believe in—if only because *this* is the world you have wrought." Everywhere, they are searching for their own answers.

For many of them, the answer may well be jail or madness or death. They may never find the faith that Kerouac believes is at the end of their road. But on one thing they would all agree: the valueless abyss of modern life is unbearable. And if other generations have lamented the fact that theirs was "the worst of all possible worlds," young people today seem to know that it is the only one that they will ever have, and that it is *how* a man lives, not why, that makes all the difference. Their assumption—that the foundation of all systems, moral or social, is the indestructible unit of the single individual—may be nothing but a rebellion against a century in which this idea has fallen into disrepute. But their recognition that what sustains the individual is belief—and their growing conviction that only spiritual beliefs have any lasting validity in a world such as ours—should put their often frenzied behavior in a new light, and will certainly figure large in whatever future they may have.

The Game of the Name   (1965)

§§ Spiritual quests to the contrary, after the initial furor about the Beat Generation in the late fifties, the public, the Media and the critics decided that when you spoke of "beatness" you were referring exclusively to the folkways of a group of urban Thoreaus who lived in those limbo-neighborhoods where the nation's Bohemias shelved off into the nation's slums. In other words, the so-called Beatniks.

That sneering diminutive, which is about all that is left of the Beat Generation today ("Among the sit-ins was the usual sprinkling of beatniks," "The moral contagion represented by juvenile delinquents, racial malcontents, and beatniks," "I certainly don't intend to support my son if he wants to be a beatnik"), was originally coined by Herb Caen, a facetious columnist in San Francisco, to describe the bearded, sandaled coffee-house loungers of the North Beach Bohemia, but it was immediately adopted by the Mass Media as a handy caricature for everyone associated with Beatness, and thereby quickly entered the smear-vocabularies of all those perceptive people who like to call intellectuals "eggheads." And for the same perceptive reason: if you can't understand them, brand them.

The notion (which became universal) that when you talked about the Beat attitude you were speaking of Caen's idea rather than Kerouac's, had the paradoxical effect of at once making the Beat Generation briefly notorious in the popular mind as a species of hip Amish, and more or less permanently obscuring the wider, and deeper, implications of the term. In my not-unprejudiced view, the Beatniks and the Mass Media, between them, succeeded in beclouding most of what was unsettling, and thereby valuable, in the idea of Beatness, and I might as well deal with this aspect of the matter before discussing the more serious critical appraisals of that idea.

The Beatniks were (and, I suppose, still are) essentially Bohemians—that is, *artistes manqués*, colony-establishers, citified Trobriand Islanders. On the run from the ant heaps of the industrial revolution, in flight from its moral cul-de-sacs, they gathered into seedy enclaves on the margins of the arts, where they immediately went about setting up a kind of parody of the society they had fled. The lifestyle described in *On the Road*, "Howl" and other books gave a direction to their withdrawal, but their dominant preoccupations remained nest-building and Square-baiting. They talked so incessantly about "the rat race" and their own group identity that, with a few changes of reference, they would have gone almost unnoticed in Levittown.

Of course, Bohemians have always, drearily, derived most of their behavior patterns from attentively watching the bourgeoisie and then doing the opposite, but the Beatniks, unlike most Bohemians, could admit that their need to shock the Squares was only the obverse side of the Squares' need to *be* shocked, and this led to such sure-fire merchandising schemes as the Rent-a-Beatnik fad, and the Do-It-Yourself Beatnik Kit. It also led to a rigorous uniformity of language, dress, tastes, attitudes and values that was almost a mirror image of the very conformity against which they were in revolt. The only difference was that the Beatniks were obsessed with the Squares, while the Squares were not obsessed with them, and a far better gimmick would have been an agency from which one could Rent-a-Square, because every pad needed one if it wanted to really swing.

Mostly, the Beatniks struck me as sad. It always seemed to me that they never realized how truly bad things were. They had reached no joy, no certainty, and small reconciliation with themselves by their secession. There was a wistful, glance-backwards quality about all their studied withdrawals, like the lonely child's contention that "they'll be sorry when I'm gone."

I have spent evenings in downtown pads that were almost

indistinguishable, one from the other (the dart board, the mattresses, the photos of W. C. Fields, the record player on the floor, the copies of *Yugen* and *Evergreen*, the day-old saucepan of spaghetti, the jelly-glasses of Thunderbird, the pathetic obscenities in the toilet); evenings during which I tried not to notice the sign tacked up over the coal stove that read "We Jell Plotz," even though, more than likely, I was there with an overweight rich boy from uptown, for whom the bearded painter in jeans, and his anemic wife in a begrimed slip, and the ubiquitous, leotarded extra girl (who was reading a comic book), were pot connections. These evenings were as ritualized as cocktail parties in Westport, though they were usually livelier. Joints went around from hand to hand, and your style in turning-on (mine was considered fortyish) was closely observed and *not* commented on; the talk centered on Superman ("Man, dig the way he's camping! Now, if my old man had ever come on like that—"); the extra girl was more or less available to take umbrage or give head, depending on whether my friend's 28-dollar pot-tab was cleared away; Coltrane skirled on and on (though not too loud), and anyone who tapped his foot was treated to glances of glacial disdain, having, after all, "lost his cool." On most of these evenings, I was successfully incognito simply because I wore a tie.

I never disliked the Beatniks, any more than I disliked the Squares. In fact, I always felt the same impulse with both; I wanted to touch their shoulders, and tell them that the condition of a man's shirt front didn't matter. I wanted to turn up the music and get drunk. I wanted enough good feelings to flow so that the mysteries of Being might venture out among us. For it was coolness, and hostility, and carbon-paper thinking, that had made me Beat, and I could see no point in trading one set of joy-killing, wonder-wilting stereotypes for another.

I suppose they thought of me as a sell-out, but it always seemed to me that they were the ones who must be selling something, because they *advertised* so much. My urge had always been to keep free of *all* the pigeonholes of society, which was best accomplished by slipping through it unnoticed, whereas they seemed obsessed with the *need* to be noticed, and thus slavishly turned themselves into so many replicas of the

Squares' image of the Beats. Therein lay their sadness to me (and, more important, their non-Beat quality), for, like the Squares, they sought a sense of their own uniqueness, not in themselves, but in others; and, so victimized were they, the only source from which they could derive this feeling of uniqueness was the aversion of the very world they had judged inadequate.

A strange sort of love affair ensued, in which the Beatniks transgressed all the taboos the Squares *longed* to transgress, and each vicariously shared the other's outrage or titillation. In a society with a fixation on cleanliness, the Beatniks were indifferent to personal hygiene; in a society that was sexually demented, they said all the "dirty" words and did all the "dirty" things; in a society that was success-dominated, they chose to live in voluntary poverty—in other words, they were irresponsible, they were hedonistic, they had more *fun*. But if the beatniks were good copy, it was because they acted out all these censored fantasies, and thereby provided a kind of voyeuristic relief to a frustrated time, and not because they were authentically Beat—at least insofar as I understood the word.

But there were serious critics who realized that there was more to the antics of the Beatniks than simply a lot of neurotic clowning; who glimpsed the state of mind of which the Beatniks were only the theatricalized symptoms; who, in other words, addressed themselves to the phenomenon of Beatness, and found it wanting. Some discussion of their objections may throw light on the subtler misunderstandings of the Beat Generation, which eventually consigned it, as a concept, to oblivion—though, as I believe, the attitude goes on. I will deal with only three such objections, each of which is representative of a different degree of sympathy. There were others, but these three were typical.

The most reiterated of these objections was summed up by Norman Podhoretz when he described the Beat Generation as a "revolt of the spiritually underprivileged and the crippled of soul—young men who can't think straight and so hate anyone who can; young men who can't get outside the morass of self and so construct definitions of feeling that exclude all human beings who manage to live, even miserably, in a world of objects." In this view, the Beats were primitivistic, anti-intellectual, know-nothing, proto-fascist sensation hunters, whose very important difference from the Rimbauds, Villons, and Genets of the past was that (in Herbert Gold's words) those "great artist-criminals were true outcasts from society: they did not pick themselves up by the seat of their own pants and toss themselves out."

One is tempted to ask just *who* tossed them out then; one is tempted to defend these Great Seceders from the implicit charge that they acted as helpless victims, rather than as defiant judges, of the world they abandoned, but there are more important considerations to be dealt with. What angers critics like Podhoretz is that the Beat attitude is apolitical, asocial, and amoral; that it concerns itself with intuitions, soul states, and affirmations of Being; that (as Podhoretz complained) "Kerouac's love of Negroes and other dark-skinned groups is [not] tied up with any radical social attitudes"; that the Beats seem to feel "that respectability is a sign not of moral corruption but of spiritual death"; that, because their casual amorous encounters "always entail sweet feelings toward the girl" and not "defiance of convention," they are a sign of "sexual anxiety of enormous proportions"; that "if a filling station will serve as well as the Rocky Mountains to arouse a sense of awe and wonder, then both the filling station and the mountains are robbed of their reality."

It is difficult to counter such charges, because, in one sense, they are all true. Given Podhoretz's values (the values of a young man who misses—and *missed*—the social activism of the thirties, and cannot understand even at this late hour why it failed either to produce great literature or change the world); given his values, his charges are all understandable. One can only wonder *who* is living in the real world, however (the post-Freudian, post-Marxist world of the 1960's): Podhoretz or Kerouac?

Podhoretz sees Negroes in terms of "radical social attitudes," and cannot comprehend (as many middle class Negroes cannot either) that what attracts the alienated white to the Negro in this century is that, having been excluded from the society, the Negro has been less stultified, in his *soul* at least, by it. To see this attraction as "an inverted form of keeping the nigger in his place" (as Ned Polsky believes it to be), rather than as a sign of how completely the modern world (by starving our intuitive faculties) has aroused a hunger in us for the spontaneities of the spirit, is to confess an inability to conceive of any problem that is not a cut-and-dried social "issue."

Podhoretz can see nothing behind the need for "sweet feelings" but the blight of "sexual anxiety," which (to men like him) is the emotional equivalent of social disenfranchisement, and nothing more. What can one say to such astonishing myopia? Need one mention that human beings are more than just bellies to be filled and egos to be gratified? That there *is* something graver than "moral corruption"? That its name *is* "spiritual death"? And that an unexamined life can lead to it? Need one repeat, after all the Dachaus and the Budapests, that there is something in all of us that is infinitely larger than the mechanisms of impersonal logic that we have manufactured to explain ourselves?

But, above all, Podhoretz cannot comprehend the nature of "awe and wonder," and he wants things firmly in their places, so that when he sees the Rocky Mountains he will know what to feel, and when he sees a filling station he will know what *not* to feel. Blake's ability "To see the world in a grain of sand/ And heaven in a wild flower" is not for him, and it is not for him because "awe and wonder" are not for him either. For as he says, "Whenever I hear anyone talking about instinct and being and the secrets of human energy, I get nervous."

But at the last, views such as Podhoretz's criticized the Beat Generation because it refused to see all problems, social and psychological, in coherent, rational and responsible terms. There is no arguing with that; it is absolutely true, and therein lay the value of the Beat attitude, at least as I conceived it. It was a clean break with all the failed modes of thought that had solved nothing; it was an attempt, above all, to reconceive the idea of the nature of man. For Beatness tried to concern itself with the largest problem of all—man orphaned from his world, and from himself; smack up against the stubborn fact of his existentiality, with which only a further evolution of his consciousness could cope. And all other "problems" (so said the

Beats) were only symptoms of our civilization's failure to address itself to this.

Paul Goodman's view of the Beat Generation (in *Growing Up Absurd*) is at once friendlier and more critically perceptive. He is certainly not offended by it, but he doesn't take it entirely seriously either. Still, no better analysis of the milieu and attitudes of the Beatniks exists outside his book, and, if anything, Goodman is more tolerant of some of their stunts and whimsies than I am. He finds them, on the whole, "sweet, independent, free-thinking, affectionate, perhaps faithful, probably sexy." Though he mostly dismisses their art works, he thinks it is "admirable that the Beat Generation has contrived a pattern of culture that, turning against the standard culture, costs very little and gives livelier satisfaction." And, above all, he knows that there is a larger dilemma to which the Beat attitude is a viable response—even though (Goodman-like) he will go no further than to say, "The organized system is the breeding ground of a Beat Generation," which, if it does not suggest that the Beats themselves are a social disease, at least implies that they are the victims of one.

But again, it is their spiritual preoccupation that makes him impatient. Unlike Podhoretz, he understands that "the Beats regard themselves as in a metaphysical crisis," and that "if there is *always* an emergency, it must imply that the danger is internal as well as external." And also unlike Podhoretz, he is perceptive enough to realize that the principle by which they cope with this "is the traditional one of classical mysticism: by 'experiences' (= kicks) to transcend the nagged and nagging self altogether and get out of one's skin." But, social critic that he is, he cannot see this as anything but the last and most hopeless extremity to which an irrational social organization can drive its more sensitive members. He doesn't really believe that there *is* a "metaphysical crisis"; it is only that work has been made meaningless, interpersonal relations are beset by moralistic shibboleths, and most of our values are unrelated to reality. But all this, he says, can be *fixed*.

Again, it is difficult to argue. Goodman is one of the most imaginative *and* realistic social observers of which our culture can boast. We are enlarged by his presence among us, and it would be unreasonable to blame him because he simply isn't much interested in a "metaphysical crisis"—to the existence of which such diverse things as existentialism, hallucinogenic drugs, Norman O. Brown, *and* Beatness, all attest.

Goodman realizes (albeit in the impatience of a parenthesis) that "the classical mystic who loses this world knows well, on returning to it, that it is a poor thing; and also that it is pointless to try to describe the Reality in terms of this world." But the fact that young men today could venture as far out, and profess a similarly enigmatic message when they return, seems to have escaped him. It has always been my understanding of the Beat attitude that it was indicative of precisely this uneasy interaction between the myriad worlds within and the single world outside. But then my *experience* has been that real, live mystics profoundly disturb most critics, to whom the "systematic derangement of the senses" is somehow heroic in Rimbaud, but is merely sordid in Ginsberg.

Most of my differences with Norman Mailer, on the other hand, are differences of future direction, and if I class him as a critic of the concept of Beatness I have been describing, it is not because he has misunderstood it. Though he came to the matter late (in the mid-fifties), he came to it as a result of "the rebellious imperatives of the self," and he brought to it the most venturesome intellect (not to mention nerves) currently at work in American literature.

As should be wearisomely clear by now, a confusion of terminology has plagued the naming of this generation, as it did those of biblical times, and Mailer's vote would probably go to Hip. I am sure all of us by now would cordially be rid of labels altogether. Certainly I have no fondness for the one with which I am associated, and am only interested in the New Consciousness for which it is a crude and perhaps misleading adjective, but nevertheless Mailer, and Hip, deserve a brief look.

As has been seen, I consider *The White Negro* to be a pioneer exploration of this New Consciousness, a document fully as important to the secret history of this age as *Notes from Underground* was to the Europe of its time. In a footnote to *The White Negro* (written somewhat later), Mailer says, "The

Beat Generation is probably best used to include hipsters and beatniks"; he then goes on to detail with fine precision the differences between the two. The Beatniks are more intellectual, less sexy; they are mystic, pacifist and neurotic, whereas "the hipster is still in life; strong on his will, he takes on the dissipation of the drugs in order to dig more life for himself, he is wrestling with the destiny of his nervous system, he is Faustian." I find little of importance to disagree with in this, as my views of the Beatniks may have made clear. But it is on this matter of "the destiny of the nervous system" where Mailer and I diverge, just as Hipness and Beatness (as I mean it) ultimately reach a crossroads of the consciousness, and must go their different ways.

Mailer's hipster goes back into the jungle of the world, where Power is the prize, and ego is the weapon, and Hip the sight through which you aim. But the destiny of the nervous system, accumulating Sensation the way Faust's mind accumulated Knowledge, is inexorably violence, just as surely as Faust's destiny was damnation, for neither the mind *nor* the nervous system is a large enough channel for the whole of Consciousness. And it is our consciousness of *more* than either our nerves or our minds can contain by themselves that is the primary fact of this half of the Twentieth century.

I have always thought that Mailer stubbed his toe on "God." He is a metaphysician snagged in the data of the senses. I do not mean to say that he is immodest when I say that he cannot seem to endure the ego-loss toward which all his finest perceptions are driving him. There is something about the "merging" that all states of heightened Consciousness precipitate that revulses him. And yet he knows, he knows—for in sex, where the dissolving of the ego is most imminent and most intense, his vision comes perilously close to a drunken fusion of the insights of Sade and Swedenborg (if that can be imagined), only to draw back at the final moment when the character armor begins to melt, and insist on once again confusing the Ego with the Self.

His version of Beat (call it what you will) is decidedly "of this world," and, as such, it has proved more comprehensible, and more attractive, than any other version. It has even suc-

ceeded in establishing a point of re-entry into the public world
(what he has dubbed "existential politics") that a serious man
can take seriously, and the consequences of which are as yet
incalculable.

Still, he goes on fighting, and fighting in the world's terms
(albeit with weapons that are closer to the truths of Being than
any that have been wielded heretofore), whereas it seems clear
to me that it is the terms themselves that must be changed if
the senseless fighting is ever to cease. It is only accurate to
remark, however, that Mailer's psychology of Hip has mostly
absorbed, in the public mind at least, the attitude of Beatness
which was, to me, the larger climate that nurtured it.

As is evident by now, the spiritual hunger, the metaphysical
quest, the new consciousness, which I considered to be the
essence of the Beat attitude, did not impress the critics over-
much, or even engage the Beatniks for very long. The times
were certainly ready for what *Life* Magazine called "the only
rebellion around," but they were ready for the bongo drums
and poetry-readings, not for a condition of expectation in the
soul; and consequently the Beat Generation, during its brief
hour of notoriety, did not move in this direction. Now that it
has all but vanished, it is clear that its contributions were social
and cultural—its ferment was fermenting—and, in the light of
this, I cannot fault its critics for failing to stress what proved to
be as superficial a part of its lifestyle as its beards.

It is clear that *my* conception of Beatness was just that—
mine; or at best a conception shared to one degree or another
by my *crowd*—Kerouac, Ginsberg, Burroughs, Corso and a few
others, like Snyder and Whalen, who turned up on the West
Coast. What I was projecting were my own bankruptcies and
aspirations, just as Jack projected his in all his novels. But it was
the blasting, beering and bumming in our work, the restless,
energetic surface of the life described, and *not* the world-and-
mind weariness, the continual moulting of consciousness, and
the spirit's arduous venture toward its own reconciliations, that
caught whatever fancies—Square *or* Beatnik—that were eventually caught.

Finally, *my* Beat Generation, like the Lost Generation before
it, was primarily a literary group, and not a social movement;

and probably all that will last out of our Beat years are a rash of vaporous anecdotes, and the few solid works that were produced. We have paid for the audacity of daring to label ourselves a "generation" by being continually ticketed with attitudes of mind and styles of behavior that were not necessarily ours, and having our work dismissed as these attitudes and styles became moribund. But thankfully a book is not as ephemeral as a beard, and, if it is a good book, it will outlast whatever quick-fading labels are attached to it. Time will tell, and not too quickly.

For the rest of it, it seems to me, the Beat Generation (and even the sorriest of the Beatniks) made contributions to the scene which deserve to be assessed—if only because they are in danger of being forgotten now, so radically has that scene changed in the last years.

Culturally, America has gone through something of a "thaw" since 1960. Part of this can be attributed to the fact that we had a President, albeit briefly, for whom culture, if it did not mean Charlie Parker, at least meant more than Lawrence Welk; a man in whose mouth the names of Faulkner and Hemingway did not sound ghost-written; a man who could speak of the inner life without somehow suggesting the digestive process. But whatever the reason, the atmosphere has changed. Among other things, the old puritan structure of censorship has been dismantled, idiocy by idiocy, and the clammy hand of Academia has been returned to the exhumation of dead works, rather than the murder of living ones. It is assumed, once more, that poetry *can* make something happen—other than a plague of exegetics, spreading through the "little magazines" like African sleeping sickness. Novels are published now that couldn't even have been written a few scant years ago. John Cage is no longer spoken of as a demented piano tuner; De Kooning is welcomed in the White House; even Iowa City has its Bergman Festival.

Off-Broadway, LSD, Ornette Coleman; the Frug, Genet, Buñuel—for the first time, the avant-garde is fashionable, experimentation is news, the far-out style is the chic style. Much of this is a mixed blessing at best, for much of it suggests the supermarket gourmand ("More, more! New, new!"), rather than the specialty-shop gourmet ("This, and this, but not that"). Still, it is a more open culture now, a culture at least trying to relate to a real and specific world, a culture in which strongly individual voices can be heard over the mindless din of the entertainment factories.

The poets, playwrights and novelists, who might be loosely associated with the Beat attitude, were among the first of these voices to be heard, and their insistence on talking in loud, personal terms (whose very negation of certain values was an implicit affirmation of others) provoked those, who were not specifically "beat" themselves, into speaking up as well. The basic *tone* of the culture has changed from the caution, irony and impersonality of the critical intellectual to the daring, commitment and diversity of the creative artist, and the Beats certainly deserve a sizable part of the credit for this.

Socially, also, America is a different land. If there has been a new tide running in the nation these past years—a tide of dissent, activism and involvement (in civil rights, disarmament, poverty and freedom of speech); a tide that bluntly calls into question the quality of our life here at home, and challenges mere anticommunism as a sane foundation for our policy abroad; a tide that has noisily erupted in the universities, the magazines, the public forums and the streets themselves—this tide is urged on by a new generation, which grew to awareness in the last half of the fifties, and was exposed to the example of a fragment of my generation, whose fixation with the idea that the Emperor had no clothes led it to proclaim the bald and unruly "No!", without which the Free Speechers, the Ban-the-Bombers, and the white (at least) Sit-Ins might not have been able to say the challenging "Yes!" we are hearing at last in the land. For if politics are back "in" among the young, they are a very different sort of politics than those of the thirties or the forties—a much tougher-minded, pragmatic, life-grounded politics, a politics of personal witness and nonviolence, a politics that tries to replace bloodless ideology with the living body interposed between the finger of the Establishment and the various buttons of the Society. All in all, it is a time of possibilities again, for which the Beat revolt is not a little responsible.

Perhaps because of all this, the fever for naming generations may be dying out of our culture at last. Perhaps the future holds no single occurrence that will prove so forming that an entire age group can be characterized by a single term. Sometimes I find myself wondering if this happened, in actual fact, in our case. But deluded though we may have been, it *was* a generation we sought to describe, and not simply a minority group and its exotic mores; it was a unique phenomenon-of-mind in all of us, and not only the eccentric behavior patterns in a few, that we felt impelled to name. And if we were wrong, it was not because we were eclectic. For myself, I believe that we perceived the new sort of consciousness that distinguished us from our elders with a clarity the intervening years have not seriously blurred.

But I cannot leave this matter of the Beat attitude without a word about the generation that has come along since mine. If, as I believe, some of its achievements, and a lot of its style, have flourished on the ground we cleared, nevertheless the differences between us may yet prove to be greater than the similarities. Existentialism, as an example, exerts a powerful influence on both generations, and probably constitutes the only philosophic point of view that is broadly typical of this time. But whereas it was existentialism's conception of the nature of man that spoke so clearly to *us*, it is existentialism's engagement in the community of men that most appeals to *them*. Nonviolence, pacifism and reverence for life are mostly means of social action to young people today, whereas, to us, they were ends in themselves: you were nonviolent not because it was one way of changing institutions, but because it was the only way of remaining a human being. Just as the improvised, individualistic onrush of *our* music and the warm, sexy mutuality of the spontaneous dances we did to it have given way to the amplified whanging of massed guitars and the squirming, jerking onanism of the Pony, the Swim, and the Watusi, so our solemn, quasi-biblical beards have been replaced by those androgynous, *fin de siècle* mops that suggest an inner dislocation more psychiatric than eccentric.

Though we recognize our own preoccupations in all these things, the unmistakable whiff of fear that seems to stand behind them (fear of life, fear of death, fear of commitment to any *private* emotion) leads me, at least, to the conclusion that this generation has yet to learn some of the uncomfortable truths that lay at the end of our road. Already the New Politics is as riddled with schisms, doctrinal hostilities, and obsession with organization as the Old. Already the new sexual candor has become more obscene than it is pornographic, and seems to be almost exclusively concerned with shocking (rather than liberating) the repressed eroticism that is as evident in J. D. Salinger as it is in Henry James. Everywhere one senses that impoverishment of deep feelings, of which the surest signs are a senseless proliferation of "causes," and a rash of artistic, sartorial, narcotic and sexual diversions—every one of which (curiously enough) involves a willed violation of *Self*, as if in the wan hope that some emotional recoil will suddenly occur out of the inner wasteland. Everywhere the very ferment and diversity in the culture seem to mask a helplessness grown so encompassing as to be beyond either anguish or outrage, a helplessness that only a leer or a snicker can express. Everywhere one sees the reign of what can only be called Anti-Values—those values of the twilight of a time. Or the hour before the dawn.

Perhaps these are inevitable reactions to a world that twenty years of Cold War have brought closer to insanity than to sense, but if that world is ever to be diverted from its present collision course with the fatality inherent in its own history (an onerous task that will fall on people who are under twenty-five today), my generation's stubborn choice of man over society, the Self over the Ego and the spirit over psychology, may have to be made all over again by those to whom we honestly thought we had bequeathed it already.

But then growing up in America has always been arduous. Our maturation rites are compounded of equal parts of nihilism and idealism, and we have always smashed our icons with *other* icons here. Young Americans have immemorially been as uncritical in their surrender to the present as they are ruthless in their repudiation of the past, and a disorderly, eruptive process of individuation, whose first requirement seems to be a weaning-by-excess, is a tradition so unbroken and so peculiar to us that America's senescence may only be said to have arrived when it no longer produces successive generations-in-revolt.

For my own part, I am weary of labels. Whatever lies ahead

for my generation will certainly make them less and less applicable to our experience, for an inevitable part of aging seems to be that one relentlessly becomes less representative of one's times, and more representative of oneself. Something like this, it seems to me, is happening to all of us who shared the Beat years—which, of course, was precisely what the Beat Generation was all about.

The Silence of Oswald

"Wasn't there anyone to give you the lecture on Cuba? Don't you sense the enormity of your mistake—you invade a country without understanding its music."

(Mailer in an Open Letter to J.F.K.)

§ § In a special sense that had little to do with his politics, John Kennedy was *our* President, the first President with whom people of my age could feel a personal identification. Whether we agreed with him or not, we assumed that we could address him as Mailer does above, without being scoffed at for suggesting that intelligence about a country's soul was as essential to foreign policy as intelligence about its Coastal Defenses. Kennedy brought a style, eloquence, taste, courage and relish for the game (perhaps the best qualities of youth) back into public life again, and I think we all became a little more interested in politics during his Administration than we had been in ten years.

If we were sometimes suspicious of his motives, critical of his accomplishments and wary of his charm, it was not because he resembled his predecessors, but precisely because he was so different from them that we judged him by different standards —standards based on reality rather than realpolitik, the standards by which we judged each other. For a brief time, America was a more exciting place to live in day to day. The rhetorical

§ 144

grunts that usually characterize our political hog-wallow were temporarily out of fashion, and a certain sharpeyed wit and grace (as distant from the locker-room wowser and the Fred Waring fox trot as Abilene is from Boston) were definitely in. For once, we had a Chief Executive and his Lady who could be viewed as sexual objects with no feeling of disrespect, and if we cavilled at the fact that Nelson Algren and Norman Mailer remained uninvited to the White House, it was not because good writers never appeared there. The persistent feeling that this man might decisively affect the quality of American public life for decades to come must have plagued even the most cynical of us. And then, with the suddenness of a rifle shot, it was over.

Probably the most universal reaction to the assassination was the shocking realization that some promise, some hope, some still-unplumbed *chance* for a shift in mood had been inexplicably lost. At least, the words that kept running through *my* head during those awful days after Dallas had nothing to do with political parties or programs: "Now it's back to America-as-usual," I thought. And yet something huge and terrible and *new* seemed to be shuddering in the air, as if a phantom Caliban had broken out of the cellars in the national psyche, and struck down our Ariel for no other reason than a desire to wreck the play. The age-old American belief in the perfectability of men *through* politics, and the bitter, violent hatred (equally age-old) which this belief can rouse in the murky corners of the soul, had collided, and the best we had to offer to this moment in history had been savagely cut down by—what? A madman? A disgruntled ideologist? A pawn in some sinister plot?

Whether out of frustrated vengeance or honest bewilderment, we turned to the figure of Lee Harvey Oswald, as you sometimes turn ahead to the last chapter of a murder mystery, acknowledging the fact that the more cruel and gratuitous the crime, the greater is the need to understand it if you are to accept a loss as stunning as Kennedy's was to us and still keep your perspective. But instead of a clear motive, an articulate gesture, and a coherent human being, we found only a further riddle, a more impenetrable silence, a man of paper. Oswald looked out at us from our TV sets—querulous, ungiving and mockingly enigmatic. We saw his death flood, with the anguish of surprise, across his face, and we saw his secrets and his reasons perish with him. I think that the suspicion that we might never know the whole truth, and that it was somehow crucial that we do if that Caliban-side of American life was ever to be disarmed (and *some* good come out of it), drove not a few of us a little off center for a time.

In any case, the necessity to understand Lee Harvey Oswald became a governmental, as well as a personal, fixation in the months that followed, resulting in the publication of the Warren Report a year later, in which most of the important *factual* questions about Oswald seemed to be answered, except in the minds of chronic skeptics and conspiracy-hunters. For despite the fact that the case against Oswald appeared to be damning as early as January, 1964, the rumors, theories, and dark allegations mounted steadily nevertheless, and the Report did little to bring these speculations to an end.

Indeed, they have continued unabated to this day. The competence of the Commission itself has been seriously questioned. Doubts as to the thoroughness and neutrality of its investigation have been raised, and it now seems likely that the Commission's work was hurried, haphazard in certain respects, and ultimately unsuccessful in accounting for gaps in the evidence and discrepancies in the testimony—to explain which, fantastic theories have been propounded (like the so-called Second Oswald Theory, which literally creates "two" questions for every one it answers). But none of these speculations, however intriguing they may be, have come up with a single scrap of positive evidence that alters the strong feeling one has after reading the Report: That despite all the gaps and all the discrepancies, in all probability it was Lee Harvey Oswald who killed John Kennedy, aided and abetted in the act by an incredible run of luck but by no one else, and that, so far at least, there is small reason to assume that the assassination did not occur more or less as the Warren Report describes it. The single most interesting question—the question of *Why?*—has not been answered by any of these post-Report theories because, quite simply, they never raise it.

Why have so many people lavished so much torturous logic

on the mostly inconsequential holes in the case against Oswald? Why have these skeptics continued to erect ever more elaborate explanations, all of which are based on nothing more damning than the conflict of recollection and the difficulty of making an airtight reconstruction of an event after the fact, that are typical of any murder case where there is neither an eye-witness nor a confession? And finally, why do most of us feel that somehow something *is* missing, even in the Report, that would make the assassination of this popular and gifted young President comprehensible?

The reasons may be more simple than the sort of subjective politicking and simplistic psychologizing to which we are all prone in moments of crisis. For an almost unbroken chain of facts *is* incomprehensible unless the man they indict is comprehensible too, and without an overriding motive all evidence remains circumstantial. The Warren Report notwithstanding, we are forced to conclude that few of the facts therein do much to answer the blunt questions: Given Oswald, why Kennedy? What was the reason for this seemingly absurd act?

Probably no one will ever be able to answer these questions for certain, and yet if we accept the broad conclusions of the Report, that Oswald was guilty and he acted alone (and I *still* see no way to avoid doing so), we are compelled to look more deeply into the life and character of Lee Harvey Oswald in the hope of discovering the psychic drives that produced his crime. Certainly I cannot have been alone in plodding through every one of the Warren Report's 800-odd pages for the sole purpose of understanding Oswald, and thus ridding myself of what had become something of an obsession. For the feeling persisted in me that somehow Oswald embodied, albeit to an extreme, a condition of Being that is growing more and more prevalent in our time.

Two kinds of motivation were ascribed to Oswald—politics and/or madness—and yet the persistent doubts, echoed in the Report itself, indicated how unsatisfactory these explanations were, to reasonable and unreasonable men alike. On the one hand, the political overtones of the assassination (a left-winger killing a liberal President) were so confused and contradictory that they supplied no really conclusive reason for the crime; and on the other, Oswald under arrest never exhibited (as did Jack Ruby) the self-aggrandizement, disassociation and rapid alternation of mood which characterize a seriously demented man. He was a psychopath all right—that was clear—but what kind of psychopath? What aggravated his condition beyond bearing? And, above all, what was the specific need in this peculiar man that demanded this particular expression?

A "deep" reading of the Report gave me, at least, a hint of an answer to these questions, for such a reading gradually made clear that Oswald's action may have been nothing less than his decisive move *beyond* politics, and *out* of mere neurosis, into that frightening existential realm from which people sometimes violently gesture back at the reality they feel has excluded them. (Camus' novel, *The Stranger*, is a chilling examination of just such a feeling of exclusion.) That people *do* act for reasons of this sort is evidenced every day in newspaper stories of cases of "meaningless" violence on the part of alienated, socially disoriented individuals (the Whitman case in Austin, Texas, 1966, is one example), and perhaps it was because the victim, in this case, was a President, and the assassin a political dissenter, that we failed to glimpse what had been under our noses all along.

Consider Oswald's human situation. His life was as unremittingly bleak, loveless and thwarting as any described in a Dostoyevskian novel. Growing up in a society that provided an unskilled but reasonably intelligent man almost nothing meaningful on which to expend his idealism, his personal environment continually sabotaged his efforts to discover his own value as a human being, and the sobering fact is that there may be almost a million people in the U.S. who are indistinguishable from Oswald, except for the crime he committed. Rootless, traditionless, fatherless, unloved by his "self-involved" mother, emotionally displaced by their peripatetic life together, moving restlessly from flat to flat, city to city, always crushingly alone, his hours occupied by TV and chance books, friendless and rejected, and so withdrawing more and more from any renewing contact with others, Oswald was that typical figure of the modern world: the anonymous, urban mass-man, who most always has the same blank, half-scornful, sullen expression on his face. Oswald's photos, as an example, are all alarmingly alike, and he always looks the same: cautious, irritable, hungry, *masked*. To him, the world was as impersonal as the camera, and he turned the same face to both.

He appears to have embraced Marxism because, in the U.S. of the 1950's, it was the most unpopular, rebellious, and socially outrageous creed he could espouse. The society which gave him no place, and did not deign to notice him *even* as a dissident, had to be spurned in its turn: "I reject the world that has rejected me," as Jean Genet has put it. Nevertheless, Oswald exhibited the neurotic's standard ambivalence toward authority: to escape from one (his mother), he embraced another (the Marines); to defy the U.S., he defended the U.S.S.R. But he was happy nowhere; the psychic heat in him intensified, demanding ceaseless changes of mind to accommodate it, and his few short years were marked by a bewildering number of conflicting political and emotional attitudes. There are those hundreds of dreary, "official" letters to the Soviet authorities, the State Department, the Navy Department, the FBI and almost everyone else, the sole reason for which was to define and get on the record his chameleon-like changes of status. Like many of us in this bureaucratized world, he searched for himself in his dossier.

Everything disappointed him; nothing gave him a feeling of his own distinct being; he tried over and over again to find a situation in which he could experience himself as alive, productive, a person of consequence, and one of the most interesting clues to his personality lies in the odd fact of his always writing about his actions (in his Historic Diary) in the present tense. The entry recording his suicide attempt in Russia is a telling example (the spelling and punctuation are Oswald's): "I am shocked!! My dreams! . . . have waited for 2 years to be accepted. My fondes dreams are shattered because of a petty offial . . . I decide to end it. Soak rist in cold water to numb the pain, Than slash my leftrist. Than plaug wrist into bathtum of hot water . . . Somewhere, a violin plays, as I wacth my life whirl away. I think to myself 'How easy to Die' and 'A Sweet Death, (to violins)'."

This is an astonishing image of a man observing himself as if he was not himself, at once self-dramatic and objective, pathetic and theatrical, but, above all, *cold.* The very precision of his account of the preparations, the alert recording of his sensory perceptions, and particularly the ironic comment at the end, form a picture of a man cruelly isolated in himself, to whom lonely communion with his own thoughts, and the sort of false, reportorial objectivity that often results, are the normal way he experiences his consciousness. Such a man often becomes a melancholic, or an artist, or a killer.

Oswald's inherent dissent soon overran his political convictions. Pinning his hopes on Russia, he was relieved for a time; losing those hopes in disappointment, he returned to the U.S., only to feel the pressure of exclusion rising in him once again. He vacillated between Cuba and Russia; he made abortive attempts to find a place for himself in various radical movements. Everywhere he was blocked, rejected, ignored. His inability to arrange an escape to Havana seems to have left him, at the last, utterly bereft, utterly placeless, finally *outside* the conflicting political solutions to his discontent. It thrust him back upon himself, reduced him to having to live with the facts of his social impotence, and his personal inadequacy, without even the illusion that he was enduring this pain in the name of something outside himself. As a result, the hammer on the rifle of his already alienated nature was cocked.

His wife never appears to have understood the sort of man he was. She comes through the Report as shallow, adaptable, materialistic, and self-centered; a simple, affectionate creature, rather like *The Stranger's* mistress, with little or no understanding of the existential attraction of underground politics to the young, disaffected American, or even of the "complex fate" of Oswald's relentlessly dispiriting life. She chides him for his failures, she complains about his ideas; she is easily accepted into the Dallas Russian Colony, while he is not; in *his* country, she finds what he has never found—friends. Oswald's male pride is constantly abused by their acquaintances, by his job losses, by their poverty, his family, and ultimately by Marina herself in the most unforgivable way: she ridicules his sexual performance. He beats her up; he is puritanical in specifically sexual ways (he flies into a fury because the zipper on her skirt is not properly fastened in front of others); he doesn't want her to smoke, or drink, or use cosmetics. He discovers her letter to a former beau in Russia, lamenting that she hadn't married *him*. The pattern of exclusion and failure becomes more and more interiorized, it reaches that pitch of psychological pressure where a man acts decisively to overcome everything, or goes under and loses his image of himself. And no matter how extravagant or idiotic that image may be, a man must have a self-image or go mad.

Viewed in this light, Oswald's crime may have been a last desperate attempt to become part of reality again, to force his way back into the reality that had ignored him, so that he could experience himself as *acting*, as living, as committed. "Men also secrete the inhuman," Camus has written. "Sometimes, in [our] moments of lucidity, the mechanical aspect of their gestures and their senseless pantomime make everything about them seem stupid." And when we are possessed by such a feeling, we have lost that sense of immediate contact with the world that is the strongest check on the violent whims that sometimes stir in all of us.

For there comes a moment when we realize that we can break through the invisible and intangible wall that separates us from the person standing right next to us; when we realize that we have been drifting along, as if under water, in the terror and *silence* of isolation; when we see things with the "hopeless lucidity" that Sartre has described somewhere, and realize that only an unwarranted act, an abrupt breaking through the wall, will restore us to reality, and obliterate that silence that imprisons us; when we realize that *they* are not mechanical dolls, automatons moving through a dream from which only *we* are excluded, but human—because they will bleed, hurt, die, and (perhaps most importatnt of all) turn toward us at the last their shocked faces, across which no hint of our existence has ever glimmered before, startled now by the abrupt recognition of our presence among them. When Marina joined *them*, when she crossed over to the other side of the wall, refusing even to talk to Oswald that last night, refusing even to consider moving into Dallas with him, she (in one sense) put the cartridge in the chamber of his life, and President Kennedy was doomed.

Still, it is possible that Oswald was not absolutely committed to his act. He may have taken the rifle to work that day merely to experience the strange and lonesome thrill of being able to hold someone's life in his hands for a single giddy moment. After all, this is why people peer through binoculars in big cities—to initiate an intimacy that is not threatening because it is an illusion. This is why people expose themselves on subway platforms, without actually planning to assault the observer, and, in some cases, hoping not even to be noticed by him. This is why people carry weapons they could never bring themselves to use. It is the urge of the outsider, the isolated, to feign a breakthrough into the unknown possibilities of on-going reality, and it is at least conceivable that Oswald intended to do nothing but *view* Kennedy through the telescopic sight of his rifle, and feel for a moment the omnipotence and self-importance that his whole life (and now his wife as well) had denied him.

Once having reached this point, however, circumstances would have pushed him over. For circumstances, the accidents of as yet unrealized Time, often create the pressure of the finger on the trigger, and psychologists believe that people always act by some logic of self-interest at their peril. What might have happened, for instance, if the Negro youth, who had eaten his lunch at Oswald's window a scant half hour before, had remained there instead of going down to a lower floor to watch the motorcade with his friends? What would have happened had someone asked Oswald to watch the motorcade with *him*? No one can say, and yet one is left with the uneasy feeling that an act of friendship, a recognition, a movement toward human contact at a hundred different junctures during Oswald's life might have radically altered the course he travelled. So why not at this most crucial of junctures? If, for instance, Marina had discussed their situation with him that last night, and perhaps allowed that discussion to lead to some sort of minimal reconciliation in their bed, would Oswald have needed this ultimate, severing act to relieve himself of the unendurable *silence* that enclosed him? No one can ever say.

Certainly, his psychopathy was real, constantly expanding and dangerous. He had tried to kill General Walker some months earlier, after planning the attempt for many weeks, only to miss a far easier shot than the apparently impulsive ones that hit the President—a clear indication to me that the first was only another muddled political gesture, whereas the second was something deeper and more mysterious. By November, 1963, his need had grown to proportions that no single annealing act on the part of any one person, much less the environment, could have dissipated. And yet there are probably thousands of people who are daily caught in psychic binds not unlike his—so many cocked rifles walking anonymously through the streets—and little or nothing in our society, or in our mostly naive conceptions of our responsibility to each other's lonely struggle to keep from drowning in it, offers any sure way by which these cocked rifles can be disarmed. At least not until they have gone off, and it is too late.

Oswald's relation to reality is succinctly described by the "we" in Camus: "A man is talking on the telephone. We cannot hear him behind the glass partition, but we can see his senseless mimicry. We wonder why he is alive?" It was this glass partition that separated Oswald from the rest of us, and made him feel that he was only a "thing" in our eyes, a piece of meaningless, uncared-for flotsam. But a man cannot exist this way, at least not a man who is the inquisitive, articulate and impatient neurotic that Oswald seems to have been. Such a man often feels that only two alternatives are open to him: to rashly insist on being his idealized image of himself, or to slavishly become the nonentity the world tells him over and over again that he is.

The fact remains that in the urbanized and impersonal America of his day, Oswald's resources were never used, his affections were never aroused, his concern-for-the-future was never harnessed, and yet, on the evidence, he seems to have been reasonably brave, potentially decisive, mostly hardworking, and certainly untiring in his efforts to break out of the deadend of his existence. At least all these qualities were present in him, in embryo, and only soured and became destructive when he could find no place to utilize them creatively.

One indication of the blistered wasteland of his human and social hopes lies in this passage, which he wrote after his disappointment with Russia: "I wonder what would happen if somebody was to stand up and say he was utterly opposed not only to the governments, but to the people, to the entire land and complete foundations of his society." We need no longer wonder, for he has given us one answer to the question, and perhaps it was this very "wondering" of his that led him (still uncommitted to the act itself) to that window. In any case, his words stand as a twisted rebuke to a society that can seem to recognize only its madmen or its heroes, but steadfastly ignores the countless millions of anonymous people yearning to feel some responsibility, some faith, some ultimate *stake* in the world around them.

In a larger sense, the two polar aspects of the contemporary American character collided that day in Dallas—a consideration which, in going beyond politics, goes far to explain why it *had* to be Kennedy. For John Kennedy was everything that Lee Oswald was not. He existed directly in the vivid center of reality, he was potent in every way, his life and personality were one continuous action and interaction; he was neither dualistic, separated, nor helpless; he had never been prevented from experiencing himself as alive and consequential. Oswald struck back at everything he was *not*, but in a sense he was performing a Kennedy-like act (as far as he could imagine one), and was attempting to *become* the sort of man he killed by the very *act* of killing. And so all that was most starved, thwarted and hopeless in our national life took its pathetic and sullen revenge on all that was most vital, potent and attractive.

The horror of Oswald's loneliness, the extremity of his hunger, the appalling facelessness and spirit-withering *silence* of his whole life exploded in a bitter and anguished threat: either he would be admitted onto life's stage, or he would pull that stage down in total ruin; he would be recognized as having that sense of uniqueness that a human being *has* to have if he is to outwit the despair that leads to madness, or he would turn his very powerlessness into a source of power. Those who are imprisoned in the silence of reality always use a gun (or, if they are more fortunate, a pen) to speak for them, and perhaps the prince and the pauper in the human spirit are doomed to meet face to face, no matter what. But certainly the job of a sane and mature society is to see that this meeting does not have to take place through the sights of a high-powered rifle.

In one sense, we are poorer for the loss of them *both*. Though we lost Oswald years before we lost Kennedy, how many losses of *any* human potential can our besieged society afford? The fact is that a man will affirm his humanity at all costs, even if it means denying the humanity of others, and the whole ghastly nightmare of modern history has been endured for nothing if we have not understood that paradox at last. Oswald's blind insistence that he *was* a man, no matter what the sum of his life might indicate, had to be made in terms that the world could comprehend, and, denied every other exit from that smothering silence, he resorted to the only language that our time seems to offer the voiceless: he took a gun, and aimed it at the center of the life from which he felt orphaned, and so broke into the stream of reality at last, by arresting it.

For a moment, he must have felt the exhilaration, the keenness to sensory stimuli, and the virile power of choice that characterize a man functioning at the top of himself as a human being. Certainly his sinister calm before the Dallas police, his refusal to be trapped by their web of logic, and his perfectly blank-faced denials of any complicity in the assassination, suggest a man whose darker conflicts are at least temporarily at rest, a man at ominous peace with his divided life.

But if all this is true, it is too harsh a comment on our world, and its attritions, to be merely a psychological footnote to a political tragedy. Instead, it should remind us that history is, at the last, only the exterior appearance of far more important inner events—such as those that Lee Harvey Oswald suffered until he could suffer no more, and so struck back out of his wound.

Revolution
Below the Belt

> "Sexuality, thought of as filthy or beastly, is still
> the greatest barrier to the reduction of man to
> the level of the thing."
>
> —*Georges Bataille*

One: 1905

§ § As Robert Lindner once pointed out, the Sexual Revolution
of our time has been mostly abortive. Though society in the last
twenty years has taken a more tolerant, not to mention sensible,
view of such things as premarital intercourse, sex techniques,
homosexuality and obscenity, it would be naive to assume that
this constitutes anything more than the kind of liberal reform
that followed the equally abortive revolution of 1905 in Russia.
Viewing sex as a social problem rather than a personal sin is
certainly an advance of sorts, but it indicates a change in terminology, not in point of view. A "healthy" attitude toward sex
is probably as much a part of the mood of the New Frontier
and the Great Society as the late President Kennedy's physical
fitness program, but this is as different from a recognition that
sex may be one of the *last* frontiers as 1905 was from 1917.
Despite such diverse breakthroughs as Kinsey, *Lolita*, Enovid
and *Playboy*, the authorities still remain to be overthrown, for
the simple reason that the authorities are internal, and always
have been.

An ideal illustration of this sort of psychological ground-
giving (as opposed to ground-clearing) is the continuing legal
argument over the censorship of literature. Viewed superficially,
it would seem that the door to the boudoir is at least ajar, if
not wide open. *Tropic of Cancer*, *Lady Chatterley's Lover* and
Naked Lunch, all heretofore the objects of suits, can now be
published openly in the United States, and the precedents
established in their cases seem to have defined for some time to

come the differences between what is called "erotic realism" and hard-core pornography. And yet the deciding factor in each of these cases, the factor attested to by all the expert witnesses and referred to in most of the judges' rulings for dismissal, was not the thorny question of the artist's inalienable right to deal with erotic desires, but its precise opposite—that, because the books under consideration did *not*, in fact, arouse erotic desires, they could not be legally banned. The courts listened to a parade of intelligent men—literary critics, college professors and novelists, all with presumably normal sex lives—solemnly testifying on the assumption that the arousal of sexual desires by a book was somehow socially reprehensible, but that in the case at issue it hadn't happened. At least, not to them. Honest.

Progress? Yes, of sorts. The author's right to take the reader into the bedroom has now been established by law, but only so long as he carefully separates behavior from emotions. His skill may be employed to describe, but never to evoke. He may write with the hands of a surgeon, but not with the eyes of a lover (the results of which sometimes make one long for the old asterisk-fadeout that at least left one's *own* imagination free to roam). The point is as simple as it is fatuous: though there is nothing wrong with describing everything from cunnilingus to pederasty, there is something very wrong indeed about arousing the desires which make this behavior comprehensible.

Of course, it should be clearly stated that very few of the witnesses in these cases accepted, in private, the assumption on which they testified in public. The law may be "a ass" (as Dickens said), but it is still the law, and it states that books appealing to prurience are bad books and may not be published. The idea that prurience is bad is one of those ideas that only applies to *other* people; leave anyone (who believes it) alone with a work of out-and-out pornography, and you will soon see how deep the conviction goes. The fact of the matter is very simple (though no one would be caught on the witness stand admitting it), and that fact is that words *do* have the power to make us realize that we are desirous, just as they have the power to make us realize that we are hungry, and (if they are ill-chosen words) that we are sleepy. But the question still remains: So what? Even the libertarians and the petition-signers

seem to be stymied by this, because they always carry on their
arguments with the book-burning maiden ladies and literary
police sergeants (who, it seems, never read *anything* but dirty
books) in terms of what *constitutes* erotica, not what's wrong
with it.

Equally, parents and educators like to think of themselves as
being very enlightened for distributing among the young all
manner of do-it-yourself sex manuals, which, like all their
brethren in an America that seems obsessed with keeping idle
hands busy, tell you in tedious detail what to do, but never
why. These chatty volumes leave almost nothing to the imagination, but carefully avoid touching on the earthier emotions
without which the more acrobatic aspects of sex must seem to
the young and inexperienced about as sensible as a trapeze act
to a blind man. The anatomical drawings in these books,
complete with helpful arrows and Latinate words, seem deliber-
ately fashioned to prepare the fifteen-year-old for the operating
room rather than the marriage bed—unlike the Japanese pillow
books which proceed on the idea that you don't have to know
it's called a vagina, you only have to know what to do with it.
As a consequence, young men memorize the graphs on the
minimum amount of time to be devoted to foreplay, and young
women know that females were given the inalienable right to
orgasm along with the right to vote, and both are prepared for
everything but the thrilling and unsettling emotions for which
all the positions, techniques and variations are only physical
expressions.

We have all had the bizarre experience of overhearing teen-
agers, who have yet to make even the most abashed, back-seat-
of-the-car love to one another, solemnly talking about masturbation or copulation, and we have probably crept away, not
wanting to embarrass them, and priding ourselves on the liber-
ality of modern society—though if we had caught them reading
a book which shamelessly celebrated these activities in their
own terms we would have intervened soon enough. For our
attitude boils down to this: healthy young people are expected
to like necking just as they like steak or tennis: because it's
invigorating, nutritious and therapeutic. In other words, it has
redeeming social value, like chaperoned rock-'n'-roll sessions or

policed drag strip races. It is a harmless release for youthful energies, which, it is clearly understood, should *never* be taken to mean that the energies thus released will be allowed to move from the level of foreplay to that of fornication. So we tolerate, and even encourage, fantasy, while the reality of sex remains under the same old injunctions.

Why? It's not really a question of morality, for though sex was once the evil half of the moral Manichaeanism of Western Consciousness (the Mr. Hyde that lay like a coiled serpent in the breasts of all Jekylls who were not vigilant, the loathsome portrait in the attic mirroring the scarlet sins that did not show on Dorian Gray's daytime face, the satanic Svengali-force that would hypnotize and enslave the better, or Trilby, angels of our nature) times have changed radically, and no one today, from Smilin' Jack to Smiley Blanton, speaks ill of sex any longer. Indeed, if anything (other than democracy and, perhaps, Albert Schweitzer) is thought to represent the good, the true, and the beautiful by most intelligent people, it is probably "healthy" sex. It is viewed as the most natural expression of love—a sort of Epoxy Glue, one drop of which will support two tons of anxiety and ethnic difference; and the day cannot be too far off when we will be reminded, on subways and in buses, that "The Family That Sleeps Together Keeps Together." Probably as many mothers worry about whether young Bobby is experiencing a healthy feeling of competition for their favors with his father, as worry about whether he will be able to get into the college of his choice; and I have seen young marrieds go off by the station-wagonful to see *Never on Sunday* and sit around afterwards enthusing wistfully over how simple, straightforward and nonneurotic sexual love could be, as evidenced by this incarnation of that sentimental folk figure, The Good Whore who is as Gay and Wise and Reassuring as—but the conversation broke off at this point, because everyone realized that they were just about to say "as mother should have been." I have listened to young matrons, freed from drudgery by appliances and from children by prep schools, confess that they knew they must be maladjusted because, though they loved sex and grabbed all of it that they could get, they still, damnably, thought of it as "dirty" instead of "beautiful and uplifting."

When reminded that you could think of farming the same way, but that this didn't mean that all 4-H Clubbers were slovenly, they looked at me as if I was suggesting that their husbands cheat on their income tax, instead of merely padding the expense account. This "healthy" attitude toward sex is as ubiquitous as the copies of *Playboy* that you find on coffee tables throughout suburbia (the wives' comments on the gatefold-Playmate usually go like this: "Last month's was sexier. I wouldn't have minded if you'd slept with her. But this one's too *fat*.") You come upon it in the laissez-faire obscenity of cocktail parties and country clubs; in the latest *Reader's Digest* article on How to Be a Mistress to Your Husband (the key to this seems to be a nap in the afternoon); and in the statements of Bennington girls that sex is the natural adjunct to a love relationship, even if that relationship doesn't result in marriage.

On the surface of it, all this sounds very advanced indeed. Certainly our grandmothers would be shocked by it (the usual rule of thumb by means of which we congratulate ourselves on how emancipated we have become), and undoubtedly they would conclude that the revolution has arrived and all authorities have been swept away. But then our grandmothers operated on the old-fogy idea that sex was a necessary evil without which marriage would be incomplete, because it would be childless. The fact that we operate on the young-fogy idea that sex is a necessary good without which love would be incomplete, because it would be child*ish*, does not occur to us, much less that it represents no radical step forward. The difference between saying that sex is all right when sanctified by marriage and saying that sex is all right when sanctified by love indicates a greater subtlety of justification, but not an abandonment of the notion that sex somehow *needs* to be justified. Both ideas assume that sexual energy is volatile, anarchic and potentially dangerous when not restrained by a "higher" emotion, and both ideas assert that the problem posed by sexual energy is primarily the problem of controlling it.

With the exception of a few wise men, like Gandhi, and a few wild men, like Mailer, no one talks about abstinence any longer as the simplest method of control (and it is interesting to note that neither of these men assumes that sex is destructive, only distracting), but people *do* talk endlessly about such things as moderation, proper outlets, normal identification and responsibility, all of which unconsciously equate sex with alcohol, narcotics, overeating and the other forms of self-indulgence by which we sometimes compensate for anxiety and inner turmoil. The fact that the very inner turmoil out of which we overindulge more often than not results from the *suppression* of sexual energy, rather than its liberation, does not seem to have occurred to them.

The reason? The reason is baldly simple: Despite overwhelming evidence to the contrary, we still assume that sex is the antithesis of the spirit (admitting that we *have* "feet of clay" is very different from trying to walk on them), that it is somehow animal-like (whether we view it as a tiger or a tabby-cat doesn't materially alter the assumption), or, at the very least, that it is merely the physical acting-out of psychological needs (why it so rarely occurs to anyone to view these very psychological needs as merely the acting-out of our damned-up sexual energy has always been a mystery). At the bottom of it, all our attitudes rest as squarely on the old Christian dualism of mind-versus-body as did the rather more austere injunctions of Saint Paul— which, at least, constituted a hardheaded counterrevolution that kept the issue clear.

The fact that there is still something grievously wrong with our sexual attitudes is as plain as the type-face in our newspapers, a good deal of which these days is taken up with statistics on divorce, promiscuity among the young and sex crimes, while the best part of what is left is used to advertise books, movies, plays or TV shows that seem obsessed with sex to a degree that not even the most uninhibited sensualist would call "normal." Social observers profess to be alarmed by this, and their explanations, when they offer any (and mostly they treat the phenomenon like an outbreak of polio, about the nature of which it is unnecessary to say anything), range all the way from the ringing of moralistic fire-whistles over the passing of nineteenth century values, to the twitter of psychiatric jargon describing the whole thing as a hangover from these very same values. The conservatives assume that all the commonality *wants* is titillation, the liberals assume that all the commonality *gets* is titillation, but both assume that there is no valid, internal reason for the preoccupation in the first place.

Nevertheless, the astonishing success of movies such as *La Dolce Vita* (which took anything but an American Legion or even a Great Books Club view of contemporary sexual life) cannot be explained solely on the basis of the degradation of, or our distortion by, an outdated moral code. What this success clearly indicates is a troubled awareness of the rigidity of current sexual attitudes, and a willingness (heretofore unknown in America) to treat the matter of sex as if it had existential, as well as social or psychological consequences. Some of the critics of *La Dolce Vita*, for instance, viewed it as a symptom of moral decay, rather than as an analysis of it; others felt that the eruptions of sex in the film indicated the degeneracy of the characters, rather than their despair; but few seemed to realize that what they were viewing was nothing less than the mirror-image of their own phantom faces, paralyzed by the ambiguity of limitless material affluence in a morally impoverished world, helpless to discover any pursuit that did not end in compromise, apathy or futility, and thus deprived of any way to experience their uniqueness, except through their own flesh. And the fact that the film could not maintain the courage of its insight (as, for instance, *La Notte* did), and fell back on baldly moralistic symbols and exaggerations which denied the dignity of the search, seems to have escaped almost everyone.

The same sort of myopia overcame the critics of such "unnormal," sex-dominated works as *Suddenly Last Summer*, *Candy*, and *Our Lady of the Flowers*, to mention only the first examples that come to mind. Their success was attributed to simple prurience on the part of the audience, and their creation to complicated maladjustments on the part of the authors, but the possibility that like-need might be calling to like-need was mostly dismissed, and what this indicated about the progress of the so-called sexual revolution was not discussed at all.

For like it or not, we are not quite ready to admit that there is a growing restiveness everywhere now concerning the internal authorities that, while they do not prevent us from indulging in sex without guilt, nevertheless compel us to justify it in any number of nonsexual ways; there is a growing suspicion that sex may constitute one of the few remaining experiences in which Jung's process of individuation can still occur; and there are disturbing signs that the psychic attritions of our time may have brought us to the brink of a sexual 1917 at last.

Two: 1917

§ § As all totalitarians discover when they allow themselves to speculate on the dynamics of control, the cheapest and most efficient way to disarm resistance is to internalize the Censor, to build the Secret Police *into* every individual. Once this is accomplished, the State can, indeed, "wither away," because (like the mite of Grace that everyone swallows with the symbolic body and blood of Christ) the State will then have been miniaturized, mass-produced and distributed to all for free, making deviation impossible and exterior authority unnecessary.

That this internalization of authority is the ultimate aim of many psychiatrists, as well as most communists, only indicates how complex modern life has become—so complex indeed that there is less and less room in it for the autonomous individual. The establishment of authority is almost always idealistic in the beginning, but because it stems from the assumption that man is basically disruptive and anarchic when left in Hobbes' State of Nature, it always ends up in the most cynical kinds of expediency. Whether one attempts to control society in the name of the intellect (as Marxism does), or whether one attempts to control the intellect in the name of the society (as Freudianism does), the result is mostly the same: a monolith of *layers* of control, one series backing up the other, until the font of resistance, deep in the psyche, has been reached and (so goes the squalid little hope anyway) sealed off. The ingenuity of totalitarians in putting fingers in the dike is only exceeded by their stubborn refusal to see that there are only so many fingers available, and that eventually the underground man, made raw to his existentiality by these very controls, breaks through in the form of the psychopath or the rebel.

There is probably no better illustration of this internalization of authority than the sexual attitudes described above, attitudes which continue to regulate behavior even though the morality of which they are a result has "withered away." But deep inside us there is something that "doesn't love a wall," and in an age that is characterized by walls that cut as deep into our consciousness as they do across our continents, that Something is growing ever more rebellious, exacerbated and desperate. It is starting to question the very nature of sexuality, just as the American colonists questioned the nature of liberty. It is indulging in self-defeating extremes of libertinism, just as the Jacobins plunged into self-consuming extremes of license. And here and there, the outraged frustration (which turned the 1905 revolutionaries in Russia into 1917 terrorists) is exiling that Something to the bitter streets and dark cellars of sadism, perversion and other forms of sexual outlawry.

Common to all these reactions is the conviction that sexuality has an intrinsic validity (in and of itself) that finally transcends the uses to which it is put. That sex is not just a kind of visceral valentine you give your beloved, nor is it something as fleeting and emptily symbolic as a handshake. That it is not so much a specific emotion directed at a specific person, as it is an objectless, steadily coursing flow of energy out from the centers of the Being which, like an underground stream, can surface in an infinite variety of places, in an infinite number of ways. The homosexual pool is different from the heterosexual river only in that it has been dammed, but both rise from the same dark, subterranean watershed, ceaselessly flowing, seeping, searching its level. "In everything living," Wilhelm Reich wrote, "sexual vegetative energy is at work." Or, as D. H. Lawrence enjoined much earlier: "Accept sex in the consciousness, and let the normal physical awareness come back, between you and other people. Be tacitly and simply aware of the sexual being in every man and woman, child and animal."

Outlandish (or outright mystical) as these statements probably sounded in their day, an approximation of the insight they contain typifies the New Consciousness of sex. The current attitude of homosexuals toward their predilection is one example. Second only to the Negro or Jew, the homosexual was once the favorite whipped-boy of the liberals, who always told you that they defended him from persecution *despite* his anomaly. But this don't-let's-be-beastly-to-the-faggots attitude (like its counterpart concerning the Germans) is actually based on the spurious magnanimity that overcomes insecure people just after they have thought, "I may not be perfect, but I'm better than you, and just to prove it I'll be *nice* to you"—with the result, in this case, that the homosexual acted more pansyish than ever, just as the Negro before him had acted more Uncle Tom-ish. For the outcast instinctively knows that when he is accepted with such a *show* of tolerance it is his very outcastness that is his meal ticket, and so he emphasizes it, secretly mocking his benefactor with the caricature, and waiting for the day of unmasking.

That that day is probably upon us is indicated by such statements as this one by Allen Ginsberg: "I sleep with men and with women. I am neither queer nor not queer, nor am I bisexual," which would have seemed gibberish to the humorless liberal of yore, whose strong suit was never satire-with-a-straight-face, and who, lost without labels, would have wondered what, indeed, Ginsberg actually *was*, then. To which Ginsberg would have replied (as he has): "My name is Allen Ginsberg and I sleep with whoever I want." This sort of Marx Brothers candor is always called "tasteless" (for which read "too pertinent") by the critics, but the fact that Ginsberg's work is singularly free of the rococo hints and minces and stifled sniggers of homosexual poetry of the past, and that he can write about women as women, rather than as so many emasculators-in-skirts or fags-in-drag, is a sign of how liberating a simple admission can be. Think of how many tedious pages of "decor and sensibility" we would have been spared if Ronald Firbank, for instance, had been allowed to make the same statement. Think of what his bizarre talent might have accomplished had he been able to admit to himself that he was homosexual but so what?

It is not so much that society has treated homosexuality as a stigma as it is that the homosexual *himself* has felt this way, that accounts for the effeminate aura of Firbank, who rarely writes overtly about homosexuality, as contrasted to the masculinity of Genet, who deals with it as candidly as if it was no more shameful than a penchant for bosomy blondes. Behind the one stands the feeling that sex is *The Flower Beneath the Foot*, something ambiguous, perverse, furtive and theatrical. Behind the other is the conviction that sex can fructify and even ennoble, that it is a recharging of the identity, and ultimately an illumination. Or as Genet puts it: "Sunk by all the woes of the world in an ocean of despair, I still knew the sweetness of being able to cling to the strong and terrible prick of a negro. It was stronger than all the currents of the world, more certain, more consoling, and by a single one of my sighs more worthy than all your continents." The homosexual of the past never got beyond the object of his desire, and his felt-necessity to either disguise that object or justify his choice of it with windy drivel about the Greeks, whereas today's homosexual realizes that it is not the cup that gives sustenance, but what is in it.

Insofar as Reich and Lawrence asserted that the important characteristics of sexual energy are its primacy, creativity and undifferentiated flow have they been unique harbingers of this revolution. Almost no one talks seriously about Reich these days, and to my knowledge no exhaustive, head-on, point-by-point refutation of his theory of sexual energy exists in English, but many people, particularly artists, feel that though he may have been scientifically wrong, he was "poetically" right when he stated that "sexuality [is] nothing else than the biological expansion from center to periphery. Conversely, anxiety [is] nothing but the reverse direction from periphery to center. Sexuality and anxiety are one and the same process of excitation, only in opposite directions." In this statement, sweeping and oversimplified as it may sound to psychiatric lint-pickers, may be found one reason for the persistent sexual preoccupation of our Age of Anxiety. For when everything else is pulverized, uncertain and relative, the consciousness automatically turns back to the cohesive, unequivocal absolute of sexual energy for relief, making (at one and the same time) a denial and an affirmation.

During the Cuban Crisis of 1962, for example, my wife and I were certainly not the only ones who found themselves obsessively making love during the three most perilous days (and also, in our case, making bad jokes about the beneficent effect of all those released orgones, that were really no more idiotic than the jokes people make to explain a binge of wine-drinking in France or a spate of intensive moviegoing in New York). Critics may feel that the inclusion of a detail like this is unnecessary, tasteless or dull-dull-dull (the accredited ploys for dealing with the erotic confessional), but then they probably also felt that the over-drinking which the anxieties of the Munich crisis brought out in people, who were caught in the double-bind of total concern and total helplessness, evidenced nothing but irresponsibility, and so they are incapable of knowing how far history and its dementias have brought us. They would undoubtedly find Lawrence's diagnosis, made ten years before Munich (not to mention Hiroshima, Hungary and Havana) incomprehensible: "When men and women are physically cut off, they become at last dangerous, bullying, cruel. Conquer the fear of sex, and restore the natural flow. Restore even the so-called obscene words, which are part of the natural flow. If you don't, if you don't put a bit of the old warmth into life, there is a savage disaster ahead."

That savage disaster had already occurred when Lawrence wrote. Mechanistic modern scientism, after destroying the old absolutes of organized religion, and then the new relatives of moral convention, went on to create the weaponry which in our time has expressed, in violence, our thwarted inability to live in the spiritual wasteland that is all that remains. Cut off from God, adrift in the baffling collectivism of a society that is itself adrift, pulverized by wars whose only noticeable result is the further loosing of inner anxiety and the concomitant tightening of outer control, man is finally orphaned from himself as well. All experiences are stereotyped and explained away; all mysteries are revealed as manifestations of misunderstood drives; until the old Rationalist Aim (the Happy Man in the Sane Society) is finally achieved, not by the light of reason, but in the dark of schizophrenia—with the clammy result that man has never *understood* himself more, and *experienced* himself less. He lives by secondhand, he watches himself living, he goes through his emotions like Dr. Frankenstein observing his monster; and all the while he struggles to believe that if you cannot abolish the instinctual beast by the imperatives of morality, you can at least tame him by the explanations of science.

Increasingly, he fails in that struggle. And increasingly he falls back on those few experiences which involve what Mailer has called "the connection of new circuits"—experiences which, because they finally elude reason, ultimately escape time (the ticking mind of life), and thereby abolish for a moment the insect-loneliness and cogwheel-futility which are perhaps the most typical modern emotions.

Once Love was one of these experiences. But Love, like Honor, Faith and Chastity, has not come through the storms of our century intact. Whether it was the emotion, or the term, that has proved too vague and general for our Age of Genocide and Overkill is not really important, but Love seems to have joined such other "secondary experiences" as Truth and Beauty, whose cerebral character gives them, in our view, connotative but not descriptive value, i.e., truth is ultimately one's *idea* of truth. But then one thing that typifies the twentieth century is a weariness with language (and the distortion of reality that it entails), for, as Arthur Adamov says: "The words in our aging vocabularies are like sick people. Some may be able to survive, others are incurable." The degree to which Love, as a word, has become "incurable" was perhaps most starkly illustrated by the final interchange between the husband and wife in *La Notte*. Having reached that emotional impasse out of which even infidelity offers no exit, she (who no longer loves him, and knows it) nevertheless begs him, "Say the words! Say the words!" to which he (who no longer loves her either, but refuses to admit it) can only reply, "I can't, I won't!" And, for the first time in the film, the deadwall that seals them off from each other produces a despair immense enough to arouse desire.

But when sexual desire becomes a sort of last stand against the deadwall in the mind (which can, literally, take the ass out of life) strange things often occur. The internal censor is challenged on its own ground by such flagrantly thrown-down gauntlets as Lenny Bruce's habit of sometimes starting his nightclub act by a meaningless stream of sexual and ethnic obscenities "just to clear the air," to exorcise these words of the dangerous power they possess when left unsaid, an example of shamanism in reverse that was unfailingly misunderstood by police department anthropologists. Bruce was known to do routines on masturbation, psychic impotence and most of the esoterica of the erotic life, and a citizen of the calmer times that are bound to come (if any times come at all) will be able to learn more about the sexual preoccupations and dislocations of this age from his work than from any number of humorless Kinsey Reports.

The outrage of club-owners and the embarrassment of audiences were the best testimony to how penetrating and accurate his perceptions were. Far from being "sick," his was a mind that was as mordantly, even obsessively, "healthy" as a latter-day Luther, who may rise to shock, but never stoops to titillate. Far from being "dirty," he assumed that the sexual life was far too important to be left in the damp hands of genteel pornographers like Dwight Fiske. For the essence of pornography is fantasy (which is socially harmless precisely because it is a substitute for action), and Bruce, as his numerous run-ins with the Law indicated, was so concerned with reality that sometimes he was simply not *funny* at all.

This feeling that the sex life has overriding importance because it constitutes one of the last frontiers is based on the recognition that the frontier experience has always caused man to transcend himself, whether that frontier was the Mississippi River or the Michelson-Morley Experiment. On the frontier, there is a disturbing but ultimately beneficial interaction between man and the unknown, which always results in a widening and a deepening of consciousness, and it is this aspect of sex which Norman Mailer, James Baldwin and others have probed most persistently.

Mailer, who is always accused by the critics of seeing sex in everything, is actually a writer so absorbed by the traditional view of the novelist-as-philosopher that the worst he can be accused of is seeing everything in sex. There is something almost Jamesian about his intention to find a level of experience on which the most complex states of being can be acted out, and such works as *The Deer Park, The Time of Her Time* and *An American Dream* may constitute nothing less than a new fictional genre, in which sexual relations are described primarily to reveal interpersonal attitudes, rather than interpersonal relations being described to reveal sexual attitudes (as was true in the psychological novel of the past that has become all but impossible to write since the War). Far from wanting to reduce life to sexuality, Mailer sees sexuality as one of the only unobstructed avenues back into the richness and creativity of the whole personality. He knows that in an age in which most human endeavors are socialized, mechanized or depersonalized, the bed is one of the last places where the triumphs and defeats, splendors and miseries, commensurate to man's essential stature, can still occur. If anything, Mailer is a puritan (as was Lawrence, as was Reich) who jealously wishes to preserve the fecund possibilities of Being from the sterile certainties of the Brain; and it is one of the paradoxes of our pulverized age that the unified vision of the puritan is most forcefully expressed these days by men who are continually mistaken for libertines.

Baldwin, on the other hand, is far less ambitious. The value of sex to him lies in its very intimacy; the opportunity it offers to express, and finally anneal, the violence and despair of Outcastness; and the best of his work vibrates with the belief that the barriers will only come down when we allow ourselves access to one another across *all* abysses, sexual and racial. His world is taut with the angry loneliness and fevered curiosities of the isolated, to whom *touch* itself is the only comprehensive act of communication. In Baldwin's novels, indeed, touching the body of the other (its strangeness, its inviolateness) is treated as the *only* way to annul its power of intensifying our loneliness simply by being out of reach. If this represents a disturbing exacerbation of consciousness, it also serves to illumine the enormous dimensions of the cul-de-sac in which we are trapped —and going stir crazy.

Portents of riot and jailbreak are everywhere. More and more people realize that the fight against censorship can no longer be waged on the censor's terms. For the definition of what is pornographic and obscene (always a misty mid-region of Weir) carries a moral stricture within it, no matter how liberal that definition may be, and it is this very moral stricture that is increasingly being put on trial. There are those, including psychiatrists, sociologists, and at least one Supreme Court Justice, who are questioning for the first time the age-old assumption, heretofore accepted by authoritarians and libertarians alike, that out-and-out erotica is rightfully beyond the protection of the law. Far from triggering antisocial acts, the evidence is mounting that the effect of pornography may be precisely the opposite: your average rapist being decidedly *not* a man who has accepted sexuality as an everyday part of his life. As a result, hard-core 1905ers are fast being forced into the position of having to argue that, yes, the ban on pornography ought to be continued, but only because it is *not* sexually exciting, and thus has *no raison d'être*—an example of prejudice torturing logic into syllogism that is classic in its absurdity.

If it is the first sign of a society's maturity when it can see some difference between children and adults (a distinction that has so far been impossible for a nation that has decided most matters of taste by the categorical imperative: would you want your sheltered twelve-year-old daughter to do it, see it, read it, think it?), one indication of our coming of age may be that, increasingly, the dispute over pornography is revolving around the problem of how to keep it from the young—a thorny question indeed, but one which we have solved on other levels without closing all the bars or banning the automobile. The day may not be too far off when representations of erotic desire, as an adjunct to that desire, may be as legal as gourmet cookbooks, which have never been under a ban, though far more people have exotic sex every day than are overpowered by the urge to whip up a *boeuf bourguignon*. The use or abuse of an appetite is ultimately beyond the reach of the censor, as would be immediately apparent to everyone if an attempt were made to blame America's obesity on Clementine Paddleford and her colleagues. Pornography may be caviar for the General, but it is certainly far less poisonous than the garbage served up by Mickey Spillane or Harold Robbins, and perhaps the strongest *negative* argument for instantly legalizing it is that no one who could obtain the one would ever again be satisfied with the other.

Far more significant, however, are the signs that more and more of us are asking the sexual experience to compensate for the aridity of most other experiences. Nowhere is our era's ambivalence of values and standardization of futility better illustrated than by our preoccupation with aspects of sex that until recently were thought to be forbidden, or at least suspect, even by the most uninhibited. "But to do the forbidden, in order to transgress limits that *seem* unnatural, is normal and innocent," as Paul Goodman once said, "and if the limits *are* unnatural it is often necessary and admirable."

As a consequence, the Era of the Orgy may finally be here, but what it evidences is neither a moral collapse nor a Late Empire decadence; rather it is a sign of an existential crisis, a crisis of ultimate personal identity, a specifically religious spasm in a godless world. In any case, the orgy, heretofore a ritual naughtiness for the rich and twisted, has become at least as widespread in New York as Zen lectures and LSD sessions, and, more often than not, the same people attend all three. The Firbankism of the Black Mass, on the other hand, which equated sex with evil, and embraced it *because* of that, has caused it to fall into disfavor these days, for what we seem to need so desperately now is not a blasphemy, but a transcendence. It is not a given code of morality that we seek to deny, as much as it is an outlawed conception of Being that we seek to affirm, by such excesses. Joyless and mechanical as an orgy may be, it opens up unknown territory where one goes armed only with one's own body, and no mass-observer or visiting-psychologist attitude will get you through it. It seems to hold out hope that if we do not discover unknown predilections, we may at least reinforce well-known aversions, and thereby emerge with a sharper sense of ourselves. For how can we recoil backwards out of our prurience and excess until we have established where our revulsion truly begins? How can we propose even a minimal limit to sexuality until we have gone *beyond* that limit? This is as true of sex as it is of swimming: we cannot finally know our capability until we are in over our heads.

Beyond this, most of us have probably known couples, trapped in the kind of marital desert depicted in *La Notte*, who made it flower, at least temporarily, by such divergings of the sexual stream as the mutual adulteries of *Les Liaisons Dangereuses*, the erotic charades of *The Balcony* or a simple *ménage à trois* involving one sex or the other. Boredom and satiation are certainly involved in sophistications such as these, but they can best be understood against the background which Mailer has put into the image: "A whore practicing fellatio looks up and says, 'Are you a Communist?'—that's what the modern world is all about in a way." For a crippling drought always awakens dreams of the Flood, and in a flood nothing is saved but the barest essentials. Sometimes, in ages such as ours, the only deeply illuminating moral experience is immorality.

Most modern revolutions have been followed by a period of civil chaos, and there are signs that this sexual 1917 will be no exception. The sudden revival of interest in the Marquis de Sade is as unmistakable an indication of upheavals under the surface of "healthy" sexuality, as the interest in Dostoyevski before the First World War was of similar upheavals under the surface of the easy going optimism of that time. Dostoyevski, once thought of as the Russian Sade (by people who had obviously never read the Frenchman), established that man cannot be reduced to a mere "organ handle" at the mercy of his "interests"; Sade, on the other hand, established that man *would* not be reduced to a mere "interest" at the mercy of his organ. But the key to Sade's fascination for people today lies in his conception of the sexual act as the ultimate existential situation. Fearless and consistent atheist that he was, he knew that the only way to experience oneself (in a reality from which the linch-pin of a transcendent faith has been removed) was to exert power over others, which, at the bottom of it, meant power over their bodies; which, in turn, demanded the continual lashing of the sexual instinct by the very anxiety to which it is opposed.

That Sade had the courage of his insight, and thereby provided us with a detailed map of the perils of the territory ahead, is exhaustively (and exhaustingly) documented in his works, which describe the relentless progress toward impotence that results from the libertine's forced marches on his sexuality. Nowhere can the tragedy of rationalism be more keenly felt than in Sade, who (alone in that Age of Reason) was brave enough, and logical enough, to turn rationalism itself to the service of the instincts. He was a veritable Napoleon of sex, but in the psychic debris that our scientific and political Napoleons have so zealously created out of the temples and parliaments of the recent past, he stands as a prophetic warning of the sort of nightmares to which the Dreams of Reason can lead. After Sade, we are at a point where a protest against the lockstep meaninglessness of modern times can only be lodged in our own flesh.

The dislocations of sexuality which can be felt everywhere today (the aforementioned orgy, *ménage à trois*, tentative forays into lesbianism or homosexuality, the psychic impotence that is as common to sensualists as it is to prudes) may be as much a result of our demand that this one emotion carry the weight of all the failed emotions of modern life, as they are of the so-called "feminization of America," the cause of which is certainly the breakdown of virility under the burden of being the sole reliable support of the male ego. Nevertheless, there are skirmishes along the frontier that bear watching, such as the upsurge of militant feminist manifestoes, ranging all the way from the NAACP-gradualism of Betty Friedan's *The Feminine Mystique* to the Black-Muslim-extremism of Elizabeth Mann Borgese's *The Ascent of Women*. Whether these books are a response to the sexual difficulties of men or are evidence of a female attitude that is the cause of those difficulties does not matter very much beside the fact that women, like men, are growing restive in their sexual roles, albeit from the other side of the frontier.

What is happening, however, is far more complicated than a simple exchange of roles. If there are more homosexuals, there are probably more "sexual engineers" as well, and for every feminist, demanding Instant Equality in the board room, there are probably fifty women experiencing it in the bedroom. The profoundest change is a change in consciousness, in the traditional conception of sex as a charade, in which roles *must* be played.

Yeats, speaking of another revolution, said: "The beggars have changed places, but the lash goes on," as neat a description of a failed revolution as one could possibly hope for. But it is precisely this idea (that sex is power, and power is eternal, and thus we are doomed to struggle over it eternally) that the New Consciousness is questioning on all levels, for a real revolution does not merely seek a transfer of power from one hand to another, but a metamorphosis in the nature of power itself. Men and women, when they struggle for sexual dominance, may be engaged in the politics of an erotic *coup d'état,* but this has nothing to do with the revolution of Being which our dehumanized times demand, a revolution which (in these early days) is unfortunately bound to be extremist, antirational and even dangerous.

That it can be dangerous is often forgotten by the staunchest advocates of this revolution (Hugh Hefner and Lawrence Lipton are examples), who insist on treating sex as if it was nothing but a simple hunger, who do not appear to understand that contemporary sex-obsession is symptomatic rather than "normal," who fail to realize that it is the *fact* that we have lost our old perspective about sex that is important, not the new perspective we have gained. Everyone is agreed that the old morality must go, that the inner censor must be disarmed, but some of the rasher revolutionists seem so preoccupied with the idea that unlimited sexuality is life-enhancing that (like the reactionaries who insist that it is life-debauching) they sometimes overlook the complex nature of eroticism itself. They resemble anarchists who are so intent on destroying the current *regime* that they take to attacking the idea of any society at all. For there is good reason to believe that eroticism, like atheism, is dependent on the Gods that it denies—in this case, the taboos it seeks to transgress. Georges Bataille, in his book *Death and Sensuality* (the only phenomenology of the erotic impulse of which I know, and a volume of such disturbingly seminal insights that it has been resolutely ignored by libertarians and authoritarians alike) warns that our contemporary insistence on denying the psychological *importance* (as well as the moral necessity) of all taboos, far from accomplishing the fulfillment of sensuality, may succeed in emptying it of its primary existential significance—which is the experience of the freedom of Being. For freedom exists only in relation to necessity; it continually defines itself in opposition to a social compromise; it maintains that dialectical tension between a conflict of drives that is the healthiest human condition. As far as eroticism goes, Bataille tells us that we must face the fact that we derive the intensest pleasure from the *act* of transgression itself, and that we diminish that pleasure by insisting that no real barriers are there to be crossed.

"A transgression is not a back-to-nature movement; it suspends a taboo *without* suppressing it . . . For it can happen that unless we see that transgression is taking place we no longer have the feeling of freedom that the full accomplishment of the sexual act demands, so much so that a scabrous situation is sometimes necessary to a blasé individual for him to reach the peak of enjoyment."

If man's consciousness protests his fate through sexuality, this very transgression of the taboo (this law that is *broken*, but not rescinded; this prohibition that is maintained, at the exact moment that it is violated, in order that some psychic benefit can be gotten out of it) may have to be protected as much from those who see sex as nothing more than a pleasurable natural function, as from those who look on it as demeaning and aberrant. As Norman O. Brown, Bataille and others have seen, sexuality and spirituality are so entangled that it is almost impossible to separate the urge toward one from the urge toward the other, for both involve the desire to transcend the limits of "rational" life. Thus sexuality, in this godless age, has become a religion, and no one who has experienced the erotic seizure, and trembled as he exulted, can doubt the *sacramental* nature of the emotion. Still, it is an open question whether the sexual revolution, having toppled the old tyrants, may not yet be undone by the new anarchists, whose desire to take the moral form out of sex all too often seems to result in taking the existential content out of it as well.

Above all, however, the basic aim of this revolution is not merely to supplant one side of man's nature by another, but to abolish this illusory duality altogether, and to do this, the cannibal mind, swollen to gigantic proportions by centuries of over-thinking, arrogant with the bloodless logic of the computers it has fashioned in its own image, must be drenched in the passions once again. For like a dictatorial regime that controls the police, the army and the press, the mind allows no free elections to the instincts, but instead stages all manner of titillating and harmless circuses to distract them. It is one of the sorry truths of our oppressive era, in which freedom all too often takes the form of anarchy, that such a regime can probably only be overthrown from the darkest cellars of the consciousness. But that the Mind Alone has failed is as evident on the couches of analysts as in the ovens of Auschwitz, both of which hold victims of the berserk Rationalism of our civilization. For what is more rational than a concentration camp, given its assumptions? And what is more rational than paranoia, given its? In each, the mind, like a demented Dr. Huer, concocts solutions which create two problems for every one they solve—on and on and on, until half the world is mad, and the other half is dead.

More and more, something whispers to us that we are doomed to this nightmare of insanity and murder if we do not become whole again. More and more, something whispers that one source of that wholeness lies in the mysterious sexual energy through which we can still experience our uniqueness, even when anxiety has most obscured it. And more and more, are we willing to assume (with Lawrence) "that people would [not] be villains, thieves, murderers and sexual criminals if they were freed from legal restraint," rather than assuming the opposite, as totalitarians of all persuasions have always done. For the essence of the New Consciousness, in sex as in everything else, is the simple insistence that man is more creative than destructive. And a more revolutionary creed, given our world, would be hard to imagine.

The Raw Materials

§ § Why confess? Why *not*? I am talking about consciousness, not history. The raw materials, not the pure products. There is a need to establish *who* has been speaking which, in these babbling times, is often the better part of *why*.

Through the head falls a tumble of images, an avalanche of bottles, old absolutes, old socks, doorkeys, dead certainties and dried roses, strings of used-up words, a mouth oh-ing a lipstick, eyes foreclosed by the mind, movie stubs, headlines, clocks; a rockslide of gimcracks gathering momentum as it approaches the abyss of the future. Time swallows everything but a few disconnected images that are thrown to the side, images of love and death mostly—for these are the realities—retrieved for *no* reason (life has its own reasons) from time relentlessly hurtling over the precipice into—what? Who can say what they mean? Except that they mean more than anything I can *understand* about them.

What follows, then, might best be viewed as an appendix to what has come before; as the raw material out of which the ideas and impressions of this book have been fashioned; as a personal evocation of the last twenty years, but *not* an autobiography; and, finally, as a prose-piece which I have attempted to control by the associative method usually employed in poetry. If the first section, dealing with the forties, is elliptical and discontinuous, it is because one's memories of youth are rarely chronological, but move from image to emotion to idea, back and forth across a stretch of time. And if the second, dealing with the fifties, is at once more analytic and more subjective, it is because a personal crisis (such as occurred in me during that decade) is usually recalled more or less in sequence. The source in both cases, however, has been solely my own recollection of those years (working as recollection works, veering where it veers), and my aim has been to create a facsimile of consciousness (my consciousness *now* of my consciousness *then*), still seeking the meaning, and the shape, our times persistently deny our awareness of ourselves.

This appendix in the form of a memoir is included here because I felt I owed some sort of private testimony to the public character of these pages, if I was decently to clear my inner decks. For if the problem posed by contemporary existence is how we can manage to survive our losses, and still move on with less, it could be said that we remember in order to be *able* to forget. In any case, I have written these fragmented chronicles of the forties and the fifties in that hope.

The Forties

§ § Those big elms stirring in the summer wind; that little depot platform on Long Island where the rails glinted in the late-morning sun back toward New York; those other dischargees waiting quietly there near the gum machines, oddly self-absorbed, quits now with the immense, chaotic event that had held us all together; that canvas bag containing everything I owned—the ludicrous Jack Tar duds that condemn a man to looking like a boy, and a couple of books, *You Can't Go Home Again* and *Mrs. Dalloway* (after six months of night duty on ambulatory wards, I was down to the W's in my self-imposed reading program); the unsettling realization that I might be anywhere that night, just anywhere the hours took me; consciousness of a beginning—

Behind me, the ornate stuccoed 1920's Lido Beach Hotel, now, in the mid-forties, a Navy discharge center, its lounges full of bored gobs waiting the last wait of their war, its verandas stacked with already obsolete gear, its lawns trampled by months of final musters. It seemed impossible that the chock of croquet balls, the clink of ice against good crystal and the delicious laughter of tanned women would ever again echo there in the long, orange twilights of whatever kind of peace had come. I was nineteen, medicaled-out for chronic migraine, and I didn't care. Whatever world there would be was down the rails.

Immediately ahead was a room and kitchenette on West 96th Street just off the Park, and the wife I had married impulsively on boot leave, and—I didn't know, except that I would never go back to the house in Westchester from which I had been inducted so many pulled-roots, so many self-discoveries ago. That house was broken up, my mother in California, my father in Washington, my sisters, who knew where; everything dispersed, sold off, in storage. I had nothing but time and myself; it seemed enough.

The trees that warm summer of 1945 were very green, moving like lush ballgowns in a waltzing breeze full of coal smoke and the odors of mown grass. The train dawdled through sunny towns toward the huge shimmering haze standing over New York. I bought that day's *PM* from a vendor with a weary limp, and didn't read it. I sat there on the rattan seats of that jiggling car, thinking of the light-blue double-breasted suit I would purchase an hour later.

Whatever happened to that suit? Whatever happened to that day?

Mislaid, mislaid.

1945, fall term at Columbia: the veterans could be identified by their polyglot garb, their old copies of *Transition, Metamorphosis,* or *Fear and Trembling,* and by the whiff of sweat and sulphur they introduced into abstract bull sessions.

Diplomaless, I lied my way into a schedule of graduate courses. Irwin Edman, an absent-minded Harry Langdon, okaying me for a seminar in philosophy I had no right to take, said, "Oh, yes, haven't I seen your face around the campus?" All our faces looked alike by then, only the uniforms were missing, and our hair was growing back: I'd never seen *his* face before. All the seminars were filled with Jungian ex-lieutenants, girl Marxists in analysis, internationalists from Emporia.

I did a paper on the relation of poetic form and social chaos, which insisted that pentameter was as dead as Petersburg, and Marx had outmoded the lyric along with laissez-faire. Two years later, composing Audenesque ironies, I could acknowledge that form was only another dike against anxiety; and four years more, described by an academic friend as "that most anachronistic American type—the minor poet," I would turn in my wand for the shovel of prose.

Being continually busy (a poem a day, a story a week, devouring twenty books at once, movie-ing, partying, on the sniff for life), of course there was time for everything. Churchill came to the Low Memorial Library after Fulton, Missouri, and we picketed his cherubic face, on which all that history had somehow left no scars. He seemed to enjoy our taunts, which grew more strident and disgruntled because he made them seem no less inevitable in the young than the gloomy Nietzsche-ism of all college cafeterias. . . . "Well, they threw old Winston *out* anyway," an acned YCLer said, unhappily echoing almost exactly what Pound had written in Pisa—for in those days the confusion was such that you often found yourself having to agree with people you wanted to hang, a truth about the myopia of politics that would come home to us later.

Double-decker buses came to swaying stops beside the Hudson River, disgorging girls attached to armfuls of Psych; Chock Full O' Nuts was hazy with talk of existentialism; the V-12ers, playing that autumn's last sets of tennis in white flannel shorts, were hooted by the veterans in their square prewar suits.

The overloaded mind, like a computer being fed a psychosis on a punch card, bogged down in those endless, solemn *Partisan Review* symposiums on "Socialism" or "Religion and the Intellectuals," longing for a clear, impatient statement like "A spectre is haunting Europe—" or "There flashed upon my mind the phrase, Reverence for Life": the overloaded mind gagging on jargon, but somehow keeping it down, like a peyote-initiate to whom nausea is uncool.

I remember talking about William Empson, and reading Whitman on the sly. I remember *serious* articles on Ross Lockridge, and Morganthau's plan to make a pasture out of Germany, and arguing with a girl student, whose skirt I wanted to explore, that Sartre was more relevant than Malraux, and having her taunt me with Gide. I remember the secret intuition that sex was a mystery, a source of "mana," existing side by side with the public conviction that all mysteries, all "manas," were the cellophane of the mind.

"A short note," I wrote that same girl student. "I've tried to call you for three days and no luck. I can't seem to write at all, except to you. . . . The river doesn't work for me any longer, or I'd walk over to it. Perhaps a movie or something. . . . I can't seem to work things out so that I can write. One of my bad days. I want to call you and have something definite, and there is no answer. Maybe I'll walk up past 34 West 76th, but that won't accrue anything. You are not there, and ringing doorbells on this kind of a day is a grisly business. I could kill somebody. But who?" (Letter—December 15, 1945)

I remember old loves, lost girls, solemn tireless wooing: I kept reaching out from my marriage during those first years, still greedy with the war, though the war was over, because my marriage and my wife—but, no. First follow the galloping thought to that girl student, that dark-browed Nastasya Phillipovna, but once removed from rickety Russian village stiles, in plaid slacks on Morningside Heights (stockings on *under* the slacks, a fact on which I brooded hungrily), her moist slash of mouth full of the words of a passionate, quirky mind, full of dialectics and transferences, who was "sick" and couldn't walk through the streets anymore, whose 76th Street door I haunted through a chilly postwar winter (married though we *both* were), unable to ring the bell for fear an outraged Ralph Bellamy would appear, or she would say, "What? You? Why?" hoping that she would simply come out and find me, fancy that, passing by. Me, in my DP overcoat and earnest double-breasted suit, head aching with Hart Crane, making poems on the IRT, Goethean unscanned lines to an impossible love, "I go to meet a lady I will never meet."

Sad Bulgarian snow fell on No Parking signs; there were ominous psychoanalysts everywhere in her neighborhood; the air had a taste of bakery in it on the slushy street corners; my feet were always wet, socks worked down into my collapsing shoes.

She thought me a silly Dolgoruky when I sent her notes in philosophy class, confessing love in that false Byronic tone that seems so true to young men. She tried to take me in hand, "Now, Holmeses," merciless in trying to be gentle, "I can't stand any messiness right now. I want a comrade, not a lover.

And what we describe as love is only a manifestation of imbalances, viscera, bourgeois sentimentality," her eyes yearning for warmth over the bitter knowledge on her lips. Of course, I agreed to everything, and drowned her in a river of ink during the two years she was too sick to see my pale twenty-odd-year-old face, even over coffee.

"Angst, angst," she wrote back. "Such a funny word. It rules my life—," phantoms of North Jersey, parental phantoms of Hackensack, clothing manufacturer and melancholy daughter phantoms: Chagall would have seen how far the cow had overshot the moon.

"Yes, my mother's death meant a great deal," came the careful scribble from a sanatarium later. "The funeral was the most terrible thing—I hated it so bitterly, her coffin there in front of me, my mother in it. Where? I don't know. Where is she? . . . It snows today and I can't help wondering if she's cold. That's the dreadful part. I've forgiven her, but *her* vengeance is terrible."

My glasses fogged up in steamy coffee shops reading the likes of this: the dead were merely dead to me, awesome lumps you didn't look at beneath hospital sheets that didn't move. But then, I weighed 140 stripped, shaved only twice a week, read Engels on the subways, longed to move to the Village but had to settle for Lexington and 56th instead (it was cheaper); and, rhetoric aside, wanted only the tenderness of sex with her, the mirror of assent in which to glimpse myself ten pounds heavier, without need of hornrims, as certain of myself as Alan Ladd, or as obsessed as Myshkin, odd perhaps but attractive.

It all foundered, it was unreal (Frau Von Stein, Dulcinea del Toboso—I made everything gravely "literary" in those days), and I never had a glimpse of her methodical disrobing in a stuffy west side room amid the smells of wet newspaper, too much cologne, burnt coffee. I know she would have unsnapped her bra without putting down her cigarette. Instead, we went to movies on the sly, ashamed to be so moved by *Brief Encounter*; huge-headed children full of Menninger, James Mason, Mayakovsky.

She vanished into her own mind (where only those she feared were nude), and years later I hurt her to save my wife, and can't excuse it now, but our Age of Choices often comes down to choosing *who* we'll victimize. She's still in the phone book, I looked her up five years ago, and had a funny feeling, and dialed her number, but when she answered—the same startled, "Yes? Yes? Who?"—I hung up. What would I have said to her anyway?

"Are you all right? Weren't we moody idiots though? Have you read Suzuki?"

The tyro writer, conducting his love affairs by mail, bricked into the cellars of his talent by rejection slips, and having to live on the stale bread of whatever dedication or oddity he can salvage, often composes letters in lieu of literature. The ashtray fills, the mind empties, we leave the desk in disgust, and go prowl the secondhand bookstores down on 4th Avenue, and settle for an evening paper.

I remember my reckless fury at *PM*'s pusillanimous agonizing (over the hardships of being a liberal) erupting in a long scathing letter, denouncing them for "talking about navigation while the ship is going down"—not even my own phrase, but barrel-organ Auden from the thirties. I remember being startled when I saw it, crude as a goddamn in the tea-party garb of print. It seemed such a commitment, it rang with all the chuckle-headed certainty of a Saroyan-philosopher; and, suppressing a naughty giggle, I sat down and wrote two anonymous replies to it—one accusing myself of being a reactionary, the other accusing myself of being a communist, both letters perfectly logical and airtight and mutually contradictory, given their assumptions. And even at the time I think I knew that the "realistic" political alternatives that were offered to us then (Luce's American Century or Wallace's Century of the Common Man) would be about as relevant to 1947 as Astaire-Rogers or MacDonald-Eddy had been to 1936.

Bikini, Lysenko, bebop: so went the litany of our anxieties that year. *Open City*, the Beverly Theater, Original Joe's: there were fine times in each. And when Henry Miller answered my letter (only one among thousands that complained to him in those days, as if he was Sam Jaffe, the High Lama of Big Sur) with the words, "You must create the very world you wish to inhabit—down to the last detail. . . . Time spent in railing against society, laws, this & that, is wasted," I don't remember that I understood what he was saying, awed as I was by the hurried squiggles of green ink, the actual signature, the words addressed to *me*, somehow legitimatizing my name to myself. But this & that, this & that: it was a good enough description of the mood of twenty-one.

"Yes, hell must be like that," Camus has said, "streets filled with shop signs and no way of explaining yourself." I walked along 57th Street one icy evening, the solemnly radical undergraduate, certain he understood the anxiety and bewilderment of the middle class while studying the Impressionist paintings in the sparkling Christmas windows: so many menacing shadows had swarmed up out of those dappled Rues. I threw up my first real bellyfull of martinis, right over the side of the bed, after a party arguing about the "reactionary rot" in Koestler. The odor of rubbery Parmesan on a cutlet became the death of Mussolini (hung like a beef before the spitting lips of the liberated) in my aching head. A lust for order was my reigning passion then: that the world would *be* coherent, after all.

"To determine the principle in virtue of which the accused is perhaps to die, is to determine the principle by which the society that judges him lives," I used to quote Saint-Just, as I quote him still—meaning the opposite now of what I meant so fiercely then.

The forepart of my brain finally died in 1948, giving birth to an unknown grub, the truth of resurrection being that it actually happens every day. . . . Nuremburg, Wallace, the Cominform, Bongo bongo bongo I don't want to leave the Congo: so many smoky, argumentative afternoons I lived in a pathetic, imaginary pogrom! I think back with amazement, but no regret, on the time when I believed that out of street fights, Delacroix, hectic posters, surplus value, Ernst Toller (all amounting to nothing but the dim shuffling of refugees toward eternally closed frontiers) an industrial Shangri-La might come, a fine brave world that was also new.

Hideous gobbets of *Daily Worker* prose went down, and

somehow stayed down. The International Bookshop was riddled with drafts, and empty of everyone but the voice of Paul Robeson booming "Meadowland." Barley soup scorched the throat in 14th Street radical restaurants: one wore a lumberjack shirt, and hurried to make the next show at the Irving Place, where once pale-rose nipples had bobbed in the soiled light, and now only the impenetrable, somehow mocking eyes of Uncle Joe noted the winos vomiting on "Geoffrey Crayon's" front stoop up the street.

There was finally a night in Clarke's Bar when my head was in Czechoslovakia, and Alan Harrington said, "Well, no matter. You were naive to think it was going to be any different. Masaryk probably jumped because he couldn't get it up."

Such was my ludicrous Kronstadt: I fancied I understood Berdyaev's prophecy of the New Dark Ages, Burckhardt's certainty that the culture-killers had to come, Yeats' ambiguous feelings about the "terrible beauty," and I had another beer. It seemed the sensible thing to do, and my youthful Marxism came up with the belch—though not without a psychic hangover that lasted months. 1948, 1984: sometimes, if I don't watch out, I still catch myself believing in prophetic arithmetic, but after 1948 who could believe anymore that God's fingers ever pressed the buttons in an election booth? I stopped reading three papers a day, and looked for the writing on the wall.

"So my life goes on. Things happen one by one. I become involved here and there, I make a fool of myself, little gets done. I am called out into the street to understand the above-mentioned things, to fit them into my patterns, to *change* my patterns where that is necessary." (Journal—December 10, 1948)

Or the next girl toward whom I reached, out of my still-unexamined discontent: troubled, Vassar-fresh, with the well-bred face of a touchy setter, pretty and tawny, who, like me, always chose people "who were impossible." We found each other with the unerring instinct of the incomplete. The silent sitter with the sardonic eye picks out the hastily lipsticked mouth too full of words: like calls to like in the most unlikely rooms, and surreptitious luncheons in remote bars always follow.

What did I represent to her, her first year in New York? When I sent her the same old dreary Picasso-reproduction Christmas card that every smart aleck in New York sends out, she gushed: "What perfect taste!" and even *I* was a little embarrassed.

Verbal sparring in a convertible, my unsuspecting wife between, out somewhere near Manhasset in spring; fried Howard Johnson clams greasy in a cardboard container, the Gatsby-twilight settling over factory Queens; bright, shallow chatter about "truth"—how was she to know how it was done? She was groping too, but only to feel, just to feel anything, even hatred, the sharp edge of a real emotion—so she said. And, rhetoric to the contrary, I wanted from her only to lie upon her generous breasts afterwards, and speculate, and be questioned, and reluctantly say sententious things to her, for she was the first who was younger than I.

Uday Shanker at the Museum of Modern Art; Central Park where the kids were playing king-of-the-hill; the smell of leatherette and exhaust on groaning Easter buses. . . . "You want me to love you," she said, pulling on her sweater one night sometime later after a failure, "you want me to say I love you. But don't you understand? I don't know what it means, much less what it feels like. Maybe you're only one more symptom of my sickness. And I can't say 'love' ever again until I know what it is."

I suppose I did want that, as if it was realer than the way her hair was soft and short behind her ears; as if some butterscotch sentiment (that attractively had no future) was more committing than her locking of the door against possible intruders—among whom might have been my wife. But my idea-wracked body betrayed me, because the body is hip. It is only the mind that knows Nowhere.

There was Wagner on the radio the day after the failure, a rainy afternoon in my shadowy wifeless apartment (the apartment of a nervous, disenchanted youth, too many books, reproductions clipped from magazines, the douche in the bathroom, a wistful bottle of Schenley's), and I watched the rise and fall of her bosom under the cardigan, an inappropriate success bulging in my trousers, and thought windily of Nietzsche, Hans Fallada, bushels of worthless marks blowing before a chill 1926 wind in backstreet Hamburg the year that I was born, leather overcoats and Fritz Lang, Buchenwald and Schweitzer. But Dr. Mabuse ruled the only Germany I knew, and the *Liebestod* that afternoon lacked only the faint rank smell of burning Jews to be complete, that obscene smell of charred flesh that is the distinctive odor of modern politics.

Of course, she swooned to Wagner, she wanted to be a singer then, she didn't want to tussle with me, I'd had my chance, and unaccepted love turns to Death, who accepts all contributions. Later, on upper Lexington Avenue Sunday, we argued nastily, I tried to get her to come into a church so I could kiss her, and talked ironies she couldn't understand. The world was new to her, but I was beginning to wonder—so much for Time.

"We should have had a foolish, suggestive, possessive, chatty talk yesterday," I wrote to her, keeping a carbon. "We would have come away from it amused, perhaps frustrated, but certainly not as troubled as we did. The horror of the whole thing is this: we think suggestive, jealous little talks are naive."

And so the most I had of her was clumsy kisses among the copper pots in her cellar kitchen, listening for footsteps on the stairs, and a few wordy lunches, during which we tried to feel that *Other Voices, Other Rooms* really spoke for our generation, and the feel of her black lace slip against my mouth that windy midnight when she came across too soon.

Inside every Alan Ladd, Jackie Coogan plays lonely marbles, imagining the muslin drawers of Becky Thatcher. And then goes out and kills a frog.

"Thus when we pronounce the word Life," Artaud has said, "we are not to understand life recognized by the outside of things. But rather that kind of fragile, moving center which forms do not touch. If there is something infernal and truly accursed at this present time, it is the lingering artistically over forms, instead of behaving like victims being burnt at the stake, who gesture out of the flames." So images, not meanings. It is meanings which lead us wrong, for every new year has its own new meanings. The only love I could believe in in those days was a "doomed-Paris 1939" love. Why? Later, my wife was to ask me: "Whatever made you so guilty, so despairing? I'm sick of your whipped tail." Later still, Kerouac was to say on reading my first book: "I never realized before that the universe was such a horrible place to you, peeling damp walls, spiders everywhere, horror." And ultimately I would counsel myself with ponderous gravity: "To salvage from life something on which one can build more life. I know this is a truth, and I don't know what it means."

Why?

I was born in Holyoke, Massachusetts (to a revered New England name that has never brought me any ease), and had a great aunt who wore a choker, and a second cousin who could remember the date of William the Conqueror's invasion of England but not always his own name, and my father was a sentimentalist who always sang while in the movies, and my mother took me to seances where my grandfather gossiped from the other world, and I imagined trench warfare at twelve, and God went away from me while I was reading accounts of atrocities in Yugoslavia, and—no reason! These aren't the reasons. My rosy nostalgias centered around Depression-poor New Hampshire towns. I was chubby and they called me Bud for one whole summer. The schooling of my imagination took place in the Plaza Movie Theater in Englewood, New Jersey. I loved a girl called Fay Kenney when I was fourteen. I read *All Quiet on the Western Front*, and dreamed of star-shells over splintered skulls through which trench-poppies grew. I used to build movie sets (the Casbah, a nightclub, the London docks) in an attic room, and live in them for hours, being Charles Boyer, Don Ameche, Preston Foster.

I had a homeroom teacher, Miss Eleanor Harvey, who said (it was repeated to me): "After a certain point, something in him closes off, a wall goes up, and you can get no farther," an insight that was as shocking to me, in its deceptive accuracy, as a mirror-image (which is a facsimile of reality, but reversed) can sometimes be. I pondered the "closed-off" faces on the street thereafter, aware that something just like me trembled behind them, certain it was visible.

In the August-dark, delivering milk just before dawn, an all-night radio station from New York told me how immense and tireless and baffling was the world beyond the Hudson. Munich was as much a fact to me as masturbation, love was a minute stolen out of time, death came violently in the alien mud, and sex came early to anneal that wound. I started leaving home in Summer 1942. Looking for the Blues in Oklahoma. Newsreel theaters full of death and landing craft on L. A. Main Street. Coming back with crossed horizons in my eyes. Never the same again. To marry too young, to worry too much. My romances all too often derived from horrible Balkan realities. I thought a brief, candid embrace would redeem everything. A sentimental pessimist: the most witless kind.

"I want to get out in the streets and live. It is strange how we desperately cling to life, to that besieged sense of life I have been feeling lately. . . . What happens between now and next year is all that is important to me now. . . . Whether we will be alive this time five years from now I could not say. I can't find that at this moment I really care. That is what I mean by this sense of life. One wants desperately to feel things, to feel them cleanly and hardly, before one has to knuckle down to the cold dark age that is ahead." (Journal—September 9, 1948)

The paradoxes in the mind of 1947–48 led to those small and necessary deaths out of which fresh life grows. One felt the intuitive rightness of the existential point of view at the exact moment that one derided it as fascistic, metaphysical, unscientific or amoral—depending on the Svengali one was slave to at the moment. One was disturbed by Gary Davis, and wished one didn't know he was a "romantic utopian," "a simplistic obscurantist," or "an oedipal adventurer"; and secretly one hoped his action would escape contamination. One's lacquer of cynicism hardened a little when he failed, and one hated the world the more. A lot of us voted for Henry Wallace, and were incredibly relieved (sometime after midnight on the way home from parties about as gay as wakes) when Truman won; and that election ended our hangover from the thirties forever—along with the folk-singing, sloganizing, and chummy egalitarianism of that sort of politics.

One began to achieve small victories to compensate for the small deaths. I remember the first time I looked at a Negro girl in the subway, and could admit that she (that particular girl) attracted me *because* of her soft, cocoa color (rather as one is sometimes attracted to a blonde because she seems the essence of blondeness), and I remember registering this as a victory of my mind over its prejudices. I remember the first time the basic psychological truths of religion became clear to me after years of snappish, brittle atheism, and I found I could use the word "God" without sneering—just as I used the word "brotherhood": to refer to a possibility, a hope. I remember the first time I listened to a thief-and-junkie, and heard the insights which the nightside of life can give the day, and not just the phrases (like "psychotic self-indulgence" and "anti-social irresponsibility") that clattered so hollowly in my own head. I remember these inconsequentials now with the fondness one feels for the earnest follies and paltry overcomings that mark a beginning.

"Guilt gives rise, first, to individuality," or so Genet has said. Everything has its apogee, and beyond crisis lies transcendence. . . . I reached out again, and this time touched the little blonde librarian with the soft full lips belying her set ideas, pedantic, lissome, barren with her beefy husband. I was older, willing to make a fool of myself, I knew by then what *didn't* matter, and this can have a certain aura of success to it. . . . Beers in Second Avenue saloons, my knees between her knees, omnivorous eyes having to do for all the rest. I calculated that an understanding silence (while *she* talked) would do the trick. It did.

"I hope this never, never (not even when you are a great-great-grandfather—I wish to my children) gets to looking like a sordid, ugly experience," she wrote gravely. "Maybe this is the only time in my life that I will be able to say and do exactly as I feel to someone close to me."

Lovers walk, along even the most hectic slum blocks, as if underwater, at an unconsciously different pace, the pace of the inquisitive blood. And for us, tankers moved sluggish as water buffalo up the smoky February river, thieving gulls dove and swooped, we lingered on chilly benches among runny-nosed kids from Avenue A.

"I want a child by you," she said in her sad little fur collar, no squashy words of love this time, our eyes on one another's mouths. But all we could arrange was cold, wintry afternoons on St. Mark's Place talking obsessively about sex, and hot need once in Radio City Music Hall watching Marlene Dietrich (did the usherettes feel the vibrations of a *real* passion, and shudder?), she stuffing my exploring hands down into her lap, down where she was most alive and most dead, so that when we came out into the sopping day we went without a word to my fortuitously empty apartment, and had our harmless little love on a guilty bed. . . . I remember her virgin-blue petticoat, her doused eyes, her intent to have it no matter what, my wife's hairbrush twelve inches from her outflung hand with the nails bitten to the quick.

"Make a baby!" she gasped, looking away as if it was the most thrilling obscenity, the saddest words I've ever heard in love, taking everything but the sadness out of it. And afterwards, "Moonglow" on the phonograph, dancing like grave high school seniors, all of whose aches are unassuaged by fox trots. "We could run away," she kept saying in my ear. "Why not? Why not? . . . at least for the weekend."

Brooklyn nights, waterfront bars, their prim apartment where the body confessed surprising things to mambo, the great baffled sympathetic face of her husband, my friend. . . . Why didn't he grab me by the collar, and knock me down? But then no nest can be rifled of anything that is truly possessed. . . . Her slumber-party sorority-girl pajamas that I had trouble unbuttoning when he sent her woefully out to me on the daybed, and how I slept an innocent deep sleep when she went away again, back to him. The next day he was sad, not knowing how to act. But I no longer cared how to act, and went out and bought pastrami for us all, and acted naturally, and we ate as friends.

Can it really have happened? Whom did I betray? The same emptiness moved us all about.

I walked back over Crane's Bridge, cold balls, no cigarettes, Rockefeller Center stared back at me from far uptown, I imagined my wife looking through a telescope, and (say it out) I felt a bitter ecstasy, because sometimes only weird and far-out things can make us feel alive. It seemed an illustration of something. "Pour me another, Western Civilization just went plop," or "The unique and supreme pleasure in love-making lies in the certain knowledge that one is doing evil"—that sort of thing.

Actually, it was unimportant, simple, refueling. And yet in that silly moment of *ménage à trois*, who can say we were not acknowledging a lack all of us shared, and the decision to overcome it by intensifying it? Sometimes life can only seem to get on by a series of such squalid honesties.

Images, images! fragment further: this is the cutting-room floor.

Images of cheap green coffee cups with cigarette ends like dead roaches in the dregs; Napoleons, oozing sugary cream, from the delly downstairs; foggy mornings under the city-gloom when last night's thought ("Anyway, there are ten thousand places on this island where I can go and get a beer for a dime") no longer seemed so comforting; the idle typewriter and the *Daily News*; the silent phone at noon. Autumns of resolution, Aprils of excess.

Letters from Mexico City announcing the death of the spirit in the death of a bull. Only a week before, the knowledge that all creatures were sentient had grieved me with the memory of taunted cats and rejected dogs. . . . Kerouac riffing to the moon on snowy Third Avenue corners, while I railed at him for not worrying about a Europe full of DP's, to which he answered later: "The language-pathos of a Max Lerner is only a self-solace of the conscience, and not a grief." . . . Lear on Sunday afternoons: such nobility of degradation seemed forever out of reach to us, and not a little unreal, for our skies were imminent with "hurricanoes" as it was. . . . The particular fragrance of the stocking-drawer of your wife dressing *up* for love; wet Saturday two *PMs* when boredom led to acrobatic lusts; voices murmuring confidences (identical to yours) from the next apartment (identical to yours).

Italian films of those years: women in frayed slips whose unshaven armpits represented the new reality; the contemporary urban horizon forever defined by ruined apartment buildings and burned-out Chevvies; "Lenin" scribbled on a bullet-pocked Roman wall under a phone number; Magnani the only mother left; a string of smudge-kneed kids trailing through an ash pit, smoking Nazionales; a girl in sneakers and a thin dress, standing in a doorway with a carbine and a loaf of bread; rain falling over the bleak Po marshes where dead Partisans drifted among drowned slogans; starving prostitutes wearily kissing the thighs of drunken GI's; a cruel carnival of bicycles in a penniless father's eye. Did it help? Did it save anything?

Rossellini lived to film Bergman without a brassiere. So much for neorealism. War was Hans selling his sister to Ivan in Berlin, or vice versa in Smolensk. So much for war. All the rest was "issues" that sickened the dyspeptic stomach. All the rest was "history" unfolding like a rebuke.

The Hunt (Wardell Gray and Dexter Gordon): listen there for the anthem in which we jettisoned the intellectual Dixieland of atheism, rationalism, liberalism—and found our own group's rebel streak at last. . . . Past-midnight doorbells waking me from dreams, and rumpled friends imprecating us out for Jack Roses before the bars closed down . . . walking into Glennon's in bare feet after Jones Beach, Potchki the dog drunk on beer . . . Neal Cassady in a kimona and a jockstrap, rolling joints, and yelling: "That's right, that's right!" . . . Ginsberg showing me Satan in the Cardplayers of Cézanne . . . Love on benzedrine, the rod would never go down . . . "Stenka Razin" crooned mawkishly over steamers on Hoboken's River Street.

I never wore a tie; for thirteen months I cut my own hair with a comb fitted with a razor blade; someone stole the first suit I'd bought in five years, and my only suspenders. I wrote a murky novel about a hired killer who ended up killing his hire-er; I found Rose Street under the Brooklyn Bridge, mourning Melville and his century; a writer-friend inexplicably went off to Vienna to become a psychiatrist; another went mad in Connecticut; another got sane, and gave up the unequal struggle.

Spring came up through the windows every year with the flutter of sheer print dresses, and we ate in the Ritz Food Shop— chopped steak, french fries, coffee, 90¢.

Climbing on Jay Landesman's radiator to Tito Puente, announcing with a licorice-tasting giggle that there was no evil in the American night; Gershon Legman's hungry grin as he showed us the filed-teeth in the cloaca of Pop Kultch; all the streets and street corners forever memorialized in my memory by pointless arguments with my wife, who knew I was cheating but dared not mention it; all the nights of feeling guilty because I didn't feel guilty.

"I will only know my place in this Dostoyevskian New York when I hurl myself fully into it, without an escape, without a chance, making an irrevocable leap. It may absorb me, I feel I might drown in it. . . . I have had a gray vision of my life in this fathomless Petersburg of my imagination, in which everyone that I have ever known lived. They were scattered in endless, tottering, labyrinthine tenements, quartered all over this thronging city. There is no rest for me but to rush from one to the other—without time for pause or reconsideration— rushing pell-mell (for my life depends on it, it seems) in search of some message. . . . There is no time in this vision; the day, the never-ending day of my life, goes on and on, and there is always time for another frantic dash across town to see so-and-so, because he, after all, may have the urgent news—." (Journal—February 3, 1949)

I look back through old journals now to discover bitterness, complaints, self-pity, and find only this grim excitement, this bleak eagerness for everything to happen at once, this silly youth taking himself so seriously. Life is stronger than the mind, and Chubby Jackson's dervish cry echoes through those years, "Now—now—*now*—NOW!"

Fifty-second Street before the strippers drove the boppers away, hearing pretty young dykes (last year they came from East Dubuque, and now they taste the strange fruit) talking about Lester coming down, if he got eyes . . . Symphony Sid taking out his false teeth in Birdland to nonplus the squares

. . . Allen Ginsberg staring at Tibet in his York Avenue apartment, and mixing lungen stew . . . Jack K. turning up at a midnight sailing, come 3000 miles back down America's endless Main street, hiding in a closet on the *Queen Mary*, set on Paris, you listen to me . . . We got him off in time, Jacques Fath was posing like Jeanmaire for the shipnews photographers as we lurched by, and later that night we saw Shearing lift Tristano down from the stand, and *we* were blind. I came back through the dawntime streets muttering madly to myself, "Achievement, achievement!"

Allan Temko falling downstairs with a whoop . . . Louanne's flat tummy on which I played soft bongo drums to Bird . . . Carl Solomon in the New School lobby, plucking at my sleeve, to say: "Myshkin"; the countersign was "Rogozhin" . . . Alan Ansen, smirking and roaring, like a sixfoot gnome in a dusty black suit, in afternoon-Clarke's among the neighborhood Irish . . . Winifred, Big Mammy, taking off her blouse as a matter of course—how sad, how foolish, how pointless, how illustrative, how true and simple, I'm hip . . . Cannastra, roaring like a Dago God, his ravaged Garfield face, playing *Norma* through the afternoons to ironic tears, climbing the El like an urban Tarzan, or walking up the street on cartops, or kissing longshoremen in remote Chelsea barrooms. Two blocks away the liners, decked in lights, champagne, faint dancemusic, and the laughter of willing women, headed for Europe with cargoes of the fortunate gone to woo an old hag . . . Cannastra, Cannastra, who knew she could be bought, and went the other way. . . .

Finally, a cold subway platform, eleven-thirty in the morning, Bird's "Stupendous" under my arm, when it came home to me that the Underground I was close to then was an odd, perhaps unique phenomenon in American life: it was *in* it, but not *of* it, and some disengagement had finally reached the suburbs of the mind.

"Our search is, I firmly believe, a spiritual one. . . . Our search is for the Rose that we insist must become visible after the end of the night has been reached; and by the End of the Night I now think we have meant the total breaking down of oneself, the process of *admitting!* How strange if the end should be, as in Yeats' refrain, 'Daylight and a candle-end.' It has relevance." (Journal—June 10, 1950)

Provincetown where it was all supposed to be new: staggering with bottles of kerosene, quarts of beer, gallons of Petri Red back across the Race Point dunes to our shack, like some lost patrol in a John Ford Sahara, visions seeming plausible at last . . . The Old Colony jukebox that had a Billy Eckstine record (!) . . . Benzedrine strips out of the inhaler wadded with Juicy Fruit; feeling my heart; talking for seven hours; no music for two months; throwing up in the Atlantic . . . Seeing my wife, who couldn't swim, walking abstractedly out into the surf one night, getting to her nipple-high; "I thought it looked so pretty, so cool"; the unreality lasting through the next noon, love collected in a glass under the eaves . . . Writing bad poetry ("Now in the reign of Fall—"), distracted by the northwest-wind sea, white-capped all the way to Cherbourg . . . Skinny-dipping as the beach-taxies came by full of school-teachers . . . Cannastra's cottage with the toilet seat splattered red, such a dreary gag to shock the girls, watching him pedaling wildly out of town on a stolen bicycle, leaving a Boston girl with a black eye, who said, adjusting the hamburger, "Tell me about this person" . . . What was there to tell? He would be dead in a year (CLIMB FROM SUBWAY FOR DRINK KILLS RIDER—*Daily News*, October 12, 1950) . . . A boat that would not sail, playing Hearts as the oil lamps guttered, surfacing in Wellfleet's pond to find a lily-pad in my mouth, trying to concentrate on Orwell under the placid eye of "Our Brother," the Sun . . . Racing a train in Providence, New York again, August swelter so live at night, "I should go mad to write this book," make it to Labor Day, Go.

"I have been working at night. Since the third day of August, I haven't missed one. Wonderful feeling, complete concentration, cooler then, nothing to distract. I begin about eleven or twelve, go on sometimes till after five. I go out for coffee and long walks about three or so. I have thrown over everything else, do not read the papers, scorn *Partisan* and the other organs by which the self-doubting literati receive their instructions, and feel at last absolutely self-sufficient." (Journal—August 20, 1949)

Reared on Kafka, Joyce, James and Donne (this was the Age of the Literary Burke and Hare, and about all the equipment one needed to be a critic was a spade and a dead writer, for hadn't *our* Burke—Kenneth—described his critical method as a process of "de-composition"?), the things we wrote were all too often designed to elicit an as-yet-unwritten exegesis. One composed humorless parodies of Nicolas Breton ("We'd have more safety if we had less love—"), and then rushed off to smoke pot with the other poets. One slogged through that month's article on Henry James in a pad full of stolen radios. One took seriously the straight-faced "rediscovery" of Fenimore Cooper. And if one was lucky one read *The Kafka Problem* (which collected twenty-odd interpretations, by as many hands, in a single volume, enabling one to understand that Kafka was at once a communist, a fascist, a Catholic, a Hassidim, an existentialist, a satirist and a psychotic). One was lucky, because perhaps one realized that K's work was incomparably less weighty than the criticism of it, but that any horse, even the most spavined, is more interesting than the cart that tries to pull him. One was lucky, because such absurdities can be educative.

Until the day came when one said irritably: "All that's wrong with Isabel Archer is that James never slept with her in his imagination."

I wanted every fetching girl I met in those days, friend's girls, wives of friends, never did anything about it of course, but all we don't know in this life is the way we look, naked and willing. . . . The rest is only books, talk, logic, balloons, time. We all possess everything but each other. Most intense spiritual experiences are best expressed in sexual terms—"The Bridegroom cometh," "the holy fornication of angels"; and most intense sexual experiences are best expressed in spiritual terms—"the earth moved," "the wingéd thing beating just outside the

windows." The libertine and the mystic ride the same subway
ceaselessly under the City of Night. God plays His tunes
between our feet. Why aren't we all angelically nude, showing
our jewels, each to each?

There was a woman who brought me to this. I would write
her initials, E. L., to tell her that I didn't forget. . . . Older,
trim-waisted, two bad marriages behind her, passionately optimistic in her belief in "creativity," I sought to contaminate her
with my dour view, the senseless lust for consistency that is the
midnight glamor of young men, but she knew better. I remember her dark, Berlin-like apartment, heavy Von Sternberg furniture, sad and trifling paintings aped from Dufy, the good scotch
always set out for me, she was there whenever I wanted to
come.

The first night, there was one nervous dance to an old Teddy
Wilson Brunswick to get us from talk to love (music's role,
after all), and then she took me to her roomy bed, patient,
warm, reassuring: "Oh, I like it so much *that* way—"

Drinks in the Menemsha Bar, gossip of the galleries, soft
talks on the telephone, and most of all long crisp mornings in
her flat that I wasted morosely, having to have my apocalypse.
But I couldn't bear to have her cry, and yet did not feel guilty
about it if she did, and that is close to upright love. And what I
learned from her was that my heart was shriveling up into a
prune as a result of my furtive, dreary succession of infidelities,
and that only the loveless make a law of love.

"But, Johnno, I believe in art, you see," she would say, not
mentioning that I drank too much, "and love between people
who respect each other, and steaks, and good whiskey (yes, all
right), and all the exciting things. Why is that wrong? . . .
though I love your solemn frown, poor boy."

I wrote her angry letters, insisting that I had no interest in
being "merely happy," and I remember her large, old-fashioned
bathroom with the linen shower curtain, and her wide freckled
shoulders, and listening to Dylan Thomas with her—she loved
him too, and was always womanly in her loves, and had lost
everything she really cared about but her ability to sleep each
night and wake new. I wrote poems to her, saying in rhyme that
we couldn't last, but when she wanted me to copy one down for

her in my own hand I balked, thinking insanely, "She'll use it against me!"

Thank God she was stronger, calmer than I, and wouldn't let me scar her life. She saw me in Glennon's once with friends, and nodded discreetly, her bright brown eyes telling me not to worry. Later, she found her love in France, and had a child, and Time gives these gifts to those who persevere.

E. L., you were very good to your stupid 25-year-old lover. Thank you for ferreting out all my old published poems. Thank you for playing me the records that I liked, and making my drinks strong (though sometimes it wasn't in your interest), and letting me have you for those few intermittent months. You never got any benefit out of me. I know I grumbled and was refractory. But you rewarded me anyway. I kiss your dark, gay eyes with gratitude.

"Time is against us, and my stupidity. My wife is hurt again and again, and I bleed. You are hurt again and again, and I bleed. I have only so much blood. My own needs cause carnage all around me, and, really, I am not worth it. . . . Do you know this little verse by Blake?

> 'The angel that presided o'er my birth
> said, "Little creature formed of joy & mirth,
> Go love without the help of anything on earth." '

It is somehow close to me." (Letter to E. L.—April, 1951)

My wife, the wife who has remained only a word so far; not even a shadowy presence in these pages, only the blank word—wife: can I keep her out of this record any longer? What can one say about a first wife?

Distance and intimacy combine to blur the glass, and often we remember a glimpsed face better than one we lived with years ago. It is sobering to realize how much one forgets, and how little that is useful can be made of what remains, yet something must be said anyway. The open mind, and the generous heart, come too late, but thankfully they *do* come, after all.

She was small, sturdy as a sparrow, olive-skinned and fine-featured. Like the figs and lemons of the Mediterranean, an old sun was entombed down in her somewhere, hazed over by the pall of unhappy times. In sweaters and skirts, moving stubbornly through smoky Westchester autumns, an intense mite of sentience, independent and outspoken, *small*, small as a tough little kitchen bird, with almost Tuscan features (though her people had piled stones in Calabria), her translucent skin looked as if it would bruise, and the discontent behind her delicate, wide mouth roused my curiosity instantly—me, the seventeen-year-old cynic in saddle-shoes, full of Lawrencian alienation from 1942 in Chappaqua, already waiting to go into "my" war, and making a life-altering discovery every day.

She had a knee bandage on when I first saw her, she was wearing a short box-back coat, a strand of dime-store pearls glimmered in the hollow of her throat, sitting on a muddy country bus, going to work (as was I that Christmas) at the *Reader's Digest*, daring anyone to notice that her feet did not quite touch the floor. I don't remember the first time I took her out, or kissed her; I only remember the feeling of irony, recent hurt, and a certain tough-mindedness that hung around her face. I thought I saw an ally there.

We walked a hundred miles in the next year (to movies, to beers, to nowhere, to fields we found), time honing our youthful words with the imminence of change, our mouths opening to one another theatrically, as if to forestall the silence we felt certain would come sooner rather than later. We talked about it along many roads, for a long time, before making love.

"If you say you love me, you should *want* to sleep with me, that would prove it."

"I do, you know I do. Of course I do, but—"

"But, as I said, you only *talk* a good game—"

But nothing would dissuade me or my logic; she had come to love me, and love always traps the rabbit. Every idiotic boy was Herrick in 1943.

"Body and Soul" (played three times on the radio) accompanied our passionate ineptness that first afternoon in my cold room, and became our song. It was raining in the bare elms outside; the dog scruffled somewhere in the empty house, needing to go out; we were embarrassed and moved, and successful in disguising both.

Then the beginning was over: Harry James' "I've Heard That Song Before" in a White Plains pizza parlor once, with her high-school friends, from whom I remained (I fancied) intriguingly aloof with my hamburger; I remember a stream of talk whenever we were alone, I remember myself with irritation now—talking, always talking; and pensive November fields with Champ, the dog, out of which we climbed to a high, exposed hill, only a bare tree or two stunted by the wind, a ruined fence all awry, the mailman walking like a Brueghel figure far down there where we looked back at Chappaqua hazy in its valley (I saw the Midlands, being Paul Morel that month, but she saw only the ambiguous vale of home); rainy Village nights paced to the wet shriek of Pee Wee Russell at Nick's (I was jazz-mad and New York was only an hour away); seriously nursing sweet martinis in the Oyster Bar, waiting for commuter trains, when we both worked in New York the next summer. I remember reading Vivian Connell's *The Chinese Room* aloud to her, and playing her Artie Shaw's "Moonglow" two hundred times (she wouldn't dance), and going off to Miami by myself, only to discover that the Beach was empty without her, and coming back after a week.

She called me variously Johnnie, Butch, and even (fondly?) Gruesome—one of those Hi-Y, joshing-of-the-boastful-boys nicknames that leave scars anyway, for the boys never think themselves attractive, and so boast. I wrote of her (in Swinburnesque verse) as "Lan."

> "Never pledge your life completely,
>   Never give yourself to me,
>   Love me silently and sweetly:
>   Passion is a remedy.
>   Let us love and lose our sorrow
>   So when I am gone tomorrow,
>   Though bereaved, you will be free."

Which was the kind of third-hand conceit the headlines and the heartthrobs evoked in the young Werthers of those days.

She was twenty when I met her, and had already suffered the severing fact—the sudden, inexplicable death of a father to whom she still had crucial things to say. Her eyes were ringed with darkness ever after, giving her that look of gaunt chic that transformed Michele Morgan into an existential madonna during the war. At a seance in shuttered upper west side Manhattan with my mother, where she heard her father mumble painfully in Italian, guttural and terrifying, using a private name for her no one else could have known, she was sickened at the idea of the dead still suffering through consciousness, and became more stubbornly atheist than before, death having killed her faith rather than kindled it—as is mostly so in our century. . . . I remember her big bundly sweaters (she was still girlishly embarrassed by her breasts), her trim tweed skirts, silk dickies and simple blouses. I remember my impetuousness though her brothers were only a room away, my solemn intoning of the day's awful poems, my pipes and jazz records, my sense of sophomoric doom. I suppose I couldn't have been as hopelessly corny as I seem now, recalling it. But then the memory edits in mysterious ways. I know she needed order, routine, comfort, a cosiness of heart. But I know as well that I didn't want marriage, I didn't want futurity, I didn't want hope in those days. I wanted her to answer to my hungers—*now*.

Months away at boot camp made me less philosophical: twelve-dollar long-distance phone calls, feverishly graphic letters, pleadings and misunderstandings—all inflated the long uprooting that probably lay ahead. The America of 1944 had all the garish false hilarity of a seedy carnival on its last night in town: every eye was weary and indefatigable; everyone had the impatient, fatalistic mouth of a gob in transit; all our stories blurred into one dark, gathering murmur, hoarse with bus grit, train soot, and the dreck of too many cigarettes in cheerless waitingrooms at four A.M. in Joplin. Everyone took what respite the next moment offered, hurrying their nerves and their emotions toward it.

Later, she would prove brave enough in shabby San Diego hotel rooms, up all night listening in panic to the marine next door, refighting Guadalcanal (she had never been west of Peekskill); living a week on potato chips and Pepsis before I got my pay; counting Roosevelt votes till two A.M. to earn five dollars; making bus connections in St. Louis with the help of drunken soldiers, who were amorous with the foretaste of their death; somehow getting all the long way back when I was transferred East; always hungering for the certainty my silly certainty of worse nights yet to come would not allow to either of us.

What darkened those years so that the stain has never really washed out? . . . A boyhood of those graphic picture-spreads in *Life* of smashed Spanish streets; later, the clipped voices from London sobering the football twilights with the static of the raids; secondhand memories of older wars bequeathed by reminiscing fathers: all this, and—and something else. A shudder in the air, like the premonition of winter that you feel during certain wizen October five o'clocks.

And then, of course, fatalism is heady in the young. Rub a sixteen-year-old, and you uncover a natural Schopenhauer. He wants so badly not to be caught nursing an illusion, and, in our war, the illusions were eagerness to get in, partisanship about the outcome, and futurity. It seemed more realistic (and more romantic) to think of oneself as a man about to become a serial number. The hungers and the anarchies of youth! We might have passed through them smoothly enough had there been no war to make it seem urgent that we have everything now, no questions asked, no debts incurred.

As it was, my war (and thus hers) was mainly wreckage. Months in a receiving hospital on Long Island: no danger, weekend leave, good chow. There, I bed-panned, catheterized, hypodermicked, and strait-jacketed the amputated youths (rebellious and done for after a year on their backs), who went AWOL in wheelchairs, were broken by mistake in traction, got drunk on rubbing alcohol; and the hopped-up marines, invalided home, who stood truncheon-duty, ugly with boredom, on the Gestapo-brigs; and the lockward Billy Budds, with saintly smiles, who sank a fork into your arm for breakfast, and then wept, pissing. I remember the night nurse who would, and the one who wouldn't; the mad machinist's mate with the red beard, plotting joyous rape; the catatonic farmboy without teeth, mummified by some city-horror that had strayed into his barnyard; the little blonde Wave from Cincinnati, who fainted, tripping over a severed foot on the OR floor, wanting out at any cost. (And twenty years later, *where* is Seaman Robert Roska? . . . "Give me a word, Doc. Give me a *big* word to define." . . . This is my word, Bob: sociosis.)

It was a grimly efficient collection point for the thrice-sunk, the stoven-in-by-landing-craft, the fakers-out-of-had-enough, the scared-shitless, the self-inflicted, the glad-I'm-syphilitic—till eventually you caught yourself longing for flesh-fear and the simpler ordeals of combat where the duty was personal survival; until you discovered the hard truth in that age-old nutward maxim, "If you go sponge, you get squeezed," and so crusted over, the nerves dulled by the odors of formaldehyde, pus, feces and the incinerators where they burned the scraps. Sometimes when I saw my wife, I was almost dumb with the hopeless, impotent fury only reluctant-healers ever feel—that Miss-Lonelyhearts-impulse to violence that comes from having no reachable enemy to strike. I slept more than I ever slept before, and could go for days without sleep; I read Joyce, Proust, Mann on twelve-hour stretches of night duty on a quiet ward; my wife was frightened and helpless through my migraines; I had no way to tell her how the commonplaces of horror could harden, as well as destroy you. And who can assess the amount of accumulating tension that I worked out by *using* her whenever we were together? Or how much of my own chaos I transferred to her during that time?

But we lost the possibility of caution then, I think. We were too young and inexperienced to know how to husband our emotions. We went through all our reserves as if there was no tomorrow. And then, all of a sudden, there was.

What can I say? When I think of her, I think of her sleeping, I think of her petulant, I think of her listening to Yankee games as children listen to a favorite story that threatens no surprise. . . . I can't remember that she had any fun in the disorderly New York life we led after the war. I can't remember her thrilled to be there, then, that way. I can't remember her laughing, though I know she did. The times had opened us to each other; the times, in opening further with the false peace, turned us away. I was self-involved, half-formed, too full of books. She worked, job after job after job, to keep us smoking.

But I remember the way she woke, as women do in these years, nastily torn back into the grimy city-morning, too queased to keep down anything but coffee and cigarettes, just as so many women awaken in our beds—Remarque's "soldier's breakfast" having become universal in an age where all are soldiers. I remember her stuffing artichokes; refusing to go to museums with me anymore because I talked her ear off; her summer-hungers for huge, bursting tomatoes; the way she made up carelessly in a minute (two slashes of the lipstick, a pass of the comb); her pshawing, easy manner with the bragging boys of our crowd, though she disapproved of most of the people we knew, not trusting them, or me, or the beat-territories of experience into which we were venturing.

And the times. The time sitting face to face in the same swivel chair in the deserted basement office of the St. Albans Naval Hospital Newspaper on a visitor's Sunday. The time of wine-y mouths on the cold midnight cement of her front porch. The time the picturetaking led to it. The time after the bitter-sweet dinner (sad and warm with brandy we couldn't afford) at Nino and Nella's in the Village, back in our 89th Street cold-water cockroach flat. The benzedrine-time after Hoboken. The time on the too-narrow couch in the cottage behind Einstein's house in Princeton as he played his cello to the fluttering trees of that May noon. The time she wouldn't in the maze of Provincetown dunes. The time with Cousin Sid in the next room when, by accident, something seemed about to happen in the darkness that might actually illuminate it. The *Tropic of Capricorn* time. The first time I noticed that she was only pretending to be asleep.

Built to bear children in the hip, nurse them at the breast, carry them on the shoulder, the children I did not want to father into our uncertain marriage lay aborted behind her eyes—a recrimination, a source of further guilt. I bought her a red tam one Christmas that I knew, at the time, she would never, never wear. She tried to sleep during the hours when

Kerouac and I sat up with bop slamming out of the radio, oo-pa-pa-da-ing and ool-ya-coo-ing of the big, wild city-night out there.

All I knew for sure was that I had to keep pace; I had to go where the times seemed to be heading. I was impatient, and she was bossy. We began to lose.

On one of her birthdays, I rushed home, after making love with E. L. all day, to find the wife of a friend just arrived in town, to whom I nervously talked through the shower curtain, washing off the last of the alien perfume, and somehow finishing everything up just as my wife walked in the door, pale with exhaustion from work, and, unknown to her, giftless and betrayed; to scold me about the dirty dishes in the sink, and call off the meal I'd planned, and go to bed. Guilt? Of course. But in those days I was equally capable of bitter self-congratulations at adroitness in deceit.

Until she felt more whole at the office than at home; until that look came up in her eyes, that grieving, irritable, baffled look of women who have not captured their men, and for the first time realize that marriage is an armistice in the personal war, but not a lasting peace; until she beered and disbelieved as intensely as I in Glennon's Bar, at Cannastra's in the soggy dawns, in the San Remo, Minetta's, Louis', in our dusty apartment with faceless crowds and label-less bottles. Until everything had been said, except the dreary litanies—"Well, I love you too," "But do you really *have* to go out tonight?," "You never read the things that are changing my life," "Why should I have to apologize for being tired?," "Of course, you think that explains everything," and, finally, like Max Roach's stuttering ticker-ticker-boom, "That's what you always say— that's what you always say—that's what you always say"—those repetitive, meaningless Our Fathers that twitter through the broken emotional circuits of our Age of Communications; that dispiriting insect hubbub that goes on behind the frozen masks in which we face one another; those gray, tenuous strings of words we toss over the inky stretch of water, relentlessly widening between ship and pier.

Those words were said (plus the taunts, the tears, the accusations), the words from which there can never be any going back, the glimpses (given out of despair rather than trust) into the chaotic center of one person, from which the other recoils, having seen himself as the author of the wreckage there, all of it eroding the other's face until that morning when we no longer see ourselves mirrored in that face, or in our own, and realize with a start that, though yesterday may be regretted, it is beyond change, and the past is entombed and unalterable once we have survived it as the present. . . . My lies and her restraints, guilt and hostility—around, around, until the wheel broke down. Until our voices were hoarse and murky; our eyes tireless and tired; our nerves perpetually strung as tight as baling wire, and we had mercy on ourselves, and on each other, and gave it up.

I haven't seen or heard from her now in ten years, a queer fact to realize because, of course, she will always be vividly alive to me in things she did and said that had no huge meaning at the time, but make me try to imagine her mornings now— remarried, with the children her sense of continuity hungered- for, back in Westchester again where the strong Medaglia d'Oro smells as good as creosote on the clean wind. I imagine her busy (with a Chesterfield forgotten in the ashtray), perhaps out of sorts while making beds, visiting her mother in the next town for Sunday pasta, even reading *this*—out there some- where, beyond anything I can do, or fail to do, again.

But perhaps most keenly I remember that sultry twilight in Bryant Park in August, 1944 (she had met me on my return from Boot Camp), where we waited for the train back to Chappaqua. I remember her white sheer blouse through which the white bra glimmered faintly; the fine sheen of brown hair on her wide shoulders; the curve of lipstick on her piquant mouth; her primly sensual body poised on the bench with an uncon- scious grace of shoulder and hip that hinted at new emotions, as she said, "I was so scared you wouldn't come after all that I got mad at the taxidriver coming over. Then I felt that getting mad that way would guarantee I wasn't ever really meant to be happy, and I almost prayed, Johnnie, for the first time since Papa," at which I was suddenly struck wordless by her palpable presence there; I felt the actual suspiration of her breath, the stubborn life animating her small limbs; I glimpsed her con- sciousness going on and on beyond my selfish desire, and opened toward it willingly, selflessly, for once . . . for she seemed to be everything that is contained in that fragrant and unsettling word, girl. It was our closest moment, we were dumb with quiet awareness, something passed between us, something that stilled the words in my astonished mouth. We were married the next afternoon.

No cheap irony in that. We lose some things in the moment of gaining them. Still, you dare not betray a perception that enlarges your life. You have to follow it to the ground.

But I have an emotion that is too simple to be evoked by what is written here. "I have a great desire that you should be happy," as Myshkin wrote Aglaia. "Are you happy? That was all I wanted to say to you."

And finally, out of those years, images flit by that are not my own. Imagination makes all of us one. I won't ask why that is any longer, for "history" is nothing but the vision of intuitive noncombatants.

The mothers murdered on the Rostov road, dead bundles of Russian rags swinging from the winter gibbets; Aussies, in funny slouch jungle hats, wrists bound, kneeling in the rice paddies to have their heads chopped off; screaming boys falling in flames out of the Channel cumulus, no phoenix; blood and dogtags beaten into the immemorial Cassino mud; the burning Jap, flushed from his lair, running in pell-mell anguish from the hose of flame; children, nothing but great walking eyes, staring through barbed wire in Silesia; butchered horses stinking the Polish fields; Saar villages leisurely burning off to the left.

All this rioted in my head in 1944 and '45, and my own eighteen-year-old tears at dusk behind the commissary on San Diego's Navy Hill, weeping with dead seriousness for pea-jacketed boys, and their Kansas soda-fountain girls, and all the uprooted drowsing on halted trains, taking on water in Oklahoma.

"Why do they always *sing?*" I sniffled, cursing under my breath, hearing the goofy American songs rising in the clear air over the bilge of harbors full of transports, "Why, goddammit!" I'd heard them sing during coffee-stops in alfalfa-towns in darkest 1942; later, I heard them sing shattered jingles on nutwards where the quiet Long Island nights were murmurous with visions. They probably sang even on work details in Dachau where certainly the nineteenth century came to an end. I guess they sang "In the Mood" sometimes on johnless prison ships making for Manchuria. And "Horst Wessel" piled more corpses up than Adolph Hitler. It is very queer. God has heard some strange things rising faintly from our ravaged earth in my lifetime—songs of the bombers and the bombed alike. What can He possibly think of us? Images of love and death?

For it seemed to me then that the burden of my generation in those first postwar years was just this vast maelstrom of death; these corpses in the mind; those murders committed, witnessed or imagined; that feeling that something had gotten dreadfully, dangerously out of hand in our world; all the Torgaus that proved faked, and the concentration camps that proved too real; and most of all the rueful hope at war's end, which the peace debauched. The burden of my generation was the knowledge that something rational had caused all this, and that nothing rational could end it; that enemies had supplanted friends, and friends enemies; that the bombs had gotten bigger, but the politics had stayed the same. The burden of my generation was to carry this in utter helplessness—the genocide, the overkill—and still seek love in the underground where all living things hide if they are to survive our century. At least, so I thought at the time.

In any case, we came to learn to expend the exuberance of youth on the far-out, the eccentric, the twisted, the unique—anything that did not smack of the murderous logistics of Power run amok. We looked for a human face that had escaped the flattening and emptying of that pseudo-death, and found the junkie's nod, the lunatic's grin, the jazzman's rapture, and the hip girl's acquiesence—all this—would do. We ended staring at our own young faces with old eyes, until it became clear that what we were suffering was not the disillusionment that followed the others' war, but a disenthrallment from the kind of consciousness that had allowed ours.

If the difference seemed crucial to us then, perhaps it is because a disillusionment is a retreat, a narrowing, a loss, producing a mood of emotional cynicism, or bittersweet resignation; but a disenthrallment in an advance, a freeing from fantasy, a breakthrough into reality, a lifting of the very spell of which disillusionment, with all its alternating glooms and hilarities, is the final moult. Perhaps our war only ended in us when we realized that the singer was the ultimate source of the reality of the song, and so began to search the face to comprehend the words. Which seemed a strategic victory in those days.

"It's dark in this wood, soft mocker," Roethke would write. "For whom have I swelled like a seed? . . . Father of tensions, I'm down to my skin at last."

The Fifties

§ § The pivot-points of modern life are as inexplicable as cancer —or a baby. Sudden success, that one headline too many, a habit that threatens to become a vice, a hopeless rising in the Balkans, even a simple kiss: all these will serve. A word can change one man's life as irrevocably as a dam will change a river; and yet a violent death near at hand will, to another man, prove to be nothing but a ripple on the pond. But sometimes change is in the air, and seems as mysterious and unalterable as the sequence of the seasons. Some dissatisfaction, longing or despair seizes everyone at the same time, and the pivot occurs. This may bring a group of people into brief, intense conjunction. It may also disperse them. If this kind of vivid conjunction was the hallmark of the late forties to me, the mysterious process of dispersal, the quiet weakening of cohesiveness, was the dominant note of the Fifties.

For me, the new decade began one dreary winter afternoon in January of 1950 when Kerouac and I sat with beers, waiting for the night to come, as everyone seemed to wait for it in those days—certain it would prove historic. We were full of the tenor of the times (at least we thought we were), and began planning what we called "a decade of parties" to be given in a loft we would rent down on Rose Street under the Brooklyn Bridge. Outlandish as this sounds today, considering that neither of us had any spare cash, we were in deadly, or at least tipsy earnest at the time. "The door would always be open, the lights would never go out, the music would always play." Jack's first novel was about to be published, mine was well underway on my desk, and it seemed impossible that the exciting and disordered years just passed were not about to bear fruit in a period of unparalleled revelry and achievement.

I suppose the decade ended for me in December, 1960, when I wrote in a journal: "The end of an eight-year attempt to come to terms with what I used to call 'the Glittering Life,' the upper world of fame, money, cynicism, smart lunches and disbelief, Us against Them, the lore of liquor, all that. I've known for years it wasn't for me, and yet somehow went on, and only these last grim eighteen months have succeeded in burning it away."

In between the first intoxication and the final hangover came that strange period called the fifties, the moral tone of which lay somewhere between Ike's reassuring grin and McCarthy's wolfish smile; a period that began with cool West Coast jazz and a hot Far Eastern war, and the retreat from certainty that was implicit in both; a period that is best evoked by such phenomena as Commander Whitehead, brinksmanship, Brubeck, Brando in *Teahouse*, Rodgers and Hammerstein, and that Orwellian therapy for all the anxieties of the nuclear age: *Time*, Teller, and tranquilizers; a time when presidential prose accomplished the feat of being both consoling and incomprehensible; and the Broadway stage could seem to come up with nothing more heady than Miss Mary Martin and her exuberant brand of Pepsi-Cola; when the art of the film took a giant step forward by radically enlarging the square-foot area on which Nothing could be projected in full color and stereophonic sound; when the fiction of James Gould Cozzens and Sloan Wilson, taking the high and low roads respectively, nevertheless hawked the same stale fortune cookie; a time of such incongruities as the Arthur Miller–Marilyn Monroe nuptials, White House press releases dealing with bowel (rather than troop) movements, Charles Van Doren's agonizing reappraisal, and having to make a choice between Hungary and Suez, Johannesburg and Little Rock.

It was the time when everyone in Exurbia read *The Exurbanites*, and young executives in identical suits, drinking identically

dry martinis, swapped identical wives, and were fashionably
worried about conformity; when *Time* Magazine used *From
Here to Eternity* to beat Norman Mailer over the head, and
then used *The Caine Mutiny* to beat James Jones over the
head, and failed to see that this sort of oneupmanship actually
led *down*; when the twenties went through a sentimental
revival, and Scott Fitzgerald was finally canonized by girls from
Bryn Mawr for the very thirsts that killed him; when the
thirties were buried forever the day Lucille Ball (making more
money than almost anyone else in the nation) confessed that
she had once joined the Communist Party; and everyone else
sat nervously under the fateful umbrella of our nuclear deter-
rent, playing Scrabble and overeating.

The sociological eye, under its mask of objectivity, selects
those details rather than others, and so succeeds in being as
false to reality as it is to memory. For though the man
remembering may be only an acquaintance of the man remembered, nevertheless he *is* a man, subjective to the end, and
there's some hope for truth in that. So I try to remember what I
was like when the decade began, and all I can recall is boundless
energy, a capacity of self-indulgence, and that special brand of
optimism that allows the young to be pessimistic and still not
get hurt. I was fond of describing myself as a rootless radical, a
believer without a creed, a pacifist by prejudice. Every day was a
discovery, and I begrudged sleep, and slept well. I seemed to
live in a continual seethe of anticipation, and what I was
anticipating was some version of that "orgiastic future" that has
always beckoned Americans out of their good sense. My version
of this (properly dark) was an almost weekly call to all the sad
captains for one last gaudy night.

The queer nature of the decade first came home to me when
financial success and marital failure happened to me almost
simultaneously. By late 1951, the novel I had been working on
when the fifties began was finished, and so was the marriage
which in no small measure had enabled me to write it. First
novels are always written at somebody's expense, and, patrons
being extinct this century, it is often the writer's wife who pays
the tab—the last item on which is sometimes, sadly, the
marriage itself. All young writers secretly applaud the candor of

Brecht's avowal, "I, of all people, must outlive violence," but, still, somebody must suffer for the vows we take, and wives are there at hand.

I was working as a public opinion-researcher down in those cold canyons off lower Fifth Avenue, and had spent three nights in a borrowed apartment in Tudor City (to prevent further disastrous postmortems) when I got the news that Go had been accepted by Scribner's, and so there would be gin for Christmas. I went back to my wife, and we tried again, for I was possessed by the idea that my advance belonged as much to her as it did to me, and (coming at the most inopportune moment) constituted the last remaining obstacle to our separation. It seemed natural to both of us that we should clear that obstacle away by spending the money as fast and as frivolously as we could. So we made a Faustian bargain, and doom was its excitement.

After years of subways, hailing a taxi to go only five blocks can be as wicked and thrilling as champagne for breakfast, and only the impoverished can know the feeling of giddy profligacy that comes with paying the rent two months in advance. We stayed up nights at our task, we spared ourselves nothing out of either weariness or despair, we bought nothing that would last till morning, and in less than six weeks we were honorably broke again, and quits.

I found a fifth-floor railroad flat (twenty-five dollars a month) in a rabbit warren on East 48th Street, which I filled with fragments of cornice, bannister and bas-relief from demolished buildings in the neighborhood—"the ruins of New York," as I called them, fancying myself an archeologist of a city in dissolution—and there, living from hand to mouth, I did my galleys and awaited publication.

By a fluke, the book appeared at the highwater mark of the Great Reprint Hysteria, when astronomic sums were being paid for the paperback rights to everything under the sun, even first novels with as little sales appeal as mine; and, as it happened, I had three dollars in my pocket when my agent called up one day to announce, "I think Bantam will go for twenty thousand—half now, half on pub—if we don't panic." A week later I found myself possessed of a bank account of four figures where the day before there had been only two—with nothing more pressing to spend it on than a divorce.

"She wants to get the divorce in New York, probably White Plains. . . . That means adultery. . . . At first, I was dead against it in my mind. It means collusion, a permanent blot. But then, last night, I realized the aptness of it. It is fitting that I should be divorced on a charge of adultery. It is one oblique way of paying off that old debt." (Journal—September 24, 1952)

The day the money was banked, I walked down Third Avenue in a daze, feeling inexplicably estranged from everything I saw. That tawdry, cobbled street under its permanent canopy of gloom had been my night's mart for years, and now the wider, airier, glossier boulevards toward the center of the island were open to me. Nevertheless, I went into the same grimy saloon where I had been nursing beers for years, and nursed a couple more, staring distractedly at the Johnnie Walker I could suddenly afford, and realizing for the first time that it was possible to think in terms of next year, rather than just next week. All at once, I could go anywhere I wanted, and all at once I couldn't think of anywhere to go.

I was a fairly affluent writer, even by standards less modest than my own, and yet one of the paradoxes of the time came home to me a few years later when I did a bit of calculation over a much better drink in a far chic-er saloon. By then, the hardcover edition of my novel had come and gone in almost total silence, selling only about two thousand copies; and the reprint house that had paid so lavishly for it in 1952 felt that it was too far-out for 1954, and decided not to publish; and I could say that I was the only writer I knew who had received almost ten dollars for every copy of a three-fifty book sold. I inspected my unbruised Gibson, and discovered that a surprising and subtle bitterness (the bad wine of sour grapes) can ferment in such paradoxes.

But by then a lot of other things had happened. So little used to money was I that I continued to live in my 25-dollar-a-month apartment for another year, and didn't buy a new suit for three months. Instead, I got a cheap tape recorder on the theory that I could thereby save on the price of records. Everything I did was a little cracked, a little out of emotional proportion, as if my psychic needle had somehow lost its true magnetic North. For I had been prepared for fame, and I had gotten money instead, and this can be fatal to the inexperienced. But good fortune, like death, becomes real a detail at a time, and before too long I had endured that first morning when you get up, with your mouth full of old socks, and the murky memory of taxies, brandy snifters and hatcheck girls cartwheeling in your defenseless head, to realize with horror that somewhere along the way you have spent one hundred dollars in a single evening. I had gotten through succeeding mornings, identical in every detail but for the horror, and had even been amused to discover that in two months I had spent more money checking my overcoat than I had paid for it.

The ambivalence that was to be typical of the times had already started to appear. Mark Van Doren, after reading Kerouac's *On the Road* in manuscript, commented: "I only hope it's not *important*"—a revealing response to the book's point of view that would keep it unpublished for five years. I signed a telegram to *The New York Times*, along with a dozen other writers, demanding that the paper withdraw its endorsement of Ike unless he repudiated McCarthy's charges against General Marshall, and was too busy with a girl the next day to even pick up the morning edition to see if they had reported it. On election night, I watched the returns on TV from a luxurious east side apartment, full of celebrated east side people, who were supposed to be holding a wake for Stevenson, but got too gay on Chivas Regal, and somehow forgot.

Whittaker Chambers waddled down the backstreets of my mind that fall, like a dogged Javert patiently exposing all Jean Valjean's fine ideals as nothing but masks for the most cynical crimes. A high pitch of hysteria was in the air, like the metallic hum of the generators in the opening scenes of *Doctor Mabuse*, and unconsciously one made one's adjustments to it, and after a while no longer heard it for what it was. Only a certain continuing unease in the nerves throbbed on and on, day after day.

I wrote an article on the Beat Generation for *The New York Times* that fall that aroused sufficient controversy for me to find myself in a television studio, at one and the same time being made up by a Lesbian in a smock and warmly praised for the article by Mike Wallace, who, ten minutes later when we were on the air, dismissed it as "probably unwarranted."

I remember being piqued by all these things, but I also remember blaming that pique on my own innocence. It was hard to keep the fine edge of pessimism honed in that seraglio-air of affluence that crooned: "Bitterness is the cold coffee of losers. And you've won. Act like it."

It was a time of small compromises, petty cowardice, and I can list a few contributions of my own to the flab of those early-fifties years. By instinct opposed to capital punishment, I was in the bar car of a train heading for a week-long party in St. Louis on the night the Rosenbergs were executed, and, aside from ordering a double, I don't remember having any but rather secondhand emotions at the time. They were human beings, but they were also Communist spies, "so let's be realistic." After all, hadn't compassion itself become suspect? And weren't most of the people who protested the sentence rogues or dupes? The breakdown of nerve that was everywhere in those days is nowhere better illustrated than by comparing this reaction, which was typical enough, to the uproar over the Chessman execution some years later. But by then, of course, half a decade of the Dulles' devil-theory of politics had unsettled even the strongest of stomachs, and murder was no longer viewed as God's Triumph, but as man's failure.

Though I was seriously alarmed by Senator McCarthy (like everyone else, my electric bill came to sixty dollars the month of the Army-McCarthy hearings), I remember cynically defending his aggressiveness and style as an infighter against the attacks of doctrinaire liberal-friends, rather as if he was nothing more than a legislative Sonny Liston. Simon-pure moral positions were a little naive after all, and the mood of the first Eisenhower

Administration somehow encouraged separating a man's style from his ideas. And besides, who was more ludicrous and embarrassing—McCarthy, or those who toadied to him? An outright Iago, with his malice on his sleeve, seemed almost hip in that Era of Polonius.

Despite the fact that I had once ghost-written for cigarette money, and knew full well that my temperament was such that when I hacked I *got* hacked, I nevertheless took on a long two-part profile of Burl Ives (in whom I had small interest) simply because the magazine editor, who commissioned it, dropped big names and big advances before my greedy eyes, tantalizing me with glimpses of the Glittering Upper World where everyone is famous together.

"You've got to see John, and Gadge, and Max, and José. . . . And take Burl down to McSorley's, get him to tell you all those raffish stories. . . . And for God's sake don't make it so *grim*. . . ."

Months later, after traipsing around through dressing rooms, nightclubs and yacht marinas while my new novel languished, I was still trying to write the sort of bland publicity-puff piece the magazine wanted, and had squandered all the money doing it. Like every other lesson I learned during the fifties, this one was expensive.

Specifically, it cost me that new novel. From the moment I began writing it, I was afflicted by second-book problems. My binoculars were blurred with the fingerprints of chance acquaintances; I'd lost my *Weltanschauung* in a cab somewhere; I was experiencing myself mostly through other people's images of me. These conditions usually occur in a writer when the slackening of creative muscle that sometimes accompanies publication makes you think that, in some indefinable way, you have "crossed over." There is nothing more conducive to creative honesty than having nothing to lose, but somehow on the second book you *have* something to lose (if only that deference of recognition that slightly widens the eyes of total strangers), and you find yourself writing to consolidate a position already gained, instead of trying to take a new one. I worked hard, and I worked almost every day, but a lot of that work was little more than going through the motions. I walked the old neighborhoods in a cold rain, trying to recapture that stubborn self-assertion in the prison of anonymity ("I'm here; you'll see!") that is all that keeps the tyro warm. I took voluminous notes, I read "helpful" books, I bought a new typewriter. But I was trying to write about the fifties themselves, and the result was mostly as muddled as the life I was living at the time.

"I have been told that I don't believe in anything, which is patently a foul canard, since I've been seen earnestly searching for values in such places as Birdland, Alexandra's, the Bleeker Tavern, and the Museum of Modern Art. . . .

"I paid Uncle most of my loot from *Go*, what with lawyer's bills and everything, but I still owe the Bearded Gentleman in the striped drawers a big bundle. There is a weapons carrier in Korea with my name on it. . . . " (Letter to Landesman, April 28, 1953) If that bright and careless voice, darkened on the edges by an easy irony, is undeniably *my* voice, the accent is the authentic accent of those years.

By this time, money and a modest reputation had opened new doors to me, and that vision of the "decade of parties" made me incautious and uncritical. Most of the doors were in that strip of midtown Manhattan I took to calling the Martini Belt, where the taste in attitudes as well as neckwear was dictated by the relativism of a Madison Avenue giddy with its new influence in Washington, and uninterested in meanings, except insofar as they were marketable. A certain ugly veneer of "hipness" characterized the world I moved into then. Almost everyone in it was connected with what was solemnly called Communications, and their reaction to the intellectual oatmeal of the times was to mock, rather than challenge. As in all periods when the fashionable takes the place of the substantial, everyone I met knew what happened yesterday, and no one knew what happened last week.

A hungry cynicism, an eagerness to find the worm under every stone, was the prevailing mood, and you were constantly greeted with remarks like, "Did you hear the latest about

Schweitzer and Ava Gardner?" If someone said, "Say, I hear it took Lillian Roth a case of Beefeater's to finish that book," someone else was bound to reply, "Horsefeathers. Junkies don't lush." All celebrities, not known to be specifically otherwise, were assumed to be homosexuals, and some of the rumors of who was doing what, and to whom, and how many watched them doing it, were truly astounding in their inventiveness and unlikelihood. This same assumption that one's public image and one's private truth were different things, but that somehow it didn't matter much, was typical of a time when *Confidential* had a mass circulation, and intellectuals talked mostly about such pseudo-profundities as The Organization Man, Subliminal Advertising, and the Revival of Religion. Hardearned existential truths were drowned in the mushroom soup of positive thinking.

If there was a bitter humor in those days, there was often as much romanticism in it as there was cynicism; and the images of the Glittering World that I was already (even from the bleachers) starting to scribble down reflected this: a montage of such sparkling objects as Tangiers, the Little Club, Stowe, House of Lords gin, twill suits, Patachou, night swimming, silver nail polish, and Negronies; of such chick folkways as sometime-parties and most-of-the-time drinking; of so-and-so's in Aspen and I'm just off for the Coast; of no one's going to Spain anymore, but everyone's renting Greece; of she's got a year-long tan and the alimony to support it; or of course he's a fruit but his studio's in for too much to blink at payola.

I imagined a world in which somebody's agent, and somebody else's producer, and somebody else's PR man came into temporary conjunction over "cocks" in somebody's girl friend's duplex on Beekman Place one magic spring twilight at five; and by seven, everyone who had been there, drinking marts out of the same Steuben pitcher and telling cancer jokes, was dispersed to any number of other smart purlieus around late-Empire Manhattan: the agent to the bar at Twenty-One and further martinis ("Just tell him to pass an unopened bottle of Noilly Prat over the shaker, boobie, and hit me with a fresh twist") that were meant to impress (and befuddle) an already nervous starlet just off Pan Am from L.A.; the producer to an apartment on 11th Street for fettucine and a bottle of Bardolino with a young man, who was last year's fawning nonentity in an ill-cut suit, the young man who did the wrong thing that weekend in Newtown, and was an unbelievable bore in the Absinthe House, but who was this year's bright, style-setting young "comer," with the new song, the choice part, the fresh script, and the burgeoning "rep" for—well, something or other; the PR man to Leiderkrantz Hall where one of his properties was getting exposure by guesting on a quiz show that was already being fed into the teleprompters; and the hostess, with freshly applied eyes, getting into a taxi to go to Pavillon to have langouste with someone whom she will never see again, or will sleep with in four hours, or slept with four years ago, or was married to once, or knew in Paris, or hated in Hollywood, or will meet for the first time once she gets there.

With the certainty that only the uninformed can summon up, I fancied that I saw the end of this sort of life along with its beginning: the relentless toll that a continual commercial hypocrisy must take on the human personality; the tab (for having flown now) that must be paid later. I felt certain that all these people would go on and on toward the breakdown or the split-up, until the day when they moved away to Connecticut if they were lucky, or the sanatarium if they had lost their wits along with their stomach linings and bank balances, or to their family's shabby shingled house down a bad block in Streator, Illinois, where they would age without grace, and strike the neighborhood kids as "loony." The beaches and the bars, the ski tows and the theaters, the staterooms and the board rooms, would never see them again; only their golf clubs, their books and records, their old scripts or Louis Quinze chiffoniers, would turn up later: all that out-of-date refuse that people always paint white, and plant ivy in.

This vision had only a shaky relation to any reality I knew, and yet something starved in my ego quickened to it nevertheless. And some promise of celebrity, security and influence (still perhaps the dominating myth of the young and inexperienced American writer) witched me out of my reservations for that brief season. And I was not alone. A lot of once-hungry cats had a surfeit of mice.

Actually, it was Aziza Bright Eyes and Smirnoff that provided most of the glitter of the world I moved in, and the women I knew drank vodka-rocks-twist, lost twenty pairs of gloves a year, and talked a hipper game than ever they played. Most of the men maneuvered their J. Press double-vents through a reality distorted by Nembies on the one hand, and Dexies on the other (working too hard, and pretending not to; picking up checks, and secretly broke), and all the while considering themselves no more than the vanguard of a nation that would be gobbling Miltown by the gross in a year or two. My crowd seldom went downtown, and rarely lasted through the third act of a play, and never talked seriously about politics. In fact, about the only heated discussions I heard in this group concerned the merits of aging chanteuses who sang obscure show tunes, or whether the Jack Palance character in *The Big Knife* had actually castrated himself at the end of the film.

Gerry Mulligan, playing music to accompany a tipsy elephant, burbled out of hi-fi rigs everywhere, and almost nothing in the national life had a piano under it, laying down the changes that tell you where you are. The cease-fire in Korea brought with it the eerie illusion that no one was being killed for an idea anywhere in the world; and that New Year's Eve a taxidriver said to my date, "I don't care what he *says*, lady. I don't want him throwing up in my cab." It seemed funny enough at the time to bear repeating over cocktails for a month.

Perhaps *Waiting for Godot* expressed the mood of those years at its most serious: "Was I sleeping while the others suffered? Am I sleeping now? Tomorrow, when I wake, or think I do, what shall I say of today? . . . In all that, what truth will there be?" But the answer, too, had become a cliché. There would be *none*.

I was never fully at ease in this Uptown World, and maintained a surreptitious afternoon life that had nothing to do with it. I remember going out to Brooklyn to be with a young friend of mine, a conscientious objector, when he was sentenced to a year in Danbury for refusing to register for the draft, and then rushing back to a party off Park Avenue where forty people stood shoulder to shoulder, while a drunken girl had convulsions on the floor, and two ad men smoked pot in the john, and everyone else watched the TV set, making bets on how long it would take Ralph Edwards to reduce his *This Is Your Life* guest to tears.

I remember spending an evening with Bill Burroughs at Ginsberg's in the East Village, looking at photos of backcountry buses in Chile, and listening to Bill's musing, Fieldsian description of all the hangups of "getting to the interior." I was wearing an eighty-dollar suit, I was getting paunchy from too many rich sauces, I hadn't moved an inch toward my own "interior" in a year.

I remember trying to write day after day with a hangover and only three hours' sleep, and forcing myself to keep at it—at least till one o'clock when dark glasses, and Bloody Marys, and luncheon at Annette's Petit Veau would quell my unease. I remember wincing when someone down the bar said, "I'm sick of balling, let's have fun," to which his wife replied, "I'm sick of having fun, let's ball." But I don't remember remarking that this wasn't such a joke, after all.

And then one day I was writing to a friend: "I feel myself changing, but I do not know what I will be when it is finished. On top of this, I am in love. . . . This, too, is new for me. . . . I write no more poems to the Great White Goddess. . . ."

For by this time I was courting a girl in the Oak Bar of the Plaza Hotel. We had rocky divorces in common, and the same feeling that the times were somehow out of joint. Like me, she had married fatalistically; like me, she had never really given herself to it; like me, she looked on another emotional entanglement with all the aversion of the twice-shy. We promptly fell in love, wary though we were, and in a month we had progressed farther into each other than either of us had ever been before: through the batwings to the golden fountain.

Her calm, absorbed face was waiting for me on West 60th Street whenever I surfaced there out of myself; I was unused to someone who could wait . . . The radio hummed with the soft, clean riffs of Les Brown; weiner schnitzel wafted under the Venetian blinds from the Viennese restaurant down the block;

we beamed at one another like idiots demented by happiness
. . . We went to Le Downbeat on rainy, musing nights where
Billy Taylor played us "We'll Be Together Again," and Dizzy
smiled cannily to see our eyes straying over each other's mouths.
We taxied home, pleasantly mulled, and said all the words we
had both disdained to say for years—the tender words for which
no gesture is a substitute, the erotic words which are gestures in
themselves. I walked back across Central Park in the pastel
April mornings, mended and alert, and took pleasure in dogs,
and perambulators, and old men.

I liked to look at her in crowded, noisy rooms—she was so
slender, trim and capable. She played jukeboxes with discrimi-
nation, and something about the set of her lip indicated
independence of mind, taste in pleasure, and an intuitive sense.
I accumulated her life (Louisiana-genteel family, bad-girl con-
vent, flight) by that same slow process of accretion that charac-
terizes great nineteenth-century novels, until she became the
emotional money in my bank, and for the first time I experienced the kind of psychic solvency against which even an insult
from a close friend cannot overdraw. We spent days locked in,
doing nothing. I carried her warm, wry glances in my head
through numerous brittle cocktail hours without her. I felt
expansive, generous, and sometimes wise. I fancy I even *looked*
better in those days, for certainly a delight of the spirit must
show on a man's face.

I bought her earrings, books, flowers, Jack Daniels; she
wanted nothing like that from me, and so the joy of it was
lagniappe. I tried to write poems to her, and found them to be
artificial, studied, heavy with a reflex of gloom, and wrote no
more verse after that. We took on one another's debts of
anxiety from the past, and paid them off, one by one, at night.
We loved. We *made* love. The way she stood at her stove,
balancing on one hip like a dreamy antelope; the way she
crossed her bare feet, looking at once contemplative and comi-
cal, while sitting in her Roman-size tub; the way she trusted
herself to me in arguments (that most flattering of all female
ploys): all this left no room for doubt. And eventually we ran
off to East Haddam, Connecticut, where a hunchbacked J.P. got
up from his farm lunch (his massive sons went on putting away

corned beef and cabbage) to mumble the words over us, adding incongruously, "I hope youse'll be very happy," and we were legal.

Later that afternoon, changing clothes in my mother's house before going down to champagne, we looked at each other in the middle of a word, and all at once the inexplicable feat of having made it safely out of our similar pasts to that moment, against our own direst predictions, made us giddy with relief, and at a loss for words at last. Marrying her was the only intelligent thing I did during this period.

Clear emotions, keen mornings, an extravagance of small hopes: such simple things rebuild life while we're not looking. People all seemed repetitious, places all seemed noisy; we finally admitted that what we wanted most was to be alone, and took to going to Connecticut one or two days a week so that I could work and avoid the temptations of the telephone.

The lavender dusks, smoky with leaf fires, tasted of sage; the Congregational Church down the street tolled solemnly among its elms; and I wrote of a postwar Viennese winter (all that European bitterness and bad coffee) while sitting in a cozy, fire-lit room near a Victorian parlor-organ and a musty set of the Countess Muhlbach. We woke to the morning sun reflected on an ornate burled-oak headboard, and spent the afternoons in cove-bound eighteenth century graveyards, and were drowsy by ten in the evening.

Saturday-night auctions; the smell of furniture polish, old leather, and wet galoshes in a country library; November beaches of drum-hard sand and frozen tide lines: in the midst of this, I tried to evoke the raw nerves of cities, the apartment dweller's torn roots, the moral wreckage behind the distracted faces down the bar. But I was too happy to write well. My contentment showed in every swollen line and mechanical image, and the chapters rolled on months beyond the point where I had taken the wrong turn.

Then one thawing January day, the book was finished, the "exile" (as I called it) over, and I walked out a muddy path to the salt marshes on the Sound, happily making plans for England in the spring. I was thinking about the fairs, and caravans, and inns of George Borrow—I remember that clearly, just as clearly as survivors remember the trivial thing they were doing when their ship hit the iceberg. Though *my* shock was still four weeks off.

I delivered the manuscript to my agent in New York, packed a bag, closed up the apartment, and we were in Louisiana when we heard that the book had been rejected by the publisher. There was an hour of quiet panic by a bayou, at the end of which I chose not to trust my premonition, and we came back and hung around while the novel was being submitted to two other houses, and soon found ourselves part of an informal luncheon club that got together once or twice a week to spend a lot of money and kill the afternoon. These were people as centerless as we were, between jobs, between marriages, marking time on the shoals of that mid-decade year when having a lot of costly fun in restaurants where the menus are bigger than the tables seemed as sensible a thing to do as anything else.

One of this crowd was "the youngest has-been in New York," having lost a $20,000-a-year job by the time he was twenty-three; another turned on with members of the narcotics squad, and, bombed out of his skull, went along with them on pot-raids in Harlem; several more were typical of the sort of pseudo-intellectual drifter, "behind the wood this year" (bartending), with vague plans to write, or act, or make a killing at the track, whom everyone numbered among their close friends in those days; the girls were that year's crop of hip chicks, usually passed pretty much from hand to hand, sometimes transferring out of the regiment to marriage or flipsville, and always replaced by other chic recruits. For a while, we cabbed up and down town with these people, and I was their "captive novelist"—the amulet they sometimes rubbed for luck. In actual fact, I was seriously bewildered by the fate of my novel. None of the rejections made the least bit of sense to me, and, for the first time, I was wondering if I had the vocation, after all. Losers have an instinctive affinity for each other, and I felt like a loser.

Before I knew it, it was spring again. Central Park was hazy and impressionistic as I saw it one afternoon from (of all places) the cocktail lounge at the top of the Beekman Towers where I stood muddled by brandies with a bunch of people I hardly knew.

Someone was saying, "No, she cut out because she thought I lived it up too much."

And someone else replied, "Well, Charlie, you know what I always say. 'Too much' is almost *enough* for me."

I swayed against the parapet, squinting at the rivers that contain Manhattan's ferment, and discovered that I was thinking, with tipsy longing, about stone fences, run-down orchards, grass. I realized all of a sudden that New York had been getting me down for weeks. It seemed to demand more and more on my nerves simply to walk across town to my bank. Some days everyone I saw was a cripple, every doorway sheltered a derelict and his pint of muscatel, everywhere I went I overheard nasty, hopeless voices. I remember blinking in the fresh April breeze, and saying to myself idiotically: "When lunch gets to be more historic than dinner, it's time to leave, it's time to stop."

A week later, it became clear to me at last that my novel had been seriously botched, and that, as a result, we would be in money trouble within three months. That self-satisfied streak of conservatism, which flows back into American life in periods of prosperity, was everywhere by then, and "Engine Charlie" Wilson's fat-cat patriotism, together with Marjorie Morningstar's kittenish chastity, seemed typical of the complacent veneer that was hardening over everything.

In or around that time, Bird died, that sky-rocket mind brought down to the bouncing ball of TV; Calder Willingham went off to Hollywood to work on something called *The Vikings*; Dylan Thomas's corpse was fought over by rival bands of acolytes, gnashing their teeth and clutching autographed copies of *Under Milk Wood*; Kerouac worked as a brakeman on the Southern Pacific Railroad, and ate grass; *The Deer Park* was called "a garbage heap," and *Peyton Place* was compared to *Main Street*; James Dean came and went like a Cocteau version of Penrod; and eventually Sherman Adams was revealed as something hairier than a hound's tooth.

In the face of all this, the bitter witticisms and heads-up boozing of my crowd seemed pretty empty and self-defeating.

Though there were some stirrings in the Village, most of the people I had known in 1951 were gone. Ginsberg was in Yucatán, Jack was somewhere between Mexico and San Francisco, Jay Landesman had moved back to St. Louis, poor Carl Solomon was being wired as "unsound," and I discovered that I hadn't seen anyone who was swimming against the stream in months. All in a morning we decided to pick up stakes and get out of town. The roots pulled easily enough out of the cracked pavements. We simply got on a train. I felt silly for having waited so long.

With the last of the money, we put a down-payment on a large and dingy Victorian house, with neither heat nor plumbing, in a river town in Connecticut. We re-did it ourselves, making nine rooms out of thirteen. We slept amid piles of plaster; I hoisted ceiling beams with an auto jack; we always smelled vaguely of turpentine. Almost broke, we berried and crabbed for our meals, purloined stones for a terrace, and stained the cheapest roofers we could buy to look like old panelling. I foraged bathroom fixtures from "pickers" upstate, and mixed the concrete footing for the chimney in a wheelbarrow. A mass of blisters, aches, calluses and bruises, I was in the best shape that I'd been in since the navy, and happy the way only a cerebral man can be when he is too busy to think. At the end of July, I turned over the paint brushes to my wife, and got down to work on a new and ambitious novel.

"I want warmth now, I want belief with which to combat the instinctive penchant I have for looking on the depressing side. Meaninglessness has been, for years, the black angel at the end of my reasoning. . . . So it is paradoxical that I am now about to write a book which must be permeated with the imminence of atomic war, in the first really calm period in world relations that we have had since 1945." (Journal—August 1, 1955)

Resolves seemed easy in such a mood. I was just about to turn thirty, and for years I had been saying that I would give up smoking and the minor vices, when I did. The second half of one's life (I reasoned windily) should be given over to putting to use what one has learned in the first half—and besides that, renunciation can be as attractive at thirty as dissipation is at twenty. In any case, I worked hard, wanting to have the book well underway before attempting to kick the bad habits of ten frantic years—bad habits that nevertheless led me, as the summer waned, to inviting six or eight people up for the weekends, during which, late at night, I would waver out to take a piss (out of the smoke and talk and noise of the counterfeit New York they had brought to our living room), to stand on our lawn under the remote stars and the placid nightsky that was always there, immensely silent and unrebuking, astonished by the way we all lived—seeming to get no closer to whatever it was we chased, and no farther from whatever it was chased us. . . . Was it only drunken befuddlement? It still happens to me now and again. . . . Nevertheless, I usually lost Mondays due to those weekends, and progress was slow.

My drive was to finish up in a reckless spurt, get a large enough advance to escape to Europe, and enter the fourth decade of my life quits with the first three. But this is a drive out of which no significant work can be done, and I got my come-uppance one rainy October day, following a bad week of sentences that spread out across the page in a formless, syrupy ooze, when I was finally forced to confess:

"Who is Calk, after all? I haven't got his image in my head, and it is a waste to go on unless he drives the book, as Stofsky drove Go. . . . It has just occurred to me, over coffee, that perhaps he is, after all, Dostoyevski. . . . Perhaps if I copy some of D.'s letters, copy his style, his tone . . . Perhaps then—"

Two weeks later, after all such desperate and foolish stratagems had failed, I finally admitted that this particular book was not yet ready to be written. I had gone ahead in a daze, working out of the baffled reflex that occasionally keeps a writer at his paper long after he should quit, and I stared at my 30,000 words like a man who has built a doghouse, and forgotten to include a door.

I sat in my room, automatically sharpening pencils, and tried to take stock. My creative vision was badly muddled, anxiety was my middle name, I was snappish and defensive even with my wife. On top of this, we were dead broke, and I had little or nothing to show for the past three years, and no time now to massage my ego with grandiloquent austerities. I think that the illusory promise of the fifties, which I had somehow managed to carry inviolate through its first half, began to die in me that day.

It didn't die easily, or fast. It took another two or three years before I recognized how infected with the illusion I had become. It took another siege of hustling for money—this time by clanking out a series of slick little tales that were so obviously hyped-up with synthetic creative adrenalin that they netted me neither satisfaction nor cash. It took several months when I simply couldn't work at all, and stared out the window at the gloomy elms of New England, truly, calmly desperate for the first time in years.

The knife of desperation finally drew blood, and drove me to begin a novel about jazz that I had had in mind for years, wanting from it only one day's good words to remind me that I could still write a paragraph that lived on its own. I got that day, and then another, and then another, and before I knew it eighteen months had passed, and I had a book.

They were good months mostly. A man thrives on the work that demands the most of him, and this was work keyed to the problem that most vexed me then: the dilemma of the artist in America—his lonely perfectionist afternoons, the wild public nights when his truth gets soiled, his bring-down dawns. I wrote a lot of my anger, and some of my answers, and most of my irritable love for my country in her bad-mood, deep into that book—perhaps too deep, for I was worried about the surface artfulness, and unconsciously courting the approval of literary arbiters who were bound to have contempt for my subject anyway. I suppose I coated the pill.

But the days and nights had a fine tang to them, neverthe- less. . . . Walking around the North Cove in the pearl-grey sunrises, collecting bored dogs for my three-mile tour of that New England Hamlin—yap-eared dogs wanting only a human conspirator to turn the yawny morning into a jaunt . . . That keen, impersonal delight, like no other, when your daemon blows the mystery of breath into a character, and he lives—despite you, outside you, needing no stern puppeteer to make him sweat or whoop to the promptings of his own truth . . . Canoeing with my wife up an estuary off the river on a day off, to saunter, nude as Adam, around a deserted, shoreside clearing, tipsily unable to remember any longer why anyone put on shame, or chic, with clothes, and so making love right there, like Klysty-simpleton, cheap wine spilled across our sun-burnt thighs; to drowse side by side afterwards, as innocent as lechers, holding sticky hands in the illusion (sweetest that I know) that beyond a certain resolute casting-off, we might all be simple creatures to one another, and no longer try to beat the moon's watery image with our silly sticks. . . .

I wrote a sentence, as long as a Jacquet solo, to prove that America had not let all the wind out of its proverbial windbags. I felt the book take hold of me with its own fate. I sweated the summer away at my desk, often working in nothing but drawers, flogging myself with no saving sense of martyrdom, and got sick in the fall before I noticed: simply woke up one night in New York, after a binge of writing-nerves and alcohol, my heart amok with tension in my chest, the imminence of some scary, final stoppage panicking me, the revolt of my body (its faint, stubborn engine begging to be *allowed* to beat) wiping out years of indifference to health in a moment: I had always thought that I was physically indestructible.

Drink and drinking (and, in my case, cigarettes): it was only later that I would come to see the truth of Wescott's line about Fitzgerald— that he treated booze as a "fatal, moral issue," and so indulged—in terms of my own dedicated dissipations, and their kickback in my chest. I poisoned myself, I taxed myself, because I was weary, strung-up, prey to double-mindedness, but also because it was emblematic and contemporary. But the body recognizes no such reasoning, and for the next few years my body struck back at me whenever my mind pushed too far, too fast, and I lay in the dark, one huge pulse, a great nerve of fear, a trembling hypochrondriac—scolding myself for being terrified. Until eventually, like Zorba, I watched the sea gulls, and thought: "That's the road to take; find the absolute rhythm and follow it with absolute trust."

During this time, I became even more disgruntled and apolitical, for in the 1956 election even Adlai Stevenson seemed to have succumbed to the cynical logic of the image manipulators, and the whole campaign had an air of dismal charade about it that was demoralizing. And yet I still wasn't ready to admit that a writer in a cowed age must be a knocker not a booster, and we lived on among middle-class Republicans (for whom this seemed the best of times), crewing on their boats, going to their parties, and never making a nuisance—as completely exiled from any reality but that in our own heads as nineteenth century intellectuals in a Siberian garrison town. My wife went to work, we lived frugally, and now and again I experienced the subversive intoxication of a day's work that would have ruffled the town's pinfeathers if it had known about it, or cared. Mostly, however, I worked cautiously, intent on writing a book that would get us out of there, for by then the idea that I must escape from the stultifying greenhouse of America in the fifties had become something of an obsession.

In late 1957, of course, the cracks started to appear in that greenhouse, and a few small, ominous winds began to blow through the nation. News of the first Russian sputnik came over the radio while an old drinking-friend from New York days, who happened to be an aerodynamicist, was up for the weekend. The mixture of joy and apprehension on his face when he said, "Now maybe they'll realize where we are, and loosen up the purse strings," produced a strange wave of relief in me that is difficult to describe.

It was the same relief I felt when the furor over the Beat Generation broke a few months later with the final publication of *On the Road*. All at once the presence of a deep layer of discontent under the frosting on the cake became clear to everyone, and those of us, who had almost given up hope that it would ever break through to daylight, felt exhilarated and redeemed.

I felt the same relief sometime later when I was asked (on another television show) how I could account for the Beatniks, the sick comics, and all the other pustules of dissent that were erupting everywhere by then, and I could think of nothing *sensible* to say, and so blurted out, "The entire content of life in this country now accounts for it," only to glance beyond the kliegs and see a cameraman vigorously agreeing.

I suppose this relief resembled the emotion you experience on waking from an uneasy dream back into the harshness of reality—where, at least, work and will can make a difference. And for some of us, certainly, that relief was strongest of all when Kennedy, campaigning for the Democratic nomination some years later, actually acknowledged that things were going to have to get worse before they got better. Suddenly the gaseous dream seemed over, and the world was coherent again.

Now I see that if I had let that first thrill of relief fully awaken me, I might have saved myself almost two further years of frustration and soul-sifting. But once again money intervened. This time it was only a small amount (the advance on my jazz novel), but when a friend said to me, "That's wonderful, now you can put heat in your house," I realized that, in one sense, I had been putting heat in my house for years, and we promptly got on a boat, and went to Europe, even though we knew we would be poor as refugees when we got back.

Europe, Europe—to which Americans flee from some stalemate in their souls. It is our own identity that we discover there, it is a geography inside we map while changing trains and currency, we find *ourselves* at the end of every street.

Turned around on fog-shrouded Millbank somewhere near the House of Commons (Big Ben bonged in grave muffles nearby), I asked the way from a group of dim figures who turned out to be the Burghers of Calais . . . Prowling in St. Paul's chilly crypt one morning, I found on a tomb (as if led to it), "Go after that which is lost—" . . . Sheep skittered over the tumbled walls of Corfe Castle in the Dorset downs, and I felt kin to the shaggy Danes who had marauded there centuries before, because the eye you haul over a winter sea is an eye impatient for essences . . . The quai-side shops in Paris were full of hummingbirds, Quiche Lorraine and Mahalia Jackson records; the walls around our immense bed in the Bisson were draped with whorish black satin; Peruvian singers chanted and strummed at our Reveillon: Paris, full of the ghosts of eminent expatriates . . . Provence in January was all sienna, ochre, moss-green; the hilltowns over their dry riverbeds seemed to shimmer in our wine-keen eyes; the streets of Aix were a circus of baskets, cheeses, and chilly sunlight. And someone, poised over the ultimate button someday, may fail to press it, remembering the cheeses of Provence: such was my certainty for at least an hour that burnished afternoon.

It seemed heartless that Lawrence's world-saturated eyes should have looked almost their last on the vulgar orange-and-green shutters of Bandol . . . I bought de Sade in St. Tropez among the yachts and idlers, and read him, yawning, behind two-foot-thick walls in Valberg (where we iced our gin in the snow piled in the window niches), and my wife brought him back through any number of Customs in her girdle—as he would have liked.

In the Jura, they caught our supper trout in a turbid river full of black leaves; we were the only guests in that dark and soggy village; rain blew out of the mountains, pelting our windows, and, lying awake, I felt suddenly boundaryless, sentient, charged with an absolutely miraculous mortality—as if the trout, the rain, the remoteness, the big harsh wind shouldering against the shutters could, in themselves, redeem the costs of living in this treacherous century. I felt strong enough that night to endure this time without the excuses and excesses of the victimized, and brought this feeling back from Europe to the test.

"There was that law of life, so cruel and so just," Mailer wrote during these years, "which demanded that one must grow or else pay more for remaining the same." To which I would only add: by some fortuitous trick of timing, life never seems to bill us until we are able to scrape together the price. We get out with nothing, but we *do* get out. Though I knew I was drifting, and had been drifting for years, somehow nothing less than hitting the reef headon, and almost foundering, would make me change my course. Broke and without enthusiasm for the task, I sat down to the planning stages of a new book. And worked along mostly on will. And gradually descended into a personal maelstrom, only some of which is relevant here.

Certain inner slippages occurred. My father, with whom I

had never been close until the last years, lost his hand in a senseless accident on the Jersey Turnpike, then suffered a cerebral thrombosis, and lay for six weeks in a dreary room in a dismal hospital in bleak South Camden where I dawdled away the days talking to him—even though he never recognized me. Twice the doctors felt he had only a few hours to live, but somehow he rallied, and finally improved enough to be transferred to another hospital on Long Island (prognosis: good). And there, after a week, he inexplicably gave up one day, and died.

If I felt anything very much (other than a certain sorrowful irony), I closed over against it. I'd learned to think very adroitly *around* death. Or thought I had. But the fact that that cheerful, sentimental man, egotistic and good-hearted as he aged, always prey to tears and impatience, publicly conventional and privately a sensualist, with whom I had fought a silly battle-of-the-generations for years, should end up in an open casket amid the hired pieties of a funeral parlor on Queens Boulevard, intoned over by a minister (who had never known him) of a religion he had been too extroverted ever to think about, weaned me of all filial angers in an instant. He had struggled harder to stay in life than I would have done, and I realized how little of the essential strengths show in a man's face, or in his words. I wanted a quiet drink with my wife, and some brave music, and a neutral moment. Just as we left the room, however, an unknown woman, fortyish and pretty in lace, approached the casket, and touched my father's dead cheek briefly with her fingertips, in a gesture of involuntary, simple grief that indicated a keener sense of his actual life than I had ever had, and something gave way a little in me at the missed chance to have been truly his son. He had touched that woman sometime, touched the quick of her, and so she had touched him back out of the mysterious equity that governs real emotions.

I looked around my life as I hadn't looked at it before, and wasn't reassured. Words, words: easy, unexamined cynicism; glib certainties; a lazy facility of mind. My fingers were covered with ink, not blood. What did I feel about this death, *any* death? Without which there was no knowing life. I was a scribbler, and what I'd touched was paper.

Old chickens came home to roost one by one. Some writers are so intimidated by the morning's empty page, so paralyzed by the thought of filling it, that every fresh start involves a conquering of anxiety that would appall a psychiatrist, much less a storekeeper. At any rate, I am like that. In the best of times, writing for me is a trauma that is willingly instituted in the hope of a catharsis; it is self-induced schizophrenia; it is the daring of ego-loss in the name of ego. But when times are bad, a writer most resembles a man in the act of brainwashing *himself,* the Grand Inquisitor in pitiless colloquy with his mirror. And times were bad for me.

The work went daily worse, and I equivocated out of old habits. Though I automatically put into operation all the standard procedures (the keep-bulling-it-ahead gambit, the take-a-week-off routine, the go-out-and-get-drunk bit, the shift-to-another-project solution), it was all to no avail. I thought "profoundly" about Death and Time. I scolded myself, I indulged myself. I sharpened pencils, and used them up.

But nothing.

Certain I had lost my talent (Hawthorne, walking in Concord woods, haunted me), it would be over a year before I realized that what I had lost was not my talent, but my judgment. "I had become identified with the objects of my horror or compassion," as Fitzgerald put it. I literally couldn't tell good prose from bad. I couldn't *feel* a character stirring into life on the page—even Raskolnikov, even Anna. I'd lost the gift of suspending myself, without which fiction seems a pointless riddle. Words swam, grew soft, then sticky. Whole paragraphs turned to sludge.

Resolutely, I wrote hundreds of moody pages; recklessly, I tore them up. I lost twenty pounds without trying, every dawn was sour with nausea, milk punches gave a surreal tilt to the afternoons, the nights were hoarse with rages and remorse. . . . Why didn't I simply give it up? Why couldn't I turn to reality, and wait? We are ignorant in the storm of Time, our audacity is ignorance.

What I was passing through was the collapse of a years-old image of myself: the Defense Council in the Big Court, the Recorder intent on outliving violence. All my wise men (the dead writers a living writer most seeks to please) looked on in silence from my walls. I fell back on illusions put aside years ago for just such a moment, and fell flat on my face. The armatures in my personality melted down; I sagged toward self-pity; I became a shapeless, ugly lump of demeaning cravings—for approval, for respect, for instant love. My soul had a bad smell. It was a sort of sane derangement. It was a Slow Flip. It was—

Well, suffice it to say that my psyche, like that of the nation just then, suffered a series of numbing bruises to the self-esteem, and I endured the personal equivalent of the U-2 incident, the Cuban Revolution, and America's prestige-losses and space-failures. The extent to which I had muddied my personality with self-abuse and false goals impressed itself on me in a way that left no room for further equivocation. The habits and disciplines of years crumbled one after the other, I came down to some sort of private bedrock, and was (it seems to me now) actually mad for one morning, and part of an afternoon.

"Today, 2:00 P.M., rage, horror, the overwhelming desire to hurt, to cry out, no place for my emotions any longer, too big for my very frame . . . frightening thoughts of suicide for the first time in years, then an ominous calm which, of course, erupted into a worse seizure. . . . All my scruples, my principles, everything I've lived by, failing me in an instant, as they have all summer. . . . But never so strong before; how to go through the sheer hours till Shirley comes home, how to fill them; to lie quietly on the bed, hands folded, and try to sleep; to drink, to play records, to try work again; how? how? Defeated by the time to be consumed, better death than to have to go through the *time*. . . . Uncontrollable tears, insane humiliating attacks of self-pity, the invention of the wildest, most childish dramas to feed my sundered ego. . . . Sick to my stomach at myself. . . . Whole moments after that, I don't clearly remember. . . . I sit alone now, eighteen minutes to midnight, and a new day. . . ." (Journal—September 23, 1959)

Then, for several months, I did little but wait, and mend,

244 S NOTHING MORE TO DECLARE

and take stock. I went to New York alone to walk streets with enough life on them to break into, and through, my paralyzing bout of subjectivity. I kept away from the old raucous haunts. I collected little reality mottoes that I repeated whenever the attacks of anxiety returned—like Kazantzakis', "In front of us now is the pilaff; let our minds become pilaff," or Lawrence's enigmatically pellucid, "Fish, oh fish,/so little matters." I healed myself as a dog does: by keeping alone, by being patient, by licking the wounds clean. For a long while after that, I was convinced that some form of Buddhism lay ahead for the Western consciousness like a fatality; I tried to empty myself in accordance with this perception; I looked around me with the scoured eyes of Zen.

It was during this time that it gradually dawned on me that America, like me, had been in a kind of thrall for years. In my mind, the decade (just ending) took on the quality of a long, bilious hallucination—with its trivial, executives-washroom anxieties; its suspicion of any distinct personal identity; its sickening Eisenhower piety and equally revolting Nixon cant; its constant referral in all matters of taste to hypothetical twelve-year-old girls, or sheltered ancients who blanched at the word "damn"; its absolutely straight-faced insistence that all this was somehow mature, responsible, healthy and American.

It was a decade when the patronizing, whipped-cream sentiments of Oscar Hammerstein and Norman Vincent Peale wafted through a nation stupified under the pall of millions of barbeque pits, automobiles the size of gun boats, golf carts with built-in massagers, and rotisseries on which to cook precooked meals. It was a time when sane people seriously believed that rigged quiz shows at least indicated a new respect for the intellectual life; that Rod Serling and Paddy Chayevsky were fearless, probing dramatists; that the avant-garde was not just eccentric, but "square"; and that *Time* Magazine's poisonous reportage was somehow redeemed by the fact that it was "well-written." It was a decade during which Doctor Pangloss became the official philosopher of the Administration, and most professionals secretly subscribed to Lenny Bruce's mock motto, "Be a man. Sell out," and the public sat hypnotized, as before a crazy-house mirror, happily watching themselves pictured on

TV as so many dumb but lovable husbands, canny but well-meaning wives, and fiendishly mischievous children who were wiser than Socrates—the whole travesty bathed in moral pap, intellectual sloth, and the baldest banshee-commercialism. It was a decade without its Mencken or even its Fitzgerald, and most of the artists, who (in Nelson Algren's memorable phrase) should have been standing "cartless in the supermart," were either loading up like everyone else, or sulking in a corner. Still, there is nothing like complicity in a fraud to sharpen the eye, and being bilked on top of it adds a saving edge of anger to the expertise.

By the time the fifties ended, and I realized that the Gaudy Night had lasted almost half the decade, and the hangover had consumed the rest, I was as poor as I had been when they began. We were living on enormous homemade soups of bought barley and begged bones, and drinking Gallo Red and seltzer. I was foraging driftwood from the beach, writing on *both* sides of the paper, and hoarding insights in a stolen notebook. I was ten years older, and ten years wearier, and what I had gotten down on paper that was worth the time and toil I'd spent could easily have been hefted in one hand. And yet there were experiences I would never have to have again, and lessons I would never afterwards have to learn, and illusions from which I had managed to get free in time.

I would have to begin all over again in my work if I was to find a distinct personal voice to embody the besieged human being I saw all around me then—and which I had, myself, become. No more Balzacian scope, no more Tolstoian sanity, no more godless, godlike eye. Consciousness itself (contracting and evolving, distorting and defining) would probably be the subject *and* the form of any future work I did. For we are all windows, and the size and shape of the particular window dictate what can be seen through it.

To some degree, I would have to begin all over in myself as well. I would probably never again be able to believe that my experience was somehow emblematic of my whole generation, or any longer use the dark thrust of the century as a mandate for ideas or excesses that had their real source in the mystery of myself. In a sense, my life had been returned to me—its limitations, its responsibilities, its purpose or its drift: all of it was my own charge again.

Some of my illusions had been profitable. They had kept me believing long enough (in the redemptive power of love, in some essential equity in the murk of life, in art's magic ability to transform by the act of creating) to escape the bitterness that often follows disillusionment in the young; and I was relieved to discover that I was now too old and too intractable to be permanently deflected from life and work by the puncturing of these hopeful balloons. Others of my illusions—the sad captains, the gaudy night—had left me woefully unprepared for my own Actium when it came, but I found that I was still not too old to survive silence, to turn down a glass, to plan to raise another fleet.

At the end of the forties, history was still my nightmare and my daydream: if the hot war had made me (and my generation), the Cold War years had unmade us all, brought us "down to our skins at last," and prepared us (so I thought) to talk back to the times with the urgency of some sort of contemporary "God's Underground." But by the end of the muddled fifties, history had become the *setting* for action, rather than the source of it: the times had proved too schizophrenic to be talked to in an oracular voice; I had come down to the bone itself, which was nothing less than the sum total of my own inner facts, and the truth of Camus' profoundest line seemed, all of a sudden, truth enough to grow on: "To learn to live and to die, and, in order to be a man, to refuse to be a god."

In order to be a *man*. Much less a writer.

Afterword

§ § Meanwhile, the past five years seem to have been summoning me toward a break. I will be forty when this book appears, and it is safe to bet that there is more time behind me than there is ahead. Just five years ago, wallowing in that deep trough of life and work, I hung a sign over my desk that read: YOU HAVE ONLY FIVE YEARS LEFT—an alarmist goad, a wake-the-dreamer admonition, but, still, it recognized a private dead-end for which nothing less than the most urgent warning seemed a proper road sign. For I had been appalled to discover (after fifteen years of work) that the roots of the urge to write go so far down into the darks of a personal need that a man cannot pull them up, even for a replanting, without tearing up something of his character as well. And after my fallow year, I knew that it was either write again or take to the couch for me, because once you have discovered that you lack the mad decisiveness for suicide, the options in the ego game narrow down to these: Quit while you're losing, or hang on and be lost.

So one day in mid-December, 1960, I sat down before a fresh and intimidating notebook, and (terrified lest the first words I wrote would sicken me back into silence, as words had been sickening me for months, as words sicken a wordman off his feed) I put down the only hard and unassailable thing I knew that morning: "To write for two hours every day no matter what. And—to pin my life on it."

Just to write, to write anything, to transmute a notion into words, to freeze it on the page for later, to use my mind in some

§ 247

shaping fashion, to *work*. With astonishment, I realized that I had a perfectly commonplace need to be tired after a day of toil that was expensive to my energies. I had a need to be emptied so that I could fill again. I wrote for four hours, I wrote the way one runs sometimes—headlong, and without looking back; and two weeks later, having dumbly persisted day after day, and filled that notebook and part of another, I felt strong enough to begin a piece of fiction, and somehow kept going on it beyond the initial stumblings, and had the luck, and eventually made it off the reef.

Now, five years later, two books later, a stint of teaching later, so many moultings and inchings and accumulations later, perhaps more changed in these five years than I ever changed in all the years that led up to them, I feel some break is imminent at last for me, some severing of which perhaps this book is one symptom. The attitudes of youth, which die so hard in all Americans, and never entirely die in some of us (that romantic transcendentalism, that infatuation with the New, the Real, with Youth itself, that secret suspicion of inner ephemerality that is the source of our misunderstood materialism)—all this seems to be slipping behind me now, and I feel the urge to emigrate out of the Scene at last. I intend to go over into a new life, a life at once less feverish with concerns about contemporaneousness, and more conducive to that uninterrupted self-communion out of which one's best work comes; a private life of small pleasures to balance out the large anxieties; a life in which I can let the old world go for a change, knowing it will come round again, no matter how I fret. Poised at a frontier, I no longer scoff at happiness, but have come to value it as an insomniac values sleep, and what I have written in this book is by way of being a customs-declaration of the few things I have chosen to bring with me out of a disordered and a wasteful past.

So much is missing from the list, so much had to be left behind, so many personal mementos of the sort that are invariably found in the shabby luggage that is abandoned in a public locker: The carefully annotated copy of A. J. Ayer, for instance, that I cannot read anymore . . . the panic-day I wished it was Händel's world, knowing it was Mingus's . . . Cannastra's trousers left as an earnest of his return sometime . . . The oysters, champagne, and Getz with which my wife and I, old hands by then like everyone else, got through the Missile Crisis . . . The bad poem I wrote called "The Double-Think of Love," and its secret heroine . . . Madeleine and Elga, Jim and Charlotte, Orkney and the Artful Dodger . . . The awesome blizzards in Nebraska, through which I redballed three hundred miles nonstop, peril irradiating me like bliss . . . The desperate hilarity, the badgirl stockings, the existential bargain in the Ambassador Hotel in Chicago . . . The thirteenth century certainties that were beautiful, but abandoned me in a moment in 1959, and the *two* copies of Andre Previn's *Like Young* that stuck by me . . . The lipsticked words written on flesh in the Iowa farmhouse after the rabbit . . . The edition of Trollope (saved like busfare during a binge) which I never dared to open, lest it fail to get me home . . . The pretty student nurse who tried to take out my father's teeth, only to discover they were his own . . . The passed-up girls—all of whom will be younger than me from now on, *born* in years I remember in my own consciousness . . . Weathered-in Block Island dawns of nerveless euphoria . . . The tweed suit I ate my way out of in three weeks . . . Aprils of my twenties when I wished for everything, for everybody . . . The survivor's ambiance that is as unmistakable as the one man in the room who is *not* an undertaker. Though sometimes it seems I am nothing but a sentient appendage to images such as these, there was no room for them in this book, they were emblematic of nothing but my *personal* reality, and they had to go.

Perhaps, too, the themes that have surfaced again and again here (themes that will continue to haunt me, I suppose, no matter what new life may come)—consciousness, history, creativity, death and sex—have remained so embedded in this montage of imagery that no single, reasoned summing up has taken place. In any case, I am left with a strew of unrelated convictions (like so many socks without mates) that stubbornly refuse to become a credo, and yet belong in these pages in the same way that wariness of fire *belongs* to a burn.

Nevertheless, there is no room to expand on them more than I have already done. There is no room to substantiate my certainty that the crucial truths of the next ten years (aside from the Zen-psychotherapy truths out of which nothing can be *made*) are the truths of Being, mostly sexual truths. Or my belief that the leap inward constitutes the only hope for a leap forward. Or my guess that the choice ahead for us could be written in the formula: LSD or ESB (Electro-Stimulation of the Brain). There is no room to explain my feeling that love, if it is ever to come back into life again, must issue out of our total emotional *assent* to another human person. Or to justify my intuition that love for another (which is a desire that has been transformed into a contingency) will have no chance to flower until after we have risked the self-love we feel we cannot afford to lose.

Nor is there any way to settle my score with this century and its contradictions, except to record a newsreel image of some years ago, which showed a woman hanging outside the window of a building that fronted on the Berlin Wall. Suddenly, a youth from the West climbed up to help her down to safety, seizing her legs, and then, out of the window, a VOPO from the East grabbed her arms to prevent it. For one giddy moment, these two men struggled with one another over the inert body of that woman, pulling and yanking her back and forth across the abyss of ideology, as if she was nothing but an object to the dogmas warring in their city; and only when she fell to the pavement, with that graceless *thud* of hurt flesh that needs no soundtrack to be audible, did she become a living human being again—unique, and irreplaceable, and dead. Until we realize that the fight for life in our time is the fight against *all* ideologies, the horrors will undoubtedly go on producing further dogmas to avenge them, which, in their turn, will produce further horrors—until all the dogmas are swept away in that final horror no avengers will survive.

Nor is there time to explain that the concentration camps and the atomized cities (wherein the existential anguish of my generation had its start) have led some of us to the conclusion that, just as there is no elegy commensurate to the idea of the nature of man that perished there, so these places were appalling beyond any demonstrable sense of outrage *or* injustice. The same sort of ideological certainty that erected Belsen (I am right, and he is wrong, and his *death* will affirm it) demolished Hiroshima, and until we accept our complicity, as a species, in murder itself, any murder, the world will be as doomed as an athlete running the four-minute mile while a fatal cancer remorselessly devours him. For these twenty Cold War years have left me with the inescapable conviction that Gandhi's faith (that the only power left untapped in all the world is the power of a single man, refusing to hate) will continue to run like a dark, troubling stream beneath the proliferating cemeteries of our age, and we will all have to spend increasingly more and more time simply mending our intellectual dikes against it.

Nor is there a place to explain my permanent enlistment in what I call Brecht's Army, an army dedicated to the idea that a certain kind of "cowardice" in our time is far more mature and responsible than all the Hemingway bunk about courage and grace under stress, which has so pathetically obscured the fact that we are *all* noncombatants now, and our duty to the future is nothing less than to survive the present, bringing with us (even if we have to jettison everything else) the noncombatant point of view: that point of view which refuses to take sides against life; that point of view which all sides in the wars of ideology are intent on eradicating; that point of view which, alone, holds out any hope that someday the wars will end.

These are my personal convictions at this time of change, and they had to be included in any declaration that was honestly made. But I no longer believe that art (much less exhortation) can avert anything that men, in their confusions, set their minds upon. The most it can do is to remind us of what is at stake, of all that can be lost, of what is worth the saving; and the artist, I suppose, must believe the rest will somehow follow in whatever time remains.

For myself, I would make peace with my own life. I would abandon my "ideal guns" (the guns that Lawrence said Americans go down defending), the guns which have sounded as clearly these past years in the selfless dissipations of libertines and boozers as they have in the selfish renunciations of moralists and revolutionaries. Care, after all, is the only measure: to know one did not live a life *muffled* against those guns.

Those of us who have paid attention to the human predicament during these decades, a predicament that has only worsened as the Cold War has dragged on and on toward a condition of permanent stalemate, have searched in strange places for a saving sense of ourselves, and for the possibilities of further life, and everyone now has a private casualty list of friends and lovers who didn't make it. If I have not dwelt overlong on my own list here, it is because there is no real solace in such tallyings, and there is something faintly self-serving and inappropriate about the only epitaphs that one could write. Silence, in the face of certain events, is all that indicates that one is aware of what has happened.

More and more, my generation takes on the aspects of a transition generation to me. The most important things that happened to us were losses (which, as we got older, we recognized were only moultings, after all), and the process of individuation, to which I have referred now and again, was probably the one experience that was characteristic of the new and unknown life into which we all ventured so eagerly twenty years ago. Since then we have lived out, in our nerves and in our minds, the vast, qualitative shift of consciousness that makes 1945 seem, already, like another era.

For myself, I am done declaring, exhorting, generationing. There are no Gentiles anymore, and there is no further need for Apostles who will speak to them.

If I no longer stay up talking all night as I did for years, feeling that *someone* should be awake guarding the candle with a glass, it is because certain old saws have come to cut with fresh teeth—like, "Sufficient unto the day. . . ." For at the end of the night *is* light (as I thought so long ago), but it is the light of the morning, unblemished by our dreams or nightmares, and it dawns on us anyway. These days I find myself longing for the crisp emptiness of such mornings in autumn—for the briny air of cities where the squawking gulls fish the harbors, for wet wind off deep water and a dog's cold nose nuzzling into your palm as you walk. I imagine the days that follow such mornings, days of the solitary, incommunicable joy of work that is done for itself. I know the answers are in reality if we will only look for them, and I am intent on it.

Fame, ambition, ego—more and more they seem like husks to me, sad husks housing frightened twitter. Money—it can no longer buy me thirty-nine. I have outlived myself as I was in the years recorded here, and I am done—even with the celebrations of their end. Though you cannot go back on what you know, you can at least survive it (a hope mired in a fact) into the next moulting, and the next, until the two truths are indistinguishable from one another at last. And meanwhile you can persevere without rage.

What more is there to declare?